LAWMAKING AND CO-OPERATION IN INTERNATIONAL POLITICS

By the same author

PATTERNS OF POLITICAL INSTABILITY

LAWMAKING AND CO-OPERATION IN INTERNATIONAL POLITICS

The Idealist Case Re-examined

David Sanders

St. Martin's Press New York

St. Martin's Press, Inc., 175 Fifth Avenue, New York, NY 10010
Printed in Hong Kong
Published in the United Kingdom by The Macmillan Press Ltd.
First published in the United States of America in 1986

ISBN 0-312-47563-2

Library of Congress Cataloging in Publication Data
Sanders, David, 1950–
Lawmaking and co-operation in international politics.
Bibliography: p.

Includes index.
1. International relations—Research. 2. Treaties.
I. Title.
JX1291.S275 1986 327'.072 85-11982
ISBN 0-312-47563-2

For my parents

Contents

List of Tables ix
Acknowledgements xi

INTRODUCTION: LAWMAKING, CO-OPERATION AND PEACE 1

1 THE IDEALIST TRADITION AND ITS MODERN VARIANTS 7

The Origins and Development of Twentieth-century Idealism 8
The Limitations of Traditional Idealism 10
Reconstructing Idealism 20
Summary and Conclusions 27

2 BACKGROUND TO THE EMPIRICAL ANALYSIS: THE DATA AND THE DATA ANALYSIS STRATEGY 30

The Data Analysis Strategy 30
The Data: Operational Measures and their Rationale 35
The Spurious Correlation Problem 44
Summary and Conclusions 49

3 TREATY-MAKING, WAR AND PEACE: PRELIMINARY EMPIRICAL FINDINGS 51

The 'More Law, Less War' Hypothesis Apparently Disconfirmed 54
Disaggregating the Law-War Relationship: An Indirect Role for Law? 57
Controlling for Friendship/Antagonism: The Spurious Correlation Problem Considered 62
Summary and Conclusions 72

4 TREATY-MAKING, WAR AND PEACE: FURTHER EMPIRICAL EVIDENCE 74

Reducing the Complexity of the Empirical Results 75
The Law-War Correlations and International Economic Factors 80
Controlling for Economic and Political 'Friendship/Antagonism' Factors Simultaneously 86
An Application of Log-linear Modelling Techniques 87
A Predictive Model of Occurrence of War in the 1921–42 Period 98
Summary and Conclusions 105

5 A CASE-STUDY: ANGLO-TURKISH RELATIONS DURING THE INTERWAR YEARS 108

The Existing Orthodoxy: An Overview of Anglo-Turkish Relations 1920–45 109
'Realpolitik' and Anglo-Turkish Relations: A Speculative Qualification 119
The Transformation of Anglo-Turkish Relations 1926–32 122
Summary and Conclusions 128

CONCLUSION: RECONSTRUCTED IDEALISM AND REVISED REALISM 131

Appendix 136
Notes and References 140
Bibliography 154
Index 158

List of Tables

Chapter 2 Background to the Empirical Analysis: The Data and the Data Analysis Strategy

2.1 Illustrative cross-tabulation of the relationship between war/no war and referrals to arbitral settlement/not 37
2.2 The classification of treaties, conventions and agreements employed in this study 39
2.3 Bilateral trade variables 43
2.4 Contextual variables 45
2.5 'Friendship/Antagonism' control variables 48

Chapter 3 Treaty-making, War and Peace: Preliminary Empirical Findings

3.1 Hypothetical cross-tabulation between war/no war and number of arbitration/conciliation treaties signed 53
3.2 Illustrative cross-tabulation of the relationship between war/no war and arbitration/conciliation agreements 53
3.3 Summary statistics derived from 2-way cross-tabulations 55
3.4 Summary statistics (gammas) derived from 3-way cross-tabulations 58
3.5 Summary statistics (gammas) derived from 4-way cross-tabulations 64
3.6 Summary statistics (gammas) derived from 4-way cross-tabulations 68
3.7 Summary statistics (gammas) derived from 4-way cross-tabulations 70

Chapter 4 Treaty-making, War and Peace: Further Empirical Evidence

4.1 Groupings of treaty types employed to produce aggregated indices 76
4.2 Summary statistics (gammas and – in brackets – tau_b) derived from 4-way cross-tabulations 78

4.3 Summary statistics (gammas and – in brackets – tau_b) derived from 4-way cross-tabulations 82
4.4 Summary statistics (gammas and – in brackets – tau_b) derived from 4-way cross-tabulations 84
4.5 Summary statistics (gammas and – in brackets – tau_b) derived from 5-way cross-tabulations 88
4.6 (a) Cell frequencies for the 4-way cross-tabulation involving political agreements, and (b) effect parameters (λ) for the saturated log-linear model defined by the table 90
4.7 (a) Cell frequencies for the 4-way cross-tabulation involving economic agreements, and (b) effect parameters (λ) for the saturated log-linear model defined by the table 92
4.8 (a) Cell frequencies for the 5-way cross-tabulation involving political agreements, and (b) effect parameters (λ) for the saturated log-linear model defined by the table 94
4.9 (a) Cell frequencies for the 5-way cross-tabulation involving economic agreements, and (b) effect parameters (λ) for the saturated log-linear model defined by the table 96
4.10 Independent variables included in regression analysis 100
4.11 Predictive model of war occurs between 1921 and 1942/not 102

Chapter 5 A Case-study: Anglo-Turkish Relations during the Interwar Years

5.1 Listing of cases from 4-way cross-tabulation 110

Acknowledgements

I am grateful to Eric Tannenbaum, Hugh Ward, Hidemi Suganami and Graham Upton for their helpful comments on an earlier draft of this manuscript. Thanks are also due to Carole Welge for her patience, speed and accuracy in producing the typescript.

D.S.

Introduction: Lawmaking, Co-operation and Peace

Contemporary decision-makers in both the East and the West are faced with a continuing dilemma: while the necessity of avoiding nuclear war impels them towards a broad strategy of mutual co-operation, the need to prevent 'the other side' from surreptitiously gaining a significant strategic advantage typically induces a general posture of confrontation. For those observers who recommend a primarily confrontationist stance, historical experience – and especially the record of the period between the two world wars – demonstrates beyond reasonable doubt that co-operative strategies towards potential aggressors are not only unproductive but also extremely dangerous. In the view of such self-proclaimed 'realists', the idealistic advocates of an overall policy of co-operation are merely fanciful optimists, incapable of furnishing any convincing empirical evidence that co-operation between potential enemies can ever be successful in promoting international peace.

This book seeks to provide the fanciful optimists with a limited amount of empirical ammunition with which to prosecute their case that co-operative strategies in international politics are at least worth trying. It argues that realism is incorrect in its assertion that co-operation between nation-states is invariably subordinated to the requirements and constraints of *realpolitik*. It suggests, rather, that co-operation can develop an autonomy of its own which is in turn capable of producing beneficial effects independently of the raw calculus of power. In order to substantiate this proposition, the present study attempts to show empirically that even during the interwar period – when, on the standard realist account, strategies of co-operation were nothing but a form of one-sided appeasement which, if anything, encouraged later aggression – there were in fact a large number of identifiable contexts in which the pursuit of co-operative strategies by nation-states did have a discernable payoff in terms of increasing the chances for international peace. While the evidence presented (precisely because it is derived from the interwar years) obviously has no *direct* application to contemporary international relations, it does indicate that the successful pursuit of co-operative strategies is not without historical precedent. The clear implication of the findings reported here is that such strategies could continue to play a significant role even in the admittedly different conditions of the present international system.

In the insecure world of international politics, however, it is by no means self-evident how strategies of co-operation can actually serve the cause of peace. For the realist orthodoxy, a state or bloc confronted by conditions of Hobbesian fear[1] simply cannot afford to drop its guard and pursue a co-operative strategy towards its presumed opponent in case that opponent – either overtly or covertly – maintains its confrontationist stance and thereby gains a significant security advantage over its rival. Moreover in view of the possibility that 'being at a serious disadvantage' can conceivably lead to the destruction of the state (or bloc) itself, realism concludes that in any given security complex[2] both sets of adversaries must inevitably pursue strategies of confrontation, with all the attendant material costs and increased risks of future conflagration which those strategies entail.[3]

For critics of the hard-line realist position, however, the logic of mutual confrontation is neither so compelling nor so clear-cut. On the contrary, if it is possible to devise a strategy of partial co-operation which is *non-fatal to either side, even if it is unsuccessful*, then (for reasons discussed later) such a strategy may provide the basis for further co-operation on more fundamental security questions, thus enhancing the prospects for both peace and security in the future.[4]

The problem, of course, is how to identify 'non-fatal if unsuccessful' co-operative strategies which nation-states (or blocs) can possibly pursue. Although there are a number of other options,[5] the present study is based on the assumption that *the most obvious and potentially fruitful 'non-fatal if unsuccessful' co-operative strategy available to nation-states in the contemporary international system is the bilateral lawmaking or treaty-making process*. By using this process, states can engage in a highly structured form of co-operation across as wide or narrow a spectrum of issues as both parties see fit, without necessarily prejudicing the security interests of the state. The extent to which each party is prepared to compromise in the construction of any particular treaty, moreover, can be varied to a considerable extent: in this sense, participation in treaty-making potentially provides a remarkably sensitive instrument for signalling co-operative intent.

This is not to suggest, however, that the signing of treaties necessarily denotes good intentions on both sides or that such an activity will of itself promote peaceful international relations. There are far too many historical examples of nation-states entering into treaty commitments which they have no intention of carrying out to sustain the belief that treaties of themselves will solve any of the great dilemmas of international politics. As Richard Nixon, an almost stereotypical practitioner of realist philosophy, has commented:

> History is a pathetic junkyard of broken treaties . . . 'friendship treaties' do not necessarily express or create friendship . . . International relations are . . . like entering a snake pit where good intentions . . . adhered to slavishly in the face of your enemy's malevolence, are bound to be distinct hindrances . . .
>
> Unless agreements are self-enforcing they will not last. It is a reflection of the great difficulty of meaningful negotiation between adversaries that such agreements, amid all of history's friendship treaties and nonaggression pacts, have been few and far between.[6]

This widely-held *realpolitik* view of 'paper treaties', however, fails to recognise that treaty-making is an enterprise that can go far beyond the negotiation of security agreements which – for whatever malevolent motives – may subsequently be violated. Nation-states engage in a wide range of bilateral and multilateral agreements that attempt to regulate their mutual relations. Indeed it is quite possible, in principle, to adopt a co-operative stance towards a potential aggressor by negotiating a series of treaties concerning economic and social – and even political – matters whilst at the same time (1) avoiding paper *security* agreements and (2) maintaining a strong (*realpolitik*) defensive military posture. The question that immediately arises, of course, is whether such a strategy of partial co-operation can ever have a positive payoff in terms of increasing the chances for peace in the future. For Nixon and the realist academic orthodoxy, the answer is simple and unequivocal: it cannot. Where there are real conflicts of vital interest, *realpolitik* is always and everywhere the supreme determinant in international affairs: co-operation in areas that 'do not really matter' invariably leads nowhere.

The question as to the value of such co-operative strategies, however, is essentially an empirical one which requires an empirical evaluation that is not based solely on the use of illustrative examples drawn selectively from 'history's junkyard'. The present study seeks to show that even during the interwar years – the period most frequently employed by realists when they are dredging the junkyard for empirical corroboration for their position – there were a number of contexts in which the pursuit of co-operative treaty-making strategies *did* produce a positive payoff by reducing the probability of war occurring between the states involved.

This limited conclusion does not in any sense seek to remove realism from its dominant position in the hearts and minds of contemporary politicians and students of international politics: to do so, in view of the tentative and qualified nature of the reported findings, would be both immodest and ill-advised. What it does suggest, however, is some support for the old familiar theme that realism would not suffer – and indeed might derive enormous benefit – if it were to be tempered with a liberal dose of idealism. Admittedly, the injection of idealism that is being proposed is not the legalistic idealism of 'peace through law' which was prevalent in the early interwar years. It is, rather, a 'reconstructed idealism' which squarely confronts the inadequacies of international law as a direct vehicle for maintaining international peace, but which still recognises that the lawmaking process – treaty-making – can exert a profound indirect influence on the relations between nation-states and thereby make a distinct contribution to the cause of peace.

Chapter 1 is concerned primarily with theoretical matters. It examines the development of traditional 'peace through law' idealism in the early part of this century and the attempts to put its principles into practice in the period after 1918. It then reviews the historical experiences which led to the general rejection of idealism and outlines the realist critique which replaced it. In the final section of the chapter, a number of recent attempts to rehabilitate international law as a force in world politics are examined. The indirect effects of international law cited in these studies, however, are not considered to be as important as the effects of the process of *lawmaking*. It is hypothesised that co-operative treaty-making strategies contribute to peace primarily by increasing the sense of mutual *trust* between the parties involved and that this sense of trust is subsequently critical, first, in any *realpolitik*-motivated transformation of bilateral relations (from, say, enmity to friendship) and, second, as a *realpolitik* resource which can be employed in the event of some later crisis in relations.

Chapter 2 describes the (dyadic) data drawn from the period between the two world wars which are analysed in Chapters 3 and 4. These data involve a specification of the treaty-making record of each pair of nations (dyad) which had contact with one another during the years 1920–42; whether or not each pair went to war in the same period; their patterns of bilateral trade; their prior record of 'friendship 'or 'antagonism'; and a number of contextual variables such as geographical proximity, cultural differences and inequity in power status. Chapter 2 also outlines the data-analytic strategy that is subsequently employed: taking pre-existing patterns of 'friendship' and 'antagonism' explicitly into account, it seeks to establish on a dyad-by-dyad basis how far a greater commitment to the treaty-making process reduces the probability that pairs of nation-states will subsequently go to war with one another.

Chapters 3 and 4 present a set of empirical findings which show that in certain limited contexts in the interwar period – where the pairs of nations concerned were culturally dissimilar, geographically remote from one another or significantly different in power status – there was a clear and consistent tendency for dyads which participated extensively in co-operative treaty-making strategies to be significantly less likely subsequently to engage in warfare than those which did not pursue such strategies. It is also shown, crucially, that this general finding cannot be dismissed as a spurious correlation resulting from the possibility that if dyads already enjoy good relations, then they will be both more likely to engage in treaty-making and more likely subsequently to avoid war.

In Chapter 5, a detailed examination of Anglo-Turkish relations in the interwar period is undertaken. The main purpose of this case-study is to ascertain whether a somewhat different approach to the question as to what constitutes 'appropriate evidence' for evaluating the 'reconstructed idealist hypothesis' yields a similar conclusion to the approach adopted in Chapters 3 and 4. The review of the historical evidence provided does indeed indicate further support for 'reconstructed idealism', the thesis that lawmaking can – through the generation of an increased sense of mutual trust – contribute significantly to the creation and maintenance of international peace.

The immediate conclusion suggested by these diverse empirical findings is that even in the crisis-ridden period of the 1920s and 1930s, when calculations of *realpolitik* predominated in the strategies pursued by nation-states, the process of lawmaking still played a significant role in international affairs. To be sure, the effects of lawmaking only operated in those contexts where the states concerned were different in power status or not geographically close; and these contexts were clearly *not* the most important ones in terms of the broad flow of world events. However, the general conclusion usually derived from the interwar period is that law, treaty-making and co-operation ill served the cause of peace. The realist orthodoxy still maintains, moreover, that such co-operative gestures remain essentially futile – if not actually damaging – and are inevitably doomed to failure. That lawmaking played a limited role in the interwar years, when political crisis was both endemic and ubiquitous, suggests the possibility that even in the admittedly different but equally dangerous conditions of the contemporary international system, co-operative strategies of lawmaking could be employed as a vehicle for increasing international trust. Such strategies could accordingly make a distinct contribution to the maintenance of international peace.

1 The Idealist Tradition and its Modern Variants

Idealism or, to its critics, 'utopianism' – the view that international law can and should be constructively employed to reduce nations' ability and willingness to resort to violence – was a pervasive influence upon international organisation during the decade after 1918. By 1939 – or even earlier on some accounts – the dramatic failures of the 'twenty years' crisis' had led to a drastic revision in the role which law was considered capable of playing in international affairs. The new (or, perhaps, the old) realism of E. H. Carr, Hans Morgenthau, Nicholas Spykeman and Georg Schwarzenberger allowed at best only a minor function for law in the presence of the deep-seated forces of power politics. Indeed, almost half a century later realism remains an important influence upon the descriptions and explanations advanced by both scholars and policy-makers in the field of international politics.

As a preliminary step towards the rehabilitation of international lawmaking as a force worth considering in international politics, this chapter briefly reviews the origins and development of twentieth-century idealism. It then examines the major reasons – both juridical and political – for the inability of idealism, during the period of the League of Nations, to provide a satisfactory system of international organisation. In addition to providing a useful historical backdrop to the empirical analysis which is subsequently undertaken in Chapters 3 and 4, this identification of the limitations of interwar idealism is essential in the development of the argument subsequently advanced which attempts to re-establish the notion that law – and more particularly, lawmaking – can play a significant role in international politics. Specifically, in the final section of this chapter, it is suggested that while international law is clearly incapable of performing the *manifest* function which some interwar optimists ascribed to it, lawmaking – or, more specifically, treaty-making – may nonetheless perform an indirect, *latent* role in the maintenance of international peace.

THE ORIGINS AND DEVELOPMENT OF TWENTIETH-CENTURY IDEALISM

Although modern idealist thought dates from at least the early seventeenth century,[1] the crucial principle of arbitration – the referral of disputes between nation-states to an independent judicial tribunal – was not given formal institutional expression on anything more than an *ad hoc* basis until the establishment of the Hague Court for International Abritration in 1899.[2] Following the juridical principles advocated by the contemporary legal positivist orthodoxy,[3] however, the Hague Court was restricted to dealing only with 'justiciable' or 'non-political' disputes. The reasoning behind this restriction was simple: in order to escape consistent violations of the Court's decisions, since states would almost certainly ignore any judicial ruling which might adversely affect their security, sovereignty or 'vital interests', it was desirable to avoid submitting disputes which affected vital interests to arbitration in the first place.

If the arbitral activities of the Hague Court were to have any meaning, therefore, it was clearly necessary to delineate a class of 'political' disputes that were intrinsically 'nonjusticiable'. Defining 'justiciable', however, proved difficult. One definition – that justiciable issues are those matters which 'concern legal rights' – foundered on the problem as to whether it is the sovereign state or the international judiciary which decides when a dispute concerns legal rights. Another definition – 'enumeration': the advance detailed specification of all contexts in which disputes should be referred to arbitration – failed to resolve the problem as to who determines when a dispute falls into one of the enumerated categories. The definition which the Hague Conventions of both 1899 and 1907 finally adopted was that justiciable disputes were those which both parties were willing to submit to judicial decision. However, since such voluntary arbitration would obviously mean that judicial decisions would only be requested when relatively minor issues were at stake, the Hague arbitration model not surprisingly elicited considerable criticism from a number of idealist protagonists who believed that compulsory arbitration was a prerequisite of an effective international legal order.[4]

Following the First World War, the idealists set about the task of constructing an institutional order capable of promoting the peaceful settlement of international disputes with renewed vigour.[5] The foundation of the new politico-legal order was to be the League of Nations Covenant which in 1920 replaced the Hague Court with the Permanent

Court of International Justice. However, although the Statute of the Court itself provided a more precise enumeration of justiciable disputes than had existed previously, referral of disputes to the Court remained voluntary: 'The Court shall be competent to hear and determine any dispute of an international character *which the parties thereto submit to it*'.[6] Of potentially greater significance, the League also made the well-known provision under Articles X, XI and XVI for 'collective security'. Not only was 'any war or threat of war a matter of concern to the whole League' (Article X), but any 'resort to war in disregard of . . . (the League) . . . Covenant shall . . . be deemed . . . an act of war against all other members of the League' (Article XVI). Of central importance in the creation of this new system of collective security was the role of the League's Council. In addition to the political task of 'mobilising the hue and cry' against transgressors of the Covenant by acting as a vehicle of communication among the Great Powers,[7] the Council was also charged with the quasi-legal responsibility of acting as mediator in the event of any unresolved nonjusticiable dispute affecting members of the League, through a process of enquiry and conciliation.[8] Because most serious disputes were indeed likely to be nonjusticiable ones, the success – or otherwise – of the League was from the outset intimately bound up with that of the Council. It is largely for this reason that the subsequent failures of the Council were widely perceived as indicating the general failure of the League system as a whole.

For the time being, however, collective security was apparently given an added boost by the Locarno Treaties of 1924–5. As Charles Fenwick pointed out, under the Treaty of Mutual Guarantee the signatory nations[9] took it upon themselves to carry out the provisions of the Covenant by establishing a number of bilateral Permanent Conciliation Commissions.[10] The logic behind these commissions was that they helped to fill the gap in the existing machinery for pacific settlement created by the voluntary arbitration provisions of the Permanent Court's terms of reference. While the Permanent Court could handle all (unimportant? nonpolitical?) justiciable disputes, the conciliation commissions could supplement the activities of the Council by providing a more specialised vehicle for dealing with the nonjusticiable ones.

The high point of idealist influence upon international organisation was the General Treaty for the Renunciation of War in August 1928[11] in which the signatories renounced the use of aggressive war as an instrument of national policy.[12] In the same year, the General Act for the Pacific Settlement of International Disputes extended the Locarno conciliation principle to almost the entire state system. Justiciable issues were to be referred for arbitration either to the Permanent Court itself or to some expressly established judicial tribunal. Nonjusticiable issues – questions (presumably affecting state security, sovereignty or vital interests) which either party to a dispute was unwilling to have settled by judicial decision – were to be referred to the appropriately constituted conciliation commission. If any nonjusticiable disputes thus referred remained irresolvable, they were to be sent to the Court for an arbitral decision: they would be redefined as justiciable.[13]

By 1928, in short, the idealists had in principle apparently devised the means of independently adjudicating all manner of international disputes: the justiciable ones were to be resolved by arbitration; the nonjusticiable, by conciliation. They had also, in the form of Articles X, XI and XVI of the Covenant, acquired the potential coercive capability – collective security – to enforce the binding decisions of the independent adjudicators. That the Great War had indeed been a war to end wars seemed a possibility. Serious reservations, however, were already being expressed. As Swanwick noted, at the time of the signature of the Pact of Paris in 1928, 'No-one rejoiced, there were no bells . . . no-one believed that the pact would be kept . . . the cynicism of it was devastating'.[14]

THE LIMITATIONS OF TRADITIONAL IDEALISM

The Juridical Critique

There can be no doubt, in restrospect, that the new apparatus of pacific settlement assembled between 1920 and 1928 was little more than a façade, and in this respect the failure of the League system to maintain world peace was entirely predictable. One set of arguments advanced in order to explain that failure focuses on the contention that the legal machinery of the Covenant, Locarno and the General Act was actually based on *faulty jurisprudence*. In what is still one of the definitive studies of the period, Alfred Zimmern commented on the inability of the Hague/League system to make adequate provision for *treaty revision*, citing the major weakness of contemporary international law as its lack of derivation from a formal and agreed constitutional source. The Covenant, together with its subsequent progeny, was 'a legal system with no constitutional system on which to repose . . . it [could at best] . . . only ensure the observance of law and not its change, still less its growth'.[15]

In an era in which the pressures for revision were immense, this inability adequately to accommodate change was almost an invitation to disaffected powers to resort to the *fait accompli* rather than to use lawful procedures as a means of alleviating their grievances. Both to Germany (forcibly shorn of its Great Power status at Versailles) and to Italy (nominally part of the winning coalition in 1918 but strongly of the opinion that the postwar settlement had cheated it of territories promised three years earlier)[16] the need for urgent and extensive treaty revision was paramount. The revisionist Powers, in addition, found their inability to effect peaceful change particularly galling in view of the widely held suspicion, later articulated by Corbett, that 'the body of international law . . . [was] . . . so vague and debatable that justification . . . [could] . . . be found in it for any award a reasonable . . . [person] . . . would be likely to make'.[17] While it seems unlikely that a more satisfactory capacity for treaty revision on the part of the Hague/League system could ever have prevented either Germany or Italy from pursuing the expansionist path which they subsequently took, the fact that these Powers – and their apologists – could legitimately use the League's inadequate provision for revision as an excuse for their actions was a testament to the poor jurisprudence of the principles upon which the League system was based.

The Locarno system of regional security agreements, a logical extension of the Covenant which was subsequently copied in a number of other security complexes throughout the world, was also heavily criticised as 'bad law'. Perhaps the strongest attack on such 'partial treaties' ('partial' because each treaty was restricted to a limited number of Powers) was delivered by Swanwick who pointed out that any given Locarno-style treaty, if properly constituted, implied that detailed military preparations would have to be made against each possible aggressor:

> [partial treaties] . . . overlook the fact that plans of campaign are not evolved against an imaginary foe. They must be devised against a specific Power or Powers. As these specific Powers become aware of this preparation, they inevitably prepare against it on their side . . . [producing] . . . in effect, a reversion to the old system of alliances under the polite fiction of 'regional agreements in support of the Covenant'.[18]
>
> [T]he guarantee given at Locarno was common to France and Germany: Britain undertook to guarantee Germany as well as

> France. It was impossible for Britain to make detailed military plans with France against Germany, unless she at the same time made detailed plans with Germany against France; which was absurd.[19]

While Swanwick may have exaggerated the extent to which detailed, mutually contradictory, military plans needed to be made under the Locarno agreements, his general point – that Locarno did little or nothing to enhance collective security – must be conceded. As Corbett noted later, the actual provisions of the Locarno guarantees in any case contained a 'get-out' clause which negated their value as a means of achieving collective security: under the terms of the guarantees, a state was only obliged to resist aggression '*to an extent which is compatible with its military situation and . . .* [*which*] *. . . takes its geographical position into account*'.[20] It hardly required an effort of great imagination to arrive at the conclusion that such a qualification rendered the Locarno declaration of mutual commitment almost meaningless from the outset.

On this same theme of the inability of the League System to provide effective collective security, Henig identifies a third sense in which that system failed the test of good jurisprudence. Contrary to Walters' claim that the League failed primarily because the collective security provisions of the Covenant were not properly *applied*,[21] Henig argues that Articles X, XI and XVI never constituted a collective security system in the first place. To suggest that collective security under the Covenant could ever have worked, she contends, attributes powers to the League that it never possessed. Even if sanctions were agreed against a violator of the Covenant, they were only *recommended* to member states by the Council: there was thus

> no provision . . . in the Covenant to deal with a potential aggressor who waited the requisite number of months, read the League's recommendations and then proceeded on his expansionist path . . . [this lack of institutional provision] . . . reflected the British government's view that no machinery in the world would stop an aggressor who really meant business.[22]

Henig's criticism in this context echoes one of the most common themes in all assessments of the failure of the League: its consistent inability either to threaten or to use force in order to support its collective decisions. Despite several French attempts to provide the Council with the coercive capability to enforce its decisions, the League never acquired the political or military resources necessary for this purpose. Leon Bourgeois' plan of 1919 included specific proposals for an international 'police force' which would be employed to 'ensure the execution' of the decisions of the Council. The plan foundered, however, in the face of strong opposition from the British Government which refused to allow coercive powers of such a magnitude to be given to any supranational institution.[23] In a similar vein, War Minister Tardieu's proposals at the 1932 Disarmament Conference for an international police force which – at the behest of the Council – would have at its disposal the weapons discarded in the disarmament process, was met with determined opposition from all of the other Great Powers.[24] From its very inception, therefore, the League was never in a position to resolve hostilities between member states simply because it lacked the physical means to do so: it had no troops of its own and no power to call on members' troops in the event of a Council decision being flouted.[25]

The real problem in this regard was that the Great Power member governments of the League – the French excepted – were unprepared to cede any part of their sovereignty to the League institutions: they insisted that the nation-state should remain the final arbiter in all matters affecting vital interests. This insistence, moreover, was continued even in the General Treaty for the Renunciation of War of 1928. Under the terms of the treaty 'Every nation alone . . . [was] . . . competent to decide whether circumstances require[d] recourse to war in self defence',[26] a situation which created obvious problems of interpretation as to the definition of aggressive war, the very form of unilateral action which was supposedly being renounced.

Perhaps the most powerful juridical critique of the Hague/League system, however, was developed by Hersch Lauterpacht. Though strongly committed to the principle of employing international law as a means of achieving pacific settlement, Lauterpacht was equally firmly convinced that the extant formulations of interwar idealism were wedded too closely to legal positivism – the belief that the express commitments of states are the only source of international law – to be of any real value in the cause of international peace. Contrary to the prevailing positivist orthodoxy, Lauterpacht contended that a direct analogy can and must be drawn between international and municipal systems of law.[27] To Lauterpacht, the prevailing notion that these systems are qualitatively different – with municipal law involving hierachical '*sub*ordinate' relationships, but international law involving '*co*-ordinate' relationships among sovereign states[28] – was erroneous. Rather, both international and municipal law are essentially subordinate systems in the sense that even though a legislature and an executive exist in only embryonic form in the international system, in both international and domestic spheres the judiciary can and has assumed a creative legislative function.

As a matter of juridical principle, Lauterpacht believed that if contemporary international law was to merit being described as a *system* of *law* at all, it must by definition be *complete*. Completeness does not mean, however, that all forms of deviant behaviour or all kinds of dispute are covered in advance by express statute, custom or precedent: even municipal law (and certainly international law) cannot *expressly* provide for all contingencies.[29] Rather, in the domestic context at least, the judiciary can and does 'legislate' – in effect, create new law or modify old law – in the light of changed circumstances by applying generally acknowledged legal principles to novel situations. Completeness in municipal law, therefore, refers to the fact that judges will never pronounce *non liquet*: they will never refuse to give a decision when confronted with a dispute; they will never declare 'we are not competent to resolve this dispute'. Indeed, Lauterpacht contended that the ability and willingness of judges to adjudicate *all* cases 'is an *a priori* assumption of every system of law'.[30]

Since for Lauterpacht there was a strong analogy between international and municipal law, in his view the principle of never declaring *non liquet* needed to be extended to international law: the international judiciary should be empowered to apply 'general principles of law' to disputes between nations; to enact 'judicial legislation'.[31] The creative role which the international judiciary could thus play would in effect counter the criticisms which, as noted earlier, Zimmern was subsequently to make, that contemporary 'international law . . . [was] . . . law without a constitution'.[32]

Lauterpacht's central argument, then, was that interwar idealism had been insufficiently bold in its application of juridical principles to international relations: the possibilities for judicial action had been too heavily circumscribed. In order to achieve a *complete* international legal system, the false justiciable/nonjusticiable distinction which 'recognizes state sovereignty as being above the law' had to be rejected and the international courts empowered to make compulsory arbitral decisions binding upon all parties to any dispute.[33] In Lauterpacht's view, the subsequent disregard for international law during the 1930s could be traced largely to the inadequate capacity for action awarded to the international judiciary under the League Covenant Locarno and the General Act.

Within its own terms of reference – the relative merits of different principles of jurisprudence – Lauterpacht's 'judicial idealist' critique of idealism was a powerful one. What is extraordinary, however, is that he barely mentioned the central problem – referred to above – of both the idealist and the judicial idealist approaches to international law: enforcement. In the absence of some sort of international police force, how was a 'judicially binding' decision to be enforced if the losing party to the dispute failed to comply? Lauterpacht's only refuge in this context was unsubstantiated assertion:

> within the state the peace promoting function of courts is enhanced by the fact that there stands behind that impartial ascertainment of legal right the physical power of the state. In international society the compulsion is less direct; and frequently the only guarantee of the effectiveness of the legal decision is the impersonal authority of the law. *This factor reduces, but does not substantially impair its function as an instrument of peace.*[34]

Lauterpacht appeared to ignore the fact, moreover, that it was precisely the problem of enforcement that had led to the nonjusticiability provision in the first place. The framers of the League Covenant and the General Act had realised that if the 'judicially binding' decisions of the Permanent Court were to be consistently flouted, the law would be debased to the point of irrelevance: they accordingly attempted to limit the scope of law to (justiciable) issues capable of producing decisions that would be binding in the real sense. Lauterpacht, on the other hand, implicitly argued that if the judiciary continually in effect pronounces *non liquet* an even greater debasement of law is to be anticipated.[35] In the absence of any institutional provision for the *compulsory* arbitration of *all* international disputes, of course, Lauterpacht was in the happy position of not having his ideas tested against the harsh realities of international politics, though it is far from clear that the general adoption of his recommendations would have done anything consequential to mitigate the failings of the League system. What is clear, however, is that in addition to the juridical limitations of that system, there were also a number of more expressly *political* weaknesses that were to become increasingly exposed by the events of the 1930s.

The Disconfirming Events

Within three years of the promulgation of the General Act, the weaknesses of the idealists' institutions started to become apparent.

Increasingly during the 1930s the recommendations of arbitration and conciliation commissions were either intrinsically ineffectual or consistently ignored; collective security, the means by which the principles of the League and the General Act were to be enforced, was never seriously attempted.

The first major breach in the idealist edifice was the Japanese invasion of the Chinese province of Manchuria in 1931; according to Walters, a 'turning point in the history of the League and of the World'.[36] As Quincy Wright pointed out, here was a clear violation of international law yet no action under Article XVI of the Covenant was taken in support of China against Japan.[37] Although 'collective security' was a useful principle to which Great Power Statesmen could pay lip-service in order to impress each other and their respective domestic audiences, it was not to be so slavishly adhered to as to prejudice the immediate interests of states not directly affected by Japanese aggression.

The Italy-Abyssinia affair of 1934–6, 'in many respects the most clear cut case of aggression which the League had to face in the interwar period'.[38] served to reinforce all of the realist suspicions which were already gathering strength. The Italians had long harboured imperialist ambitions towards Abyssinia and in December 1934 the Wal Wal oasis in the disputed Ogaden desert was the scene of an armed confrontation between a group of Abyssinian tribesmen and Italian troops supposedly stationed in Italian Somaliland. Angry diplomatic exchanges ensued but, since a 20-year arbitration treaty had conveniently been signed between the protagonists in 1928, an independent arbitration tribunal was established under League supervision and the entire matter promptly referred to the tribunal for judicial decision. The ruling of the tribunal six months later, however, was indecisive: neither Italy nor Abyssinia was deemed to be responsible for the Wal Wal incident (what were the Italians doing in Wal Wal?) and no mention was made of the question of the legal possession of the disputed Ogaden territory. Perceiving this nondecision as an implicit vindication of Abyssinia's position, in October 1935 the Italians invaded Abyssinia in clear violation not only of the General Act but also of an 1896 treaty recognising Abyssinian independence and a 1906 Treaty guaranteeing to preserve that independence. On this occasion, there *was* a collective security response: an ineffectual 50-nation arms embargo against Italy which collapsed within six months. Whatever the reason for the lack of concerted opposition to Italian aggression (one popular explanation was that no-one wanted to push Mussolini into a tighter embrace with Hitler; another was that the Council had simply become too big to be an effective decision-making body[39]) the entire affair served to undermine further the belief that effective mechanisms of pacific international settlement could be developed in the face of determined expansionism on the part of a handful of aggressive powers. In particular,

> the credibility of the League as a coercive organisation was completely destroyed and even more importantly, the will of its members to work together was greatly weakened . . . After this successful coup it was a case of each nation protecting its own interests as best it could.[40]

The Chaco territorial dispute between Bolivia and Paraguay exemplified another major weakness of interwar efforts at pacific settlement: in the absence of effective means of enforcement, states simply ignored arbitral or conciliatory rulings which contradicted their immediate interests. In December 1933, following two years of extensive border warfare between the two countries,[41] the dispute was referred to the League for arbitration. In November 1934 the specially constituted arbitration commission ruled against Paraguay's claims to the disputed territory; three months later Paraguay withdrew from the League and the border war resumed. In March 1935 both Bolivia and Paraguay accepted an Argentine-Chilean peace formula and in January 1936 a neutral conciliation commission was accordingly established. In April 1938 the commission reported in favour of Paraguay; Bolivia promptly rejected its recommendations and warfare resumed. Without adequate means of enforcement, both arbitration and conciliation had failed to sustain peace.

The decline of idealism was further hastened by Hitler's expansionist strategems of the late 1930s. Germany's remilitarisation of the Rhineland in 1936 clearly violated the provisions of the Treaty of Versailles, but as with the Manchurian and Abyssinian episodes there was no resort to a collective enforcement of demilitarisation. Neither was any use made of the Locarno Permanent Conciliation Commission which had been expressly designed to resolve any political differences that might subsequently arise between the signatories. Moreover, as the full extent of Hitler's plans for Europe became apparent, the irrelevance of the Locarno agreements became increasingly pronounced. It was more than a little ironic, in view of the list of countries which were to suffer Nazi aggression after 1938, that at Locarno Germany had established conciliation machinery with Czechoslovakia, Poland, France, Belgium and Britain. Indeed, the irony would have been complete had Norway, Denmark and the Netherlands participated in the Locarno process. In any event, the 1930s appeared to have witnessed the comprehensive failure of law in its efforts to preserve peace. Arbitration, conciliation and collective security had failed conspicuously in the relations between a Great Power and a small Power (Italy-Abyssinia, Germany-Czechoslovakia); they had failed in the relations between two small Powers (Bolivia-Paraguay); and they had failed in the relations between two or more Great Powers (Germany-France, Germany-Britain). The stage was set for the revival of a more cynical realism.

The Realist Critique

The developments of the 1930s and of the immediate postwar era gave much credence to the realist revision: the view that international relations above all else need to recognise the imperatives of power politics rapidly became the new orthodoxy. A central element in the realist critique was that any legal order – municipal or international – is a reflection of the prevailing power configuration in which the law itself is invariably employed to rationalise and protect the *status quo*.[42] Indeed, for the realists, the global 'harmony of interest', which in the idealists' view made the 'peace through law' approach possible, was in reality the sectional interest of the dominant *status quo* powers.

The realists also believed that idealism should never have attempted to develop the analogy between domestic and international systems of law. In the first place, the international community has no effective executive, no real legislature and no coercive capability to enforce judicial decisions. Since these are prerequisites of an effective system of law, the idea that law can conceivably perform the same function internationally as it does domestically is untenable.[43] As Corbett points out,

> It is a matter of common observation that no institutions yet developed on the international plane have been able to perform the ordering and pacifying functions of the legal system in the national domain . . . the lawyer's craft can never supply the wanting social and political basis for an effective legal system . . . [the most serious limitation of international law is the lack of] . . . agreement on supreme common values, the sense of community, loyalty and mutual tolerance which within the state make compulsory institutions bearable.[44]

A second reason for rejecting the analogy between municipal and international law was expressed by Morgenthau. In his opinion the idealists misread the experience of domestic European politics in the eighteenth and nineteenth centuries. They observed a correlation between the codification of municipal law and the growth of domestic political stability and proceeded to infer (for Morgenthau, incorrectly) the existence of a causal relationship between the two: law had produced order domestically; why not reproduce the process at the international level? Morgenthau argued that if the correlation did describe a causal relationship at all, it was probably in the reverse direction. Indeed, in his view, order developed prior to and largely independently of law.[45] Law was simply required after a stable political order had been achieved to regularise and formalise the established pattern of power relations. Because the same factors which made for domestic stability were not present in the international system, Morgenthau concluded that law was virtually useless as a means of achieving pacific settlement. While it might occasionally resolve trivial differences between nations, it would invariably break down when confronted with a serious conflict of interest. In conditions of continuing crisis such as those which obtained throughout the mid- and late 1930s, the appeal to legality could only ever serve as an *ex post* justification for decisions already taken on the basis of security calculations.

It is worth noting parenthetically that Morgenthau's conclusions in this regard are strongly supported by more recent empirical analyses of crisis decision-making. One of the few studies which explicitly seeks to identify the extent to which considerations of legality played either a direct or an indirect role in the course of a number of prominent postwar international crises, is the collection of essays by Scheinman and Wilkinson.[46] With the (perhaps predictable) exception of the contribution by Richard Falk, each of the constituent papers strongly confirms Morgenthau's conclusion that in any major international crisis, where the protection of the nation-state's long-term security interest is paramount, the requirements of *realpolitik* are so strong as to render the question of legal rights and obligations virtually irrelevant both at the decision stage of the crisis and in terms of how the crisis is resolved.

Scheinman, for example, in his discussion of the 1948 Berlin crisis concludes that during the affair, 'law became principally a tactical device for manoeuvring through the crisis[47] . . . [it] . . . serve [d] . . . more as a justification than as a determinant'.[48] Similarly Friedman and Collins, in their examination of the 1956 Suez Crisis, provide almost a classical statement of the realist view of the irrelevance of law in crisis decision-making:

> the convergence of interest . . . [of the two superpowers] . . . rather than the strength of the international legal order account[s] for the final outcome of the Suez episode . . . The acid test of the precedence of international legal norms comes when fundamental interests risk being undermined by adherence to such norms . . . [The Soviet and American responses to the Suez crisis represented nothing more than] . . . the calculation of cost, risk and interest couched in the language of the law . . . International law is, in times of crisis, still not the controlling factor in the use of force . . . the USSR and USA got away with their unilateral actions (unlike Britain, France and Israel) because their power could not be effectively challenged'.[49]

The final element in the realist critique was that the idealists never specified how in practice – in the absence of a permanent international 'police' force – international law could possibly help to secure international peace. E. H. Carr's well-known characterisation of this problem bears repetition. The idealists' 'explanation' of the impact of law on international order, he suggests, is analogous to the man who at the time of the Great Lisbon Earthquake of 1775 went about selling anti-earthquake pills. When challenged: 'What good will they do?' the salesman responded: 'Who can tell, but what else would you do?'[50] In effect, Carr contends, the idealists argued: 'We must try using law to achieve world peace even though we don't know how or why it might work'.[51]

Regardless of the reservations one might have about Carr's method of attack upon idealism, his central criticism has to be accepted. The idealists never addressed the central problem inherent in their position: the question as to what specific mechanisms of compellance or of self-discipline might induce sovereign states to abide by unfavourable judicial or supranational decisions. Indeed, partly for this very reason, insofar as there is any longer a debate between the idealist and realist positions, realism clearly dominates. It is generally regarded as a utopian fantasy to suppose that states would be prepared permanently to cede any significant part of their sovereignty either to an international judiciary or to a supranational council. It is similarly recognised that international law is most unlikely to acquire the independent coercive capability necessary to enforce judicial or supranational political decisions.

RECONSTRUCTING IDEALISM

The main point that any defence of idealism must immediately concede to the realist position is that experience does indeed demonstrate that international law cannot now or in the foreseeable future perform the *manifest* function for the international community which the interwar idealists claimed for it. The international judiciary cannot make binding decisions in major disputes between nations and back their decisions with coercive force. When vital interests are at stake nation-states do not determine their foreign policy strategies on the basis of what is deemed to be legally correct. There is, in short, no *direct* connection between international law and international peace.[52] The defence of idealism which is proposed here, therefore, is really a 'reconstruction' of idealism based upon the *latent* functions which law can perform. It centres upon the *indirect* effects which law might have in the creation and maintenance of international peace.[53]

In many respects there is nothing new in the suggestion that law plays a positive but indirect role in international relations. The point has been well made on several occasions that in contrast to the position in municipal law, a relatively small number of violations of international law tend to be viewed (somewhat unreasonably) by its critics as evidence that international law is unworkable.[54] Defenders of the role of law also point to the fact that most states most of the time abide by the generally understood rules of international law,[55] a tendency which Higgins attributes to the simple mechanism of reciprocity.[56] The protagonists of international law, however, are frequently less articulate in their specification of the *way* in which law contributes to international order or peace. Indeed, modern advocates of the efficacy of international law – though they do attempt to answer Carr's charge that idealism failed to specify *how* law could contribute to peace – do not go far beyond the interwar idealists either in identifying specific mechanisms through which law promotes order or in providing clear supporting evidence that law does indeed have a positive role to play in the maintenance of peace.

Richard Falk, for example, identifies at least four general mechanisms through which law might indirectly reduce the chances of violent international conflict occurring. First, '[nations] . . . avoid a clear violation of law so as to discourage . . . [world] . . . community responses in favour of the victim'.[57] Second, law provides national actors with 'a regular and highly articulated procedure . . . [which] . . . if they wish it can moderate conflict before it generates devastation'.[58] Third, law supplies 'Standards to help with the determination of whether a particular claim is reasonable. This serves to civilise the process of conflict by revealing a concern with community approval'.[59]

Finally, after reviewing the conflict between Indonesia and Malaysia in the 1960s, in which both sides consistently issued mutually agreed statements summarising their previous efforts at settlement, Falk suggests that

> [D]epartures from these agreed statements were later perceived as 'violations' by the aggrieved party . . . [This injected a 'law element' into the situation without which] . . . the encounter would more easily . . . [have] . . . degenerate[d] into unmitigated conflict resolvable only by the clash of wills and arms; *with this law element there is a braking mechanism that allows the disputing parties a certain flexibility to accelerate, decelerate, or even halt the conflict.*[60]

For Hedley Bull, law contributes to international order principally by 'stating the basic rules of coexistence . . . [and by] . . . mobilising the other factors making for compliance . . . [to widely accepted norms]';[61] while for Corbett, international law – especially arbitration – can encourage peaceful conflict resolution by serving 'as a means of enabling one side to surrender without a politically costly loss of face'.[62]

In the light of his study of the Berlin crisis cited earlier, Scheinman, though extremely sceptical about the overall utility of law in international politics, finally concedes that international law can play a limited but perceptible role in the sense that even when there is a serious conflict of interests, 'legal contentions serve as a means to probe the other side's commitment (a substitute for force) and *by obscuring the underlying political confrontation in the jargon of the law, they blanket the volatility which characterises* . . . [a crisis] . . . *situation*'.[63]

Two additional mechanisms have been hypothesised by international lawyers to provide indirect links between international law and international peace. Their contentions are predicated on the assumption that if a pair of nations have developed an extensive network of mutual treaty rights and obligations, this legal framework may permit the resolution of a series of relatively minor legal or quasi-political disputes (perhaps at the boundary of the justiciable and the nonjusticiable) which divide the countries. A series of such resolutions may reduce the probability of a later violent confrontation between the countries in two ways. First, as Louis Renault suggested at the second Hague conference, the resolution of a series of minor disputes through the legal process may create a 'habit of compliance', thus increasing the chances at some later date of securing compliance with judicial decisions that are concerned with more serious matters.[64] Second, the resolution of minor matters by legal means may serve to pre-empt or defuse more serious disputes before they emerge as a 'serious clash of interest'. In the opinion of Manley O. Hudson, a limited amount of empirical support for this latter proposition could be derived from the experience of the Permanent Court:

> The judgements and opinions given by the Court . . . [some 32 Judgements and 27 Advisory Opinions were laid down between 1920 and 1942] . . . led to the settlement of a large number of disputes. None of them was flouted; in no case was challenge offered to the Court's authority. No-one can say that any of the disputes might otherwise have led to armed conflict, yet some . . . might have proved disturbing if they had been permitted to simmer.[65]

While all of the mechanisms identified above seem moderately plausible, it has to be admitted that none of them makes a particularly compelling case for a clear linkage – however indirect – between international law and international peace. Moreover, in view of the observations about crisis decision-making already made, it could be argued that in the context of crises – perhaps the most important situations in international politics – it is extremely unlikely that *any* of the mechanisms would work. Indeed, given (1) this relative lack of conviction inherent in the mechanisms cited, (2) the general absence of firm empirical evidence showing that the mechanisms operate to any significant degree, and (3) the appeal of the alternative realist interpretation, the chances of constructing a convincing argument – in which international law could reasonably be hypothesised to contribute significantly to peaceful relations between states – appear very slim indeed.

The essence of the 'reconstructed idealism' that I would wish to defend, however, does not focus on the *static* aspects of international law which are emphasised in the mechanisms cited above. These mechanisms are characterised here as being concerned with international law in a static sense because the operation of each of them presumes that, at any given point in time, international law provides a fixed body of rules that nation-states – for whatever reason – can invoke or follow as and when they see fit. In the case of each mechanism, it is the invoking or following of a specific rule or set of rules derived from the (at any specific time, fixed) general body of international law that is hypothesised to contribute to peaceful international relations.[66]

What matters more to 'reconstructed idealism', however, is the *dynamic* aspect of international law, the process of lawmaking itself. This perspective on the indirect effects of law, which derives partly from the work of Schelling and of Bilder,[67] is based on the assumption that the process of international lawmaking, for reasons specified below, slowly encourages the development of a greater sense of trust between or among the parties involved. The emphasis on the process of lawmaking, moreover, shifts the focus of analysis away from the decisions of the international judiciary and the activities of would-be supranational bodies such as the League Council. It similarly shifts attention away from the question as to whether there is increasing or decreasing adherence to particular international legal norms or conventions, and away from the possible effects of the overall growth in the acknowledged body of international law. Rather, an emphasis on the process of lawmaking assumes that the international legal system as a whole matters less than the extent to which pairs or groups of nation-states actually engage in the lawmaking, or treaty-making process.

The broad hypothesis which represents the theoretical core of 'reconstructed idealism' can accordingly be stated as follows: the more that nations participate with one another in the treaty-making process over time, the more likely they are, *ceteris paribus*, gradually to develop a sense of mutual trust in each other's intentions and ambitions; and consequently the less likely they are subsequently to engage in violent conflict with one another. The value of the treaty-making process in the context of this hypothesis derives from the possibility that the increased communication (even of markedly different positions), negotiation, compromise and (admittedly sometimes ambiguous) agreement which lawmaking necessarily entails all contribute towards breaking down the mistrust and sense of Hobbesian fear that frequently divide nations and which can lead directly to violent conflict between them. Even if the language of a treaty agreement is equivocal – making use of a deliberate ambiguity to permit different interpretations of the agreement for the benefit of different domestic audiences – the lawmaking process is still capable of assisting in the long-term build-up of trust, if only because the parties involved have developed enough of a rapport to agree to disagree. There is, of course, no *guarantee* that even the construction of an extensive network of mutual rights and obligations between a pair of nations will necessarily do anything at all to foster mutual trust and good relations between them. Nonetheless, in the sense that numerous diplomatic exchanges and *compromises* must have preceded the signing of each of the treaties which comprise that network, the extensive use of the treaty-making process undoubtedly increases the chances that a higher level of inter-nation trust will be achieved.

The idea that recourse to treaty-making can over time help to promote trust between nations and that trust can in turn make a positive contribution to peaceful bilateral relations, therefore, does not describe anything more than a probabilistic tendency. It was perhaps no accident, however, that Israel – the state most justifiably plagued by a sense of Hobbesian fear in the contemporary international system – made the assumption that precisely this kind of mechanism had some chance of success in its 1979 peace treaty with Egypt. As Mr Abba Eban observed in his explanation of why, in 1976, the Israeli government decided to participate in the 'peace process', 'When you descend to earth from an exceptionally tall ladder, it is often prudent to use the intervening rungs, rather than to seek posthumous glory by a single leap'.[68] This is perhaps the most important of the indirect functions that international lawmaking (even equivocal lawmaking) can perform: the provision of rungs on the ladder; a tentative step in the direction of reducing mistrust which might lead later to a more solid foundation for a lasting peace.

However, even if participation in the lawmaking process does lead to a build-up of trust between the parties involved, how can that greater degree of trust serve to promote the cause of peace? It seems likely, for example, that if a serious security crisis subsequently develops – affecting either of the parties which have previously enjoyed, as a result of their treaty-making activities, a build-up of mutual trust – considerations of *realpolitik* will rapidly assume a position of pre-eminence in the decision calculus of the states involved. In these circumstances, it might well be concluded that the previous build-up of trust would be unlikely to exert any real influence either on the strategies adopted during the crisis or on its eventual outcome: trust, it might be argued, would have no more effect than considerations of legal rectitude; that is, virtually none at all.

While the paramountcy of *realpolitik* motivations in conditions of international crisis cannot be denied, the view that the effects of trust are negligible in such conditions seriously underestimates the role that the gradual development of mutual trust can play in international politics. In order to appreciate the extent of this role it is necessary to recognise the very obvious fact that the relations between nation-states change radically over time: at the extremes, a former enemy can in some new situation be transformed into an ally; a former friend into a dangerous potential aggressor. It is indisputable that the forces of *realpolitik* – the result of the unending search for material advantage and security in a changing and threatening environment – are crucial in these transformations; especially, and obviously, in the transformation of a former ally into an actual or potential enemy. It is somewhat less clear, however, how enemies become transformed into friends. To be sure, *realpolitik* is inevitably at the root of such a change, but in practice the establishment of unequivocally friendly relations between nation-states – whether in the form of some sort of tacit mutual commitment or of a formal alliance – always requires a prior build-up of mutual trust and understanding. Whatever the role of the treaty-making process in this build-up might be, the build-up itself is essential: without it, friendship cannot exist; mutual suspicion and mistrust will continue even in the face of an apparent convergence of material and security interests. The fact that two nations have a community of security interest is useless if neither can trust the other to pursue strategies which will maximise that community of interest. It is only as a reservoir of trust is developed that a genuine transformation in relations can occur.

Once bilateral relations have been transformed, moreover, the reserve of trust previously assembled can itself become, in the event of a later crisis, an important element in the *realpolitik* calculations that are subsequently made. Consider, for example, a nation-state (A) which is imminently threatened by external aggression. The confidence – born out of an increased sense of mutual trust – that a former antagonist (B) will not align itself with the source of the current aggression in this situation, will inevitably serve, *ceteris paribus*, to increase A's ability to resist any threats or blandishments which the new aggressor might make. This ability to resist, moreover, may in turn reduce the chances that the new aggressor will resort to overt violence. In contrast, without that confidence born out of trust, even though the *realpolitik* logic of the security situation might point to a community of interest between A and B, A's greater uncertainty as to the stance B will adopt in the event of actual aggression necessarily proscribes the range of strategy options from which A must choose in order to determine its response to the external threat. Trust in the relatively benign intentions and objectives of a former enemy, in short, can be a vital ingredient in determining the range of *realpolitik* strategy options which nation-states have at their disposal in crisis situations.

The importance of the process of lawmaking, then, is that it provides a means of effecting a genuine transformation in the relations between nation-states. With some notable exceptions – most obviously, armistices and similar treaties which seek to establish a new postwar settlement – nation-states are rarely coerced into treaty-making. On the contrary, lawmaking is a voluntary act of considerable symbolic importance. It signifies that the parties involved have to some degree decided, at least for the time being, to opt for a co-operative approach to the issues which divide them. Moreover what has been suggested here is that the pursuit of co-operation thus engendered can have a real payoff in terms of the positive effect which it has on the probability of subsequent peaceful relations between the states concerned. That this positive effect will not always – or even, perhaps, in the majority of cases – occur, does not mean that co-operative strategies are not worth trying. Indeed, quite the reverse implication is intended: following Abba Eban's logic, they *are* worth trying, even though they might not always be effective.

To confirmed realists, this interpretation may seem outrageous: where is the *evidence*, one can hear them ask, that any of these 'mechanisms' or 'processes' actually operate? In the firm belief that some such evidence is essential if the 'reconstructed idealist' hypothesis is to be sustained, the ensuing chapters attempt to show empirically that even in the interwar years – the period in recent history most closely associated both with the failure of idealism and the attendant rise of realism – there were still a number of specifiable contexts in which the pursuit of co-operative treaty-making strategies did play a significant role in the transformation of relations between states: in these contexts it is not unreasonable to conclude that lawmaking did contribute to the cause of international peace.

SUMMARY AND CONCLUSIONS

It is hardly a matter of contention to suggest that the international idealism of the early interwar years was excessively optimistic – and even simplistic – in its single-minded belief that a lasting peace could be secured if only the correct politico-legal framework of pacific settlement could be constructed. The events of the 1930s – most notably the acts of outright aggression perpetrated by the Axis Powers – proved beyond reasonable doubt that international peace could never be achieved by a combination (however inventive) of judicial decision, arbitration and conciliation unsupported by coercive force.

It was not surprising, therefore, that in the late 1930s a hard-headed realism, derived partly from an understanding of nineteenth-century balance of power politics,[69] should reassert itself and form the new orthodoxy in the analysis of international relations. The failure of the idealist experiment served simply to reinforce the view that international law was clearly incapable of performing the manifest function for the international community which its over-optimistic protagonists had ascribed to it. Moreover the widespread perception arose, which correctly remains with us today, that in the foreseeable future peace is most assuredly never going to be achieved through the 'legally binding' decisions of international courts or arbitration tribunals, or by the recommendations of conciliation commissions.

The interwar idealists' main error, in essence, was to overemphasise the formal, the direct, the manifest (one might even venture, the 'legal') role that law could play in the international community. Indeed it could be argued that had they concentrated more on the informal, the indirect, the latent, the 'political' effects of international law, they might have been more assertive (even when confronted with the alarming events of the 1930s) in their defence of the utility of law as a long-term instrument for achieving peace.

This theme has in fact been expressly pursued by a number of recent scholars who suggest that if too much is not expected of it, international law can still perform a limited, indirect role in international politics. However, in the context of the indirect effects which international law might have on the chances for peace, not only do these writers fail to provide any systematic empirical evidence showing that law does indeed contribute, however indirectly, to peace, but they also supply theoretical arguments (or 'mechanisms') which seem unlikely to be of great relevance in the event of a crisis occurring in the relations between nation-states.

These attempts to rehabilitate international law as a force in international politics, moreover, though they correctly emphasise the latent rather than the manifest functions of law, still base their analysis on mechanisms which concentrate primarily on the static aspects of international law. This perspective, it has been suggested here, fails to recognise that the crucial latent contribution which international law can make towards peace is in terms of the effects of the law*making* process itself. What has been described as 'reconstructed idealism' accordingly contends that participation in treaty-making – in lawmaking – has the distinctive effect of increasing the sense of mutual trust between the parties involved. It also contends that this increased trust constitutes a valuable resource which can be drawn upon in any subsequent crisis which might arise, thereby potentially shifting the balance of *realpolitik* calculation towards a more peaceful crisis outcome.

The critic of this argument, of course, could immediately point out that the wild overoptimism of 'reconstructed idealism' thus displayed, with its faith in the value of 'trust', is matched only by the overoptimism of interwar idealism, with *its* faith in the capabilities of the formal legal process. In an attempt to pre-empt this criticism, the remainder of this study provides empirical evidence which shows that the optimism of reconstructed idealism is not entirely without foundation. The formal data analysis presented in Chapters 3 and 4 indicates that there were indeed a number of identifiable contexts in the interwar period where lawmaking, though not necessarily the major influence (how could it be given the ubiquity of *realpolitik*?), certainly appears to have been a critical factor in the maintenance of peace. In Chapter 5, a detailed study of interwar relations between Britain and Turkey is undertaken. This case-study provides evidence strongly consistent with the notion that the build-up of trust, which arose out of the mutual treaty-making activities of the two countries in the mid-1920s, was crucial in determining the subsequent course of Anglo-Turkish relations throughout the period, and in particular in sustaining peace between them in the difficult years after 1936. Though the evidence which is reported by no means furnishes conclusive proof of the validity of 'reconstructed idealism' as a theoretical postulate, it certainly suggests the need for realism to make some sort of concession to the idea that co-operative treaty-making strategies in international politics can make a positive contribution to international peace.

2 Background to the Empirical Analysis: The Data and the Data Analysis Strategy

In Chapter 1 an attempt was made to identify a number of mechanisms through which international law and lawmaking might contribute to the maintenance of international peace. Chapters 3 and 4 offer an empirical analysis of the latent role of the treaty-making process during the interwar period. In this chapter, the rationale underlying the data analysis strategy is discussed and the data employed in the investigation are described.

THE DATA ANALYSIS STRATEGY

The choice of the interwar period as the empirical referent for testing assertions about the positive role of lawmaking and co-operation in international politics is by no means accidental. As has already been intimated, the interwar period is regarded by many commentators as providing the most vivid demonstration of the irrelevance of international law to the world of *realpolitik*; a perfect illustration of false expectations about the capabilities of a thoroughly imperfect instrument being deflated by harsh realities. The interwar period on this account was where international law met its greatest failure both in terms of the dismal record of the many broken bilateral treaties and in terms of the inability of the legal and political apparatus erected under the auspices of the League of Nations to resolve effectively any of the major conflicts which developed in the years after 1918. Since this realist view holds powerful sway in contemporary academic and political circles, it is essential that any attempt to defend a reconstructed, more 'realistic' version of idealism must begin on this, the most difficult terrain; for if it can be shown that even in the circumstances of the 1930s, law in fact played a limited but positive role in the maintenance of peace, then the case for its possible contemporary relevance is considerably strengthened.

A second reason for choosing the interwar period is that the years 1920–42 represent, in the lexicon of quantitative international politics, a discrete 'historical subsystem'. A considerable amount of empirical research in the last 20 years or so has attempted to test generalisations about international relations by partitioning historical time into a number of different segments according to the dominant structural characteristics of the state-system. On most accounts, the interwar years constitute one of these subsystems[1] and, for the purposes of empirical investigation, an exclusive focus on this period accordingly (and desirably) holds constant a number of systemic factors, as 'polarity', 'level of military technology', 'capability distribution' or 'the extent to which there is a normative consensus among international statesmen', any of which might otherwise perturb the conclusions arrived at by statistical analysis.

Even if there are good reasons for focusing upon the interwar period, however, it is less clear how it could ever be demonstrated that international lawmaking has some sort of reductive effect on the propensity of nations to wage war on one another. This problem is best confronted initially by posing what superficially appears to be rather a familiar question (with an equally familiar answer): on what basis has it generally been concluded that international law failed to affect the prospects for peace in the 1920s and 1930s?

The general strategy followed by orthodox historians and mainstream students of international politics has been to select the high profile, 'significant', most 'visible' events of the interwar period and then to assess the possible manifest and latent consequences of the international legal commitments of the participant nation-state actors. In terms of the potential *manifest* effect of law, the research task has been relatively simple: in the event of a (serious) conflict of interest between two or more nation states, did the relevant parties refer the dispute to law and accept the judgement of the appropriate legal tribunal? In contrast to the implications of one recent quantitative study,[2] the verdict of history is clear and uncontentious. As indicated in Chapter 1, in relation to the 'great events' of the interwar period, law transparently failed to perform its major intended manifest function of legislating peace.

An analysis of the 'high profile' events, however, does not need to limit itself to an investigation of superficial legal formalities. It is also possible to ascertain whether law had any *latent* 'political' effect on nation-state behaviour in any given conflict by engaging in a detailed documentary analysis of the motives and justifications for action that were employed by prominent key decision-makers: did questions of legal rectitude appear to constrain decision-makers in their choice of strategy when they were confronted with situations which threatened either the general or the vital interests of the state? Again, the position of the orthodoxy on this issue, derived from a large number of historical and contemporary case studies, is clear: crisis decision-making invariably subordinates legal niceties to the realities of power politics; legal commitments are discarded if there is any danger that they might constrain decision-makers' ability to maximise the security prospects of the states which they represent.

While it is reasonable to conclude that in the context of the 'high profile' events of the 1930s law failed to play a significant manifest or latent role in sustaining peace, if a somewhat broader view is taken – incorporating both 'high' and 'low' profile events – then a rather different conclusion emerges. This does not mean that I wish to revise the orthodox view of the (irrelevant) role of law in the most prominent world events of the interwar years; neither do I want to deny that a selection of empirical materials always has to be made when a particular substantive theoretical problem is being confronted. Rather, I would suggest that in focusing largely on the most visible, high profile conflicts, existing empirical analyses – both quantitative and, especially, qualitative – have distorted our picture of the role that law and the lawmaking process may have played in less prominent contexts. After all, the increased interest in the possibilities of international law in the 1920s and 1930s was not confined to the small group of Great Powers and their immediate allies. In a sense it is odd that on the basis of a limited number of well-publicised failures, it should be concluded that the failure of international law was all-pervading. Indeed, in order to arrive at a balanced assessment of the role of international lawmaking in the interwar period, it is necessary to examine the maximum range and number of conflicts – both potential and actual – that are permitted by the available empirical evidence if a distorted conclusion about the role of law is to be avoided. It is precisely this sort of comprehensive analysis which is undertaken in the ensuing chapters.

The reasoning behind the analysis is based upon a simple, if not platitudinous, observation: although there was a dramatic increase in the number of bilateral and multilateral treaty commitments throughout the entire nation-state system in the period after the Great War, these new commitments and obligations – and the extent of diplomatic negotiation that preceded and accompanied each of them – were not distributed evenly. Quite simply, some pairs of nations, or *dyads*, were much more enthusiastic in their attempt to construct a framework of legal regulation and understanding in their mutual bilateral dealings than others; some dyads attempted to formalise their mutual relations across a wide range of military, political and economic areas of contact while others restricted their new-found mutual legal obligations to a relatively narrow range of activities and interactions.

It is contended here that the full variety of the different legal commitments which nation-states entered into in the interwar period must be recognised and taken into account in any assessment of the legal and extra-legal – the political – role of international law. Specifically, an attempt is made, *inter alia*, to relate the *different lawmaking experiences* of nation-state dyads to their chances of engaging in overt warfare with one another. In order to proceed with this endeavour, it is assumed that the content of any specific treaty commitment or the fact that its provisions were observed or disregarded are less important than the fact that a treaty commitment was made. This assumption is made not only because of the difficulties of obtaining an 'objective' assessment as to whether a particular treaty provision was adhered to or not, but also because, given the kind of arguments presented in Chapter 1, it is the process of negotiation and compromise that is involved in lawmaking which most probably furnishes the link between law and international peace. The signing of any treaty, therefore, acts as a surrogate indicator for the process of diplomatic negotiation which precedes it and which makes that signing possible. Under this assumption – and this is a theme which is returned to later – the underlying logic of the data analysis strategy which is pursued throughout this study is as follows. If idealist mechanisms of the sort identified in Chapter 1 do operate – if law and lawmaking over the long term do serve indirectly to reduce the probability of violent confrontation between nations – then, regardless of the content of any specific treaty commitments, pairs of nations which jointly sign a relatively large number of treaties – and especially those which pursue a diplomatic discourse across a number of different areas of contact – should be less likely *ceteris paribus* to engage in violent confrontation than pairs which sign relatively few treaties or none at all.

All of this means that in operational terms the empirical analysis undertaken here is based on the dyad or pair of nations: since pairs of nations vary considerably in their treaty-making experiences, an analysis of the possible linkages between lawmaking and war-avoidance necessarily requires a dyadic approach which explicitly allows for such variations. Indeed, all pairs of nations which had some form of political contact – that is, which either entered into at least one mutual treaty commitment (excluding the General Act of 1928) and/or went to war with one another – in the period 1920–42 are included in the analysis.[3]

The need to assess the bilateral lawmaking experiences of nation-states, however, is not the only reason for pursuing a dyadic approach to the problem as to how far law might play a role in international politics. A second reason for taking a dyadic perspective is that the main alternative research strategy – to focus on the international *system* itself – is subject to significant limitations. Systemic analyses, as their name suggests, generally involve regarding nation-state behaviour as the broad consequence of international system level characteristics and/or processes. In quantitative terms this typically means that the researcher is interested (1) in knowing how much 'war' or 'violence' (or whatever the dependent variable is) there is in the system during some given time period, and (2) in identifying the (presumably corresponding) characteristics of the international system in the same or some earlier time period which might 'explain' variations in the systemic level of war or violence.[4]

While a systemic approach frequently makes good sense in theoretical terms – as Waltz has persuasively argued, a thorough-going understanding of the role of international system structure is essential if the behaviour of nation-states is to be comprehensively explained[5] – the problem with quantitative systemic analysis is that it fails to take account of which particular nation-states are actually responsible for the occurrence of a high level of systemic violence or war at a given time; facts that may well be crucial if the theoretical problem at hand is to be properly understood.

The nature of this limitation of the systemic approach is well illustrated in study undertaken by Gregory A. Raymond into the relationship between (1) efforts at international arbitration and (2) the level of war in the international system as a whole.[6] Raymond's analysis covers the period 1820 to 1964. Using data grouped into five-year time aggregates, he attempts to show that, in general, periods in which international arbitration is widely used tend to be followed by periods in which the amount of violent conflict in the international system is relatively low. On the basis of a set of theoretical arguments which link these two empirical tendencies together, Raymond concludes that *ceteris paribus* arbitration would appear to be a useful, though by no means invariably successful, vehicle for avoiding violent conflict.

Contrary to the formal theoretical position adopted by its advocates, however, the reasoning behind such systems analysis is frequently couched primarily in terms of what might plausibly be expected to happen in *bilateral* state relations. In the context of Raymond's analysis, for example, it seems reasonable to suppose that if two countries resolve a number of their mutual differences by arbitration then this might ease tensions and in turn serve to reduce the chances of violent conflict between them. Empirical analysis at the systemic level, however, which by definition treats the system itself as the unit of analysis and which accordingly attempts to measure fluctuations in system characteristics over time in order that these characteristics can be correlated, is incapable of properly testing such reasoning. If countries A and B engage in extensive arbitration and subsequently avoid war, it is easy to see why a researcher might want to argue that arbitration contributed to the maintenance of peace. It is less easy to see why, if countries A and B consistently employ arbitral settlement yet still subsequently find themselves at war with one another, anyone would want to argue that the avoidance of war by countries C, D and E is the result of the arbitral activities of A and B; yet with system-level correlations this latter kind of argument may implicitly be adopted. Because system-level correlations do not reveal who does what to or with whom, researchers who use them consistently have to assume, if their findings are to make sense, that a system-level correlation between, say, arbitration and avoidance of war results from a tendency for dyads which consistently arbitrate to avoid war. Unfortunately, as will be demonstrated below, this assumption is frequently not warranted: in the interwar period in particular, many of the dyads which most frequently engaged in mutual arbitration procedures subsequently experienced open warfare with one another. This not only contradicts Raymond's conclusions about the general relationship between arbitration and conflict avoidance but also illustrates the value of pursuing a dyadic as opposed to a systemic research strategy in any examination of the relationship between international law and peace: dyadic analysis by definition takes account of the specific pattern of bilateral relations which must necessarily be examined if the political impact of the complex pattern of international lawmaking is to be properly assessed.[7]

THE DATA: OPERATIONAL MEASURES AND THEIR RATIONALE

The data employed in this study fall into four broad categories: (1) the dependent variable, international peace/war; (2) politico-legal variables such as treaty commitments, Permanent Court rulings and arbitration referrals; (3) economic variables, which are primarily bilateral trade data for the 1920s and 1930s; and (4) a series of contextual variables which common sense suggests might have a confounding effect on the relationship between the dependent variable and the independent variables identified in groups (2) and (3).

The Dependent Variable: International Peace/War

Since a dyadic approach is adopted in the present study, the task of operationalising the concept of 'peace' is a relatively easy one. To be sure, the condition characterised as peace can in principle vary considerably across dyads; a hostile and precarious peace, for example, providing an obvious contrast with an amicable and secure one. Nonetheless the international conditions of the late interwar years were such, given the general pervasiveness of overt hostilities after 1939, that it is far more important to make the simple but fundamental distinction between (1) dyads which managed to maintain peaceful relations throughout the period and (2) those whose relationship degenerated into war. Accordingly the dependent variable employed in this analysis simply records whether or not each pair of nation-states in the international system went to war with one another in the period between 1 January 1921 (by which time most of the overt hostilities associated with the First World War had ended) and 31 December 1941, shortly after the entry of the US into the Second World War.[8] This operationalisation provides a clear and unambiguous dummy variable which takes on the value of unity if the pair of nations comprising the dyad went to war with one another, and zero if they remained at peace. It also raises the possibility of using probability models in the statistical analysis, an opportunity which is explicitly pursued in Chapter 4, where a series of log-linear models and a dummy dependent variable multiple regression model are examined.

Politico-legal Variables

These data represent the primary set of measures designed to be used in order to test the various 'idealist mechanisms' developed in the final section of Chapter 1. The first set of variables in this category is intended to measure the *manifest operations of the international legal process* during the interwar years. Specifically, this entails: (1) a variable labelled JUDGEMENTS which indicates the number of times each pair of nations in the analysis jointly referred a mutual dispute to the Permanent Court and at least notionally accepted the judgement laid down by the Court; (2) a variable labelled ORDERS which indicates for each pair of nations the number of times the Permanent Court made an Order concerning their mutual relations; (3) a variable labelled ADVICE which indicates the frequency of Advisory Opinions given by the Court concerning the mutual relations of each dyad; (4) a variable labelled COURT which additively combines the JUDGEMENTS, ORDERS and ADVICE variables, thereby summarising the overall activities of the Permanent Court as far as each dyad is concerned; and (5) a variable labelled ARBITRATIONS which indicates the number of times each dyad referred a matter of mutual dispute to an independently constituted arbitral tribunal.[9]

Clearly these variables provide an obvious means of assessing the value of the formal legal process as a vehicle for avoiding violent conflict. Simple cross-tabulations of the variables against the 'war/not' variable readily provide an indication of the extent to which dyads that used the available legal mechanisms succeeded in avoiding violent conflict at some later date. Table 2.1 provides an illustrative indication of the extent to which the use of arbitral settlement techniques affected (or, more correctly, failed to affect) the chances of dyads going to war

TABLE 2.1 *Illustrative cross-tabulation of the relationship between war/no war and referrals to arbitral settlement/not*

	No referrals to arbitral settlement 1920–42	*At least one referral to arbitral settlement 1920–42*	*Total*
No war 1921–42	857 (89.2%)	42 (76.4%)	899 (88.5%)
War occurs after 1921	104 (10.8%)	13 (23.6%)	117 (11.5%)
Total	961 (100%)	55 (100%)	1016 (100%)

Goodman and Kruskal's gamma = 0.43
Kendall's $tau_b = 0.09$

during the interwar years. The rationale underlying the interpretation of this and similar tables is described at the beginning of Chapter 3.

As the table indicates, if there is any relationship at all between arbitration and violent conflict (and there is a strong case for arguing that the empirical relationship is in any event theoretically spurious, a point which is discussed in some detail below), it would appear that the former *encourages* the latter. Of the dyads that engaged in arbitration, some 23.6 per cent subsequently went to war; of the dyads that did not use arbitral tribunals, only 10.8 per cent went to war. Apart from contracting the results reported by Raymond which were referred to earlier, this sort of finding is entirely in line with the standard account of the manifest role of international law in the interwar period – an account which I do not wish to challenge – namely, that between the two world wars law quite simply failed to deliver the peaceful pattern of conflict resolution that its vigorous and overoptimistic advocates had promised.

The second set of politico-legal variables refers to the *treaty commitments* entered into by each pair of nation-states in the interwar period. These variables are designed primarily to measure the *latent* effects of international law in the interwar years, and reflect the full range of treaty-making activities, across a wide range of issue-areas, engaged in by nation-states in that period. Table 2.2 describes the typology of varieties of treaty commitment adopted in this study, which broadly follows the classification scheme developed by Peter Rohn in his four volume *World Treaty Index*.[10] The 'Arbitration/conciliation' variable, for example, records the number of treaties, conventions and/or agreements (excluding actual referrals to arbitration tribunals) signed by each pair of nations after 31 December 1920 and up to either 31 December 1941 or prior to the outbreak of warfare between the pair of nations, whichever came first.[11] The same principles were applied to each of the remaining treaty types. These principles have the considerable advantage of ensuring that any correlation between treaty-making and war-avoidance which might be observed cannot be artificially inflated by treaty-making which occurs *after* the outbreak of war. In this sense, the independent variables (the treaty-making records of the dyads) are *temporally prior* to the dependent variable (war/not); a condition which is essential if there is to be any possibility of sustaining the view that lawmaking might exert a *causal* influence upon war-avoidance.[12]

In order to establish why it is useful to record the number of times each dyad jointly signed a variety of treaties, it is necessary to return to some of the arguments advanced in Chapter 1. It was suggested that

TABLE 2.2 *The classification of treaties, conventions and agreements employed in this study*

Financial	Territory/boundaries	General political
General economic	Diplomatic (including *de jure* recognition)	Specific political
Specific economic	Aliens' rights/duties/limits to behaviour	General military
Most Favoured Nation	Arbitration/conciliation (excluding Pact of Paris)	Arms limitation
Short-run economic (less than six months' duration)	Cultural/medical/scientific	Military short of alliance
Transport and communications	Administrative co-operation	Non-aggression/anti-war pact
Friendship and co-operation		Reparations
		Mutual assistance
		Reciprocal neutrality
		Armistice/peace treaties

perhaps the most important way in which law affects international relations is through the process of treaty-making itself; a process which provides 'rungs on the ladder' of breaking down mutual mistrust. In this sense, law(making) has an essentially latent, political role to play in international relations rather than the conventional, legal one which the interwar idealists intended for it. It was also suggested that lawmaking necessarily involves a considerable amount of continuing formal diplomatic contact and effort. Even if the resultant treaties represent only a disagreement to disagree, the process of negotiation and compromise entailed in their creation may serve over time to develop a better sense of understanding between the nation-states involved and thereby to lessen tensions and reduce the chances of open warfare between them. In the sense, then, that an extensive network of mutual treaty commitments between any given pair of nations indicates that a not inconsiderable diplomatic effort has gone into the production of that network, it seems reasonable to suppose that a set of variables which records the treaty-making activities of the pairs of nations under analysis does provide an approximate indication of the extent of diplomatic contact, negotiation and compromise in which each pair of nations has been engaged. In short, express treaty commitments act as a surrogate indicator for the diplomatic effort involved in the (international) lawmaking process, and accordingly provide a very useful vehicle for assessing the latent role of law in the international system.

As I indicated in Chapter 1, however, the suggestion that law may play a latent role in international politics does not mean that I wish to argue that signing treaties, together with the attendant diplomacy which it engenders, necessarily makes for more peaceful international relations. It is worth re-emphasising the fact that lawmaking and diplomacy frequently fail in their long- and short-term objectives – they certainly failed to stop Hitler in the 1930s – but this does not mean that they are always and everywhere ineffective. As suggested earlier, although in crisis situations the imperatives of power politics invariably take priority over legal-diplomatic commitments and agreements (as the Second World War approached in the late 1930s decision-makers throughout the state system without exception developed their strategies on the basis of the requirements of *realpolitik*), this does not mean that *in the period before the crisis arises* law and the diplomatic process are not capable of broadening the range of peaceful options which are available, so that when the crisis does break the chances for a peaceful route through it may be marginally greater. This is essentially what the treaty-making process is capable of doing: by bringing potential antagonists together in a formal process of diplomatic exchange, it obliges them to engage in communication and negotiation and, if the treaty is to be signed, to find common ground. As argued in Chapter 1, it is contended here that without a full consideration of the appropriate evidence it is simply not acceptable to dismiss these claims out of hand: they raise empirical questions which require empirical testing. Moreover, as has been indicated repeatedly, there is evidence (reported in Chapters 3 and 4) to suggest that in certain limited contexts, even in the interwar period, treaty-making did in fact serve indirectly to help preserve international peace.

Economic Variables: Bilateral Trade Data

Given the intimate connection between economics and politics, it is clearly desirable that any analysis of the impact of law and diplomacy on nation-state behaviour should take some account of economic factors and in particular the patterns of trade which obtain among the various nation-state actors.

There are in fact two general ways in which trade data might be relevant to a study of the international political economy of the interwar period. The first derives from the simple – though contentious – observation, much propagated by proponents of Marxian political economy, that the crisis of capitalist production which precipitated the great depression of the 1930s was resolved primarily through a massive rearmament programme among the Great (capitalist) Powers. This rearmament race, it is argued – though it successfully stimulated the domestic economies of the leading capitalist countries – fostered a situation of heightened mutual hostility which itself contributed significantly to the subsequent outbreak of war. The overall collapse of international trade that accompanied the 1930s crisis of (capital) overaccumulation in this first sense, then, is regarded as a general causal factor underlying the Second World War.[13] In terms of the international system as a whole, the empirical observations certainly seem to be consistent with at least a part of the hypothesised causal sequence: there was a collapse in the volume of world trade in the early to mid-1930s; there was a series of large-scale rearmament programmes throughout the world from the mid-1930s onwards, accompanied by a significantly heightened sense of international tension; and a major international war did begin in 1939. What is less clear, however, is that it was a global crisis of capital overaccumulation which precipitated the collapse of world trade and that arms spending was either the only, or even the best, strategy for international capital to pursue in order to resolve the economic crisis. While the relevance of these two factors still awaits a convincing demonstration, it is certainly beyond the scope of this study to determine the validity of the claim that the sequence of world events beginning in the late 1920s and culminating in the 1939–45 war were to a greater or lesser degree the consequence of a Marxian crisis of capital overaccumulation.

A more modest goal, however, is perhaps attainable. The real value of international trade data for a study of this sort derives from the fact that in any dyadic examination of the potential relationship between nation-states' legal-diplomatic activities and their later predispositions to fight one another, it is clearly important to know how far the nation-states that comprise each dyad have a mutual (economic) interest in avoiding a deterioration in their political-military relations. It might be hypothesised, for example, that in situations where bilateral trade is high, the mutual economic interdependence thus engendered will of itself serve to reduce the likelihood of war occurring between the nations involved. Bilateral trade data, therefore, in the first instance provide a useful summary indication of the extent of mutual economic interdependence. This form of exchange, moreover, not only acts as some sort of brake upon nations' recourse to war (see Chapter 4), but also serves to confound the effects of some of the politico-legal variables identified above. It is also the case (as will be made clear later in this chapter) that the information provided by bilateral trade data provides an important set of control variables describing the economic context in which different dyads operate.

Table 2.3 describes a number of bilateral trade variables derived from a League of Nations source which conveniently reports the total value of dyadic trade flows throughout the world, on a cross-nationally comparable basis, for the period 1928–38. Each of these variables, potentially, might on *a priori* grounds be expected to influence the probability of war occurring between any pair of nations.

VOLUME28 provides a general indication of the level of trade interdependence experienced by each dyad in the period before the Great Depression. VOLUME38 records the (generally much reduced) level of trade interdependence on the eve of the Second World War. If trade interdependence does inhibit the resort to warfare then it is to be expected that either or both of these variables should correlate negatively with the war/not dependent variable.

VOLCHANGE indicates the extent to which bilateral trade fell during the period 1928–38 as a result of the upsurge in economic nationalism which both resulted from and served to reinforce the depression of the early 1930s. In the period after 1928, tariff barriers were rapidly erected as national governments sought desperately to protect domestic employment. In the process they counterproductively robbed themselves of the benefits of comparative advantage which the relatively high levels of international trade in the 1920s had provided, and thus exacerbated the very unemployment problem which protection was designed to remedy. VOLCHANGE, by measuring the extent of the decline in trade on a dyadic basis, permits an assessment of the impact of economic nationalism upon the growth of international tension in the late 1930s. In essence, it makes it possible to ascertain whether or not the dyads that experienced a dramatic decline in the volume of bilateral trade during the 1930s were also the ones whose constituent nation-states found themselves on opposing sides in the Second World War. If this were indeed the case, then a clear empirical linkage between economic nationalism, protection and war would have been established.

IMBALANCE28 and IMBALANCE38 measure the degree of bilateral trade imbalance (for any given dyad, A–B, this constitutes the

TABLE 2.3 *Bilateral trade variables*[a]

Variable Name	*Description*	*Predicted correlation with war/not*	*Rationale*
VOLUME28[b]	Total volume of bilateral trade between the two countries in each dyad, 1928	Negative	More trade → more mutual interdependence → less chance or war
VOLUME38	Total volume of bilateral trade between the two countries in each dyad, 1938	Negative	More trade → more mutual interdependence → less chance of war
VOLCHANGE	Change in the volume of bilateral trade between 1928 and 1938	Negative	Larger decrease in trade means greater deterioration in economic relations → greater chance of war
IMBALANCE28	Absolute value of exports – imports for one of the trading partners in each dyad, 1928	Positive	Greater imbalance → greater tension → more chance of war
IMBALANCE38	Absolute value of exports – imports for one of the trading partners in each dyad, 1938	Positive	Greater imbalance → greater tension → more chance of war

[a] All variables record the monetary value of trade exchanges measured in US$ equivalents according to contemporary exchange rate values.
[b] Separate variables for imports and exports were initially operationalised for the present study. Their pattern of behaviour in the statistical analysis was virtually identical to that of VOLUME28 and VOLUME38 and for this reason their results are not subsequently reported.
SOURCE League of Nations Economic Intelligence Service, *The Network of World Trade* (Geneva: League of Nations, 1942).

absolute difference between the value of A's exports to B and the value of B's exports to A) for 1928 and 1938 respectively. These variables were included in the analysis on the assumption that, especially in the era before Bretton Woods, a highly unbalanced trading relationship might well constitute a continuing source of resentment and discontent as far as the junior trading partner was concerned. Under these circumstances it might be expected that the probability of war again *ceteris paribus* would be greater for dyads with a high trade imbalance than for dyads with a low imbalance or none at all. In any event, the notion of a trade imbalance certainly represents an important control variable in any dyadic analysis of the relationship between international lawmaking and international peace.

Contextual Variables

Bilateral trade patterns, however, are not the only means of providing a statistical context in which the relationship between lawmaking and peace can be examined. Coplin and Rochester, for example, in their examination of the rulings laid down by international courts between 1920 and 1970, show that a number of common-sense variables – which describe very obvious dyad characteristics such as geographical proximity or cultural similarity – constitute controls which must be incorporated into dyadic statistical analysis if the results reported are to be of any value.[14] Broadly following Coplin and Rochester, Table 2.4 describes the additional control variables included in the present analysis.

THE SPURIOUS CORRELATION PROBLEM

It is now necessary to confront and resolve a major problem which has been alluded to several times already. It may well have occurred to the reader that even if a clear correlation is found between nations' treaty-making activities and their (absence of) recourse to war, it is quite possible that such an empirical relationship is not the consequence of any real causal connection between lawmaking and peace. Rather it might well be argued that, on the one hand, those pairs of countries which (1) experience no treaty-making and (2) go to war with one another do so because they are already in some sense 'enemies'; on the

TABLE 2.4 *Contextual variables*[b]

Variable Name	*Description*	*Coding values*
ADJACENT[a]	Whether or not the countries in each dyad share a common border	Share common border = 1; not = 0
NEAR	Whether or not the countries in each dyad were either (1) adjacent, or (2) separated by one other country (excluding USSR, USA and China), or (3) within 200 miles of one another	Near = 1; not = 0
POWERDIF	Whether or not the countries in each dyad were of similar power status. 'Power differential' covers all those dyads where *one* of the powers was a major power (Britain, France, USA, Germany, USSR, Italy and Japan were defined as major powers)	Differential in power status exists = 1; not = 0
CULDIF	Whether or not the countries in each dyad, in my opinion, shared a similar culture (language, major religion and/or dominant ideology); the codings are very similar to Coplin and Rochester's 'geocultural region'	Significant cultural differences exist = 1; not = 0
COLONY	Whether or not the countries in each dyad exhibited a formal colonial or quasi-colonial relationship.	Colonial relationship exists = 1; not = 0
ECDIF[a]	Whether or not the countries in each dyad in my judgement experienced broadly similar levels of GNP/capita in the interwar period.	Significant economic differences exist = 1; not = 0

[a] The findings for ADJACENT and for ECDIF are not reported here because their behaviour in the statistical analysis was virtually identical to that of NEAR and CULDIF respectively.
[b] All the data employed in this study are lodged with the ESRC Data Archive, University of Essex, Colchester, UK. The dataset is available on request.

other hand, those dyads which (1) engage in extensive treaty-making and (2) avoid war do so because they are already in some sense 'friends'. In both sets of cases, the point at issue is a classic example of a spurious theoretical interpretation of an empirical correlation. On this basis, lawmaking and the absence of war are correlated only because they are both 'caused' by a third, 'friendship–antagonism' variable. Another way of looking at the spurious correlation problem is to regard it as a reflection of the fact that in any investigation of the relationship between treaty-making and the occurrence of war it does not really make sense to assume that the probability of war is constant across all pairs of countries; to assume that nothing else is known about the dyads under analysis and their perhaps differing *a priori* predispositions to engage in warfare. Regardless of the extent of treaty-making, for example, it would be reasonable to suspect that given the historical experience of the previous (say) 150 years, the *a priori* probability of war for the Britain – USA dyad for the period 1920–42 would be significantly lower than the equivalent probability for Germany–France. In these circumstances – and they obviously extend beyond the specific examples to the general case – it is essential that systematic efforts are made to take account of the different *a priori* probabilities of war which are characteristic of each dyad.

This role is in fact partially fulfilled by the contextual and bilateral trade variables already described. Individually and in combination these measures do in effect permit variation in the *a priori* probabilities of war. This means that when the effects of law and the lawmaking process are being assessed, that assessment can in fact be based on *conditional a priori* probabilities rather than on the somewhat ludicrous *a priori* assumption that all dyads have an equal probability of going to war.

The contextual and trade variables mentioned thus far, however, are not on their own sufficiently comprehensive to allow for as full a range of conditional probabilities as is perhaps desirable. Moreover they do not adequately confront the 'spurious interpretation' accusation that might be levelled against any observed correlation between international lawmaking and the avoidance of war. A final set of measures, which will be referred to for want of better label as 'friendship/antagonism' variables, fills both of these gaps: on the one hand, these variables broaden the range of conditional probabilities that can be considered and, on the other, by effecting operationalisations of the phenomenon that is supposedly producing the 'spurious correlations', they allow specific statistical tests to be undertaken which can determine whether the observed correlations in question are genuinely spurious or not.

What specifically, though, are these 'friendship/antagonism' variables? Table 2.5 describes the main details of each of them. Using a variety of different criteria, each variable attempts to distinguish either (1) between those pairs of nations which might reasonably be construed as having enjoyed friendly bilateral relations as opposed to those which did not, or (2) between those pairs which could fairly be described, at the beginning of the time period under analysis at least, as highly antagonistic towards one another as opposed to those which could not.

The rationale behind each of the operationalisations of 'friendship/antagonism' identified in Table 2.5 is largely self-explanatory but two of them are sufficiently important to merit further brief attention. The first of these is 'Friendship/Antagonism I', which defines antagonistic dyads as those pairs of nations which had been at war with one another in the period between 1900–20. Bearing in mind that almost all of the dyads thus defined were on opposing sides in the First World War, this variable is a remarkably good indicator of which pairs of countries were distinct enemies at the beginning of the period under analysis. As such it constitutes a particularly useful vehicle for an evaluation of the claim that any empirical correlation between lawmaking and war avoidance is theoretically spurious because enemies are *ceteris paribus* likely to (1) resort to war again and (2) unlikely to bother signing many treaties with each other. Once that group of dyads defined as enemies has been isolated, it is then a relatively simple matter, using well-established principles that are outlined in Chapter 3, to evaluate the spurious correlation accusation. In essence, this involves examining specifically those dyads which can be defined as having some pre-existing enmity: any positive correlation between international lawmaking and peace within this group can hardly be adequately explained by the assertion that the dyads involved are 'already friends or allies'.

Finally, it is also worth mentioning 'Friendship/Antagonism V'. Derived from Singer and Small's study of alliance aggregation,[15] this variable identifies those dyads which over the period 1815–1920 were never enemies in war but fought on the same side against some third party at least once. By concentrating on long-term political-military friendship, therefore, 'Friendship/Antagonism V' provides a useful counterpoint to 'Friendship/Antagonism I'. While the latter allows a tightly defined group of 'enemies' to be isolated for control purposes, the former permits an equivalent isolation for a well-defined group of 'friends'. Again, as will be shown in the next chapter, this facility to determine whether or not dyads had a prior record of long-term friendship is crucial in any attempt to evaluate the claim that 'pre-

TABLE 2.5 *'Friendship/Antagonism' control variables*

Variable name	*Description*	*Comments/rationale*
Friendship/Antagonism I	Dyads defined as 'friendly' had not been at war with one another since 1900; dyads defined as 'antagonistic' had been at war with one another sometime between 1900 and 1920, in nearly all cases during the First World War	Primarily intended to identify dyads which had experienced a high level of antagonism in the years immediately prior to the interwar period.
Friendship/Antagonism II	Dyads defined as 'friendly' had (1) signed either a general military or a non–aggression treaty between 1920 and 1939 *and* (2) had not been at war with one another since 1900; dyads defined as antagonists did not satisfy (1) and/or (2)	Designed to narrow the definition of 'friendly dyads' to those which (1) had a convergence of security interest in the interwar years and (2) had no immediate prior record of antagonism
Friendship/Antagonism III	Dyads defined as 'friendly' shared a common language, at least as far as the major linguistic group in each country was concerned; 'antagonistic' dyads did not	Designed to provide a very narrow definition of 'friendship' based on inherent cultural and linguistic affinities
Friendship/Antagonism IV	Dyads defined as 'friendly' signed at least five[a] treaties of any type between 1920 and 1939; 'antagonistic' dyads signed less than five such treaties	Designed as means of testing the assertion that treaty-making is primarily an *indicator* of good relations (rather than a causal influence upon them). Friendly dyads can accordingly be identified on the basis of their signing some minimum number of treaties
Friendship/Antagonism V	Dyads defined as 'friendly' had been allies in war at least once *and* never enemies in the period 1815–1920; dyads defined as antagonistic failed to meet at least one of the two criteria	Mainly intended to distinguish between those dyads which had a long–run convergence of security interest and those which did not

[a] For reasons of brevity, the present study reports only results obtained from a cut-off point of five treaties. Similar statistical effects were found, however, for cut-offs of three, four, six, seven and eight treaties.

existing friendship' can 'explain' any observed correlation which might be found between lawmaking and peace.

SUMMARY AND CONCLUSIONS

Perhaps the least contentious observation that has been made in this chapter is that in the interwar years the newly assembled machinery of international law transparently failed to perform its primary manifest function of maintaining peace. It is nonetheless the case, however, that international law and lawmaking are capable of performing a more indirect, political role in the maintenance of peaceful international relations. Indeed, it has been argued here that it is by no means self-evident that international law failed as comprehensively in the performance of this latent role, even in the interwar period, as the existing orthodoxy might imply. The view that law and lawmaking have no real role to play in the great issues of war and peace has been derived largely from an examination of a limited number of (admittedly very important) cases. The question of the possible latent role of international lawmaking, however, is an empirical one that requires an examination of all of the relevant case materials, not just the most visible ones. It is precisely such an empirical investigation which is undertaken in the next two chapters.

This investigation is based on the assumption that *ceteris paribus* the dyadic treaty-making record provides a summary indication of the extent of diplomatic contact, negotiation and compromise entered into by each pair of nations. There are two main senses in which a well-developed network of bilateral lawmaking might be expected to influence the chances for international peace. First, extensive efforts at diplomatic negotiation and compromise may serve to foster a better sense of understanding between national leaders or representatives, thus reducing the sense of mutual fear and suspicion which frequently divides nations. Second, an extensive record of dyadic diplomatic contacts and compromise can serve to broaden the range of opportunities for conflict resolution in the event of a serious crisis in bilateral relations.

Clearly, as has been repeatedly recognised, both of these hypothesised mechanisms can easily be challenged on *a priori* theoretical grounds: diplomacy may lead to a greater sense of frustration and confrontation rather than understanding and reduced suspicion; it may simply be rendered irrelevant in the face of the *realpolitik* strategies produced by statesmen in crisis situations. The point, however, is that the question of the operation of the 'mechanisms' is an empirical one. If it can be shown that in certain contexts a more extensive treaty-making network does seem to be consistently related to peaceful bilateral relations, then the hypothesised mechanisms must gain some credence at the direct expense of the plausibility of the counterarguments.

It is in the context of this conclusion, of course, that the 'spurious correlation' argument becomes relevant. An empirical correlation between bilateral treaty-making and peace can only be used to support the notion that lawmaking plays a positive role in the international system if the obvious alternative explanation – that the dyads involved already enjoyed good relations, which explains both the treaty-making and the peaceful bilateral relations – can be discounted. This problem is systematically investigated in the ensuing chapters and, as will become apparent, the empirical results reported do indeed support the notion that in certain limited and specifiable contexts, international lawmaking did contribute indirectly to the maintenance of international peace in the interwar years.

3 Treaty-making, War and Peace: Preliminary Empirical Findings

In an attempt to assess the extent to which international lawmaking may have played a latent political role in the interwar period, the broad operational hypothesis of this chapter is that, *ceteris paribus*, more lawmaking means less chance of war: dyads which established or developed an extensive treaty network during the 1920s and 1930s, in comparison with those that did not, were less likely to engage in warfare at the end of the period precisely because of the diplomatic contact, negotiation and compromise engendered by the treaty-making process itself. In an important sense this 'reconstructed idealist hypothesis' goes beyond the Churchillian cliché that it is *better* to jaw-jaw than war-war: the hypothesis that is in effect being tested is that in certain contexts extensive and prolonged jaw-jawing–in the form of treaty-making–can serve to *inhibit* the resort to war.

This chapter commences the evaluation of this general proposition by examining a set of global correlations,[1] covering all active dyads in the interwar period, between the occurrence of war and a variety of types of treaty commitment. The correlations lend overwhelming support to the view that the reconstructed idealist hypothesis mentioned above is palpably false. The second part of the chapter, however, by disaggregating these global correlations, shows that there were certain contexts in which international lawmaking does appear to have contributed in a limited way to the cause of international peace. The final section of the chapter begins the task of reinforcing this conclusion by subjecting the disaggregated findings to more searching empirical scrutiny; a task which is continued in Chapter 4.

Before the empirical findings can be presented, however, it is necessary to make a qualification concerning the principles underlying the data analysis results reported in this chapter. The main data-analytic tool employed here is a series of (initially, 2-way; later 3-way, 4-way and 5-way) cross-tabulations between (1) whether war occurs or not and (2) the number of treaties of each of the types identified in Table 2.2 which were jointly signed by each pair of nations in the period 1920–42. Table 3.1 below provides an extreme hypothesised example of the results which might be expected if the signing of, say, arbitration/conciliation treaties had been correctly hypothesised to be a guarantee – on the assumption that the legal machinery thus established would always be used and would always settle the disputes involved to the satisfaction of both parties – that war would not subsequently occur between the parties concerned. Two aspects of the table are of critical importance. First, of the 816 hypothetical dyads which failed to sign an arbitration-conciliation treaty, some 116 (14.2 per cent) subsequently went to war. In absolute terms this appears to be a relatively small percentage, but it needs to be recognised that a large proportion of the 700 hypothetical pairs of countries in the top left cell would be likely to experience very little contact with each other and would accordingly be very unlikely to go to war with one another regardless of the fact that they had not signed a mutual arbitration/conciliation treaty. Second, and much more significant, of the 200 hypothetical dyads which signed arbitration treaties, none subsequently went to war. This substantial difference in the ratios of 'war: no war' dyads in colums 1 and 2 of Table 3.1 is reflected in the value of gamma ($\gamma = -1$) which is calculated from the table.

If such a pattern were ever to be observed with 'real' data, the inescapable implication of this particular finding (no matter how implausible it might appear given our 'knowledge' of the 'real' world) would be that arbitration/conciliation treaties do appear to exert a reductive influence on the resort to war; unless of course it could be demonstrated that some third variable(s) were operating which rendered the empirical correlation theoretically spurious.

The essential point, however, is that if the spurious correlation problem can be controlled for (which it can), any attempt to explain away as 'coincidence' the fact that all of the 200 dyads which signed arbitration/conciliation treaties avoided war, whereas none of the 116 which did go to war signed such a treaty, would look very weak indeed. In such circumstances, it would have to be conceded that there was some link between this particular form of lawmking and war-avoidance.

The results reported in this chapter make explicit use of the reasoning thus described. Obviously, hardly anywhere do the reported empirical findings correspond to the exaggerated hypothetical pattern described in Table 3.1. Nonetheless the same interpretative principles apply. In examining the relationship between war/not and the incidence of a

TABLE 3.1 *Hypothetical cross-tabulation between war/no war and number of arbitration/conciliation treaties signed*

	Number of arbitration and/or conciliation treaties signed		
	Column 1 *None*	*Column 2* *One or more*	
No war 1921–42	700 (85.8%)	200 (100%)	900 (88.6%)
War occurred after 1921	116 (14.2%)	0 (0%)	116 (11.4%)
	816 (100%)	200 (100%)	1016

Goodman and Kruskal's gamma = −1

number of different types of treaty-making activity, attention will be focused, as it was in the discussion of Table 3.1, on *differences in column ratios*. If law and lawmaking did indeed play an indirect role in inhibiting the recourse to war, then it is to be expected that for each treaty type the ratio of 'no-war: war' dyads should be greater for those dyads which signed treaties than for those dyads which did not.

For the sake of brevity, the statistical results that are presented are limited largely to the summary statistics derived from the sort of cross-tabulation described in Table 3.2. Since both the dependent and

TABLE 3.2 *Illustrative cross-tabulation of the relationship between war/no war and arbitration/conciliation agreements*

	Number of arbitration/conciliation agreements signed by each pair of nations after 1920 and prior to the last outbreak of warfare between them or up to 31 December 1941, whichever came first		
	None	*One or more*	*Total*
No war 1921–42	642 (89.4%)	257 (86.2%)	899 (88.5%)
War occurred after 1921	76 (10.6%)	41 (13.8%)	117 (11.5%)
Total	718 (100%)	298 (100%)	1016

Goodman and Kruskal's gamma = 0.14

independent variables are in effect measured at ordinal level the summary statistics reported are Goodman and Kruskal's gamma (γ) and, where appropriate, Kendall's tau_b (τ_b). Although the latter provides a more stringent test of overall association than the former, the computing algorithm for gamma has the considerable advantage of accurately reflecting differences in column percentages regardless of imbalances in row and column totals.[2] As Table 3.2 indicates – and it is in this context highly representative – imbalances are a typical feature of the cross-tabulations undertaken in the present study: as a result, rather more emphasis will be placed on the reported gamma values than on the τ_b values. Throughout this chapter and the next, however, reference will not be made to the specific magnitudes of the reported coefficients. This is not because these magnitudes are unimportant – though the absolute value of gamma can be misleading near its upper bounds if too much emphasis is placed upon it – but because what matters is the *sign* (positive or negative) of the coefficient.[3] Broadly speaking, the coefficients are interpreted as follows:

1 a zero coefficient indicates that there is no empirical relationship at the dyadic level between international lawmaking and the recourse to war. It contradicts the view that treaty-making played any role – however indirect – in sustaining peace in the interwar years.
2 a positive coefficient is even more disturbing for the claim that 'more lawmaking means less chance of war'. It implies that if treaty-making played any role whatsoever, it served to exacerbate the situation by increasing the probability that the nations involved would subsequently go to war.
3 a negative coefficient is consistent with the view that treaty-making can perform a latent political role in the cause of international peace. Obviously, the larger the coefficient, the more the observed cross-tabulation from which it was derived corresponds to the hypothetical, ideal-type pattern described in Table 3.1

THE 'MORE LAW, LESS WAR' HYPOTHESIS APPARENTLY DISCONFIRMED

Table 3.3 indicates the extent to which, considered as a global, generalised description across all interwar dyads, the 'more law means less war' hypothesis must be strongly rejected. The results reported in Table 3.3 emphatically contradict the notion that law and lawmaking

TABLE 3.3 *Summary statistics derived from 2-way cross-tabulations between (1) war occurs after 1920/no war occurs between 1921 and 1942; and (2) each of the politico-legal variables identified in Chapter 2*
(Table 3.2 provides a model for the source cross-tabulations)

	War occurs after 1920/not		*Number of dyads which used each formal legal channel or entered into each type of treaty commitment (out of 1016 dyads)*
	Goodman and Kruskal's gamma (N = 1016)	*Kendall's tau_b (N = 1016)*	
(a) Type of activity concerned with the manifest function of international law:			
Judgements	0.39	0.07	45
Orders	0.64	0.07	8
Advisory opinions	0.56	0.10	33
Court	0.31	0.06	68
Referrals to arbitration	0.43	0.09	55
(b) Type of treaty/convention/agreement concerned with the latent function of lawmaking:			
Financial	0.20	0.05	161
General economic	−0.15	−0.04	504
Specific economic	0.09	0.02	286
Most Favoured Nation	0	0	299
Short-run economic	0	0	51
Transport/communications	0.17	0.05	295
General political	0.41	0.12	141
Friendship and co-operation	0	0	194
Territory/boundaries	0.34	0.0	170
Diplomatic	0	0	178
Aliens' rights/duties/limits	0	0	326
Arbitration/conciliation	0.14	0.04	298
Cultural/medical/ scientific	0.05	0.0	176
Administrative co-operation	0.13	0.02	248
Specific political	0	0	88
General Military	0.32	0.07	99
Military agreement short of alliance	0.06	0.01	78
Non-aggression/anti-war	0.38	0.09	90
Mutual assistance	−1	−0.05	21
Arms limitation	0.42	0.07	43
Reciprocal neutrality	0	0	28
Armistice/peace	0.64	0.19	74

played any positive role in the cause of international peace. In terms of both its 'manifest' and 'latent' functions, law clearly fails to reduce the chances of dyads going to war. All of the 'manifest' variables correlate *positively* with the occurrence of war rather than negatively as they should do if recourse to law had actually been responsible for the maintenance of peace. Similarly, in relation to international law's possible latent function, across almost all treaty types, the reported summary statistics indicate either a *positive* relationship between law and war (for example $\gamma = 0.34$ for treaties concerned with territory or boundaries) or no relationship at all (for example, $\gamma = 0$ for Most-Favoured-Nation treaties). Unlike the hypothetical 'results' described in Table 3.1, Table 3.3 indicates, for example, that for arbitration conciliation treaties, the observed gamma is in fact $\gamma = 0.14$. This summary measure reflects the fact that of those pairs of countries which jointly *signed* one or more such treaties, a marginally greater proportion subsequently *went to war* with each other than did the equivalent proportion for those pairs which did *not* sign an arbitration/conciliation treaty.

The only exceptions to this consistent pattern of apparently harsh refutation of the notion that international law might have a positive role to play are the coefficients for general economic treaties ($\gamma = -0.15$; $\tau_b = -0.04$) and for mutual assistance treaties ($\gamma = -1.0$: $\tau_b = -0.05$).[4] While the general economic treaties relationship might be construed as providing marginal support for the general 'more law, less war' hypothesis, the mutual assistance coefficient is probably best regarded as an example of the kind of theoretically spurious correlation referred to earlier. It might well be argued that it is not the signing of a mutual assistance treaty, together with the attendant diplomatic activity involved, which prevents pairs of nations from going to war with one another. Rather it seems likely that nations sign mutual assistance treaties and avoid mutual warfare because they already enjoy friendly bilateral relations and share common security concerns. There is, in short, no causal connection between (mutual assistance) law and war-avoidance: both are explained by the existence of other factors.

However, if this spurious correlation argument can be applied in the context of mutual assistance treaties can it not also be applied to all of the treaty types identified in Table 3.3? Can it not be argued that any negative correlation which might be found between international law and war will always describe a spurious, non-causal relationship between them because treaty-making is simply an *indicator* of the general state of relations between nation-states? (If relations are good there will be treaties and no war; if relations are bad there will be no treaties and – perhaps – war.) There are two reasons for rejecting this interpretation. First, mutual assistance treaties differ substantially from other treaty types in the sense that they are only likely to be concluded when there is a strong convergence of security interest between the states involved: in these circumstances, a divergence of security interest of the sort which underlies most outbreaks of war is, almost by definition, unlikely to occur. No other treaty type has this strong security connotation and as a result there is no reason to suppose that these other treaty types are subject to the same dangers of being spuriously linked to the occurrence of war/not. Second, if treaty commitments did indicate good relations between countries then we would expect to find that pairs of nations which entered into such commitments were less likely – given these good relations – subsequently to go to war. We would certainly *not* expect to discover that they were *more* likely to go to war than dyads which did not make such commitments. Yet both of these expectations are confounded by the results reported in Table 3.3. Most of the coefficients are either zero (denoting no relationship between treaty-making and war) or positive (more treaty-making, *more* chance of war). In short, *treaty-making commitments are not a good general indicator of the state of relations between nation-states*: they are either useless (see the zero coefficients in Table 3.3) or else, somewhat implausibly, describe how *bad* bilateral relations are (see the positive coefficients in Table 3.3).

Even if we can firmly reject the notion that treaty-making merely indicates the state of (good) relations between countries, however, the fact remains that the coefficients presented in Table 3.3 clearly appear to refute the claim that law and lawmaking can in either a direct or an indirect sense contribute to international peace. Table 3.3, in essence, confirms the orthodox realist view of the role of international law in the 1920s and 1930s; that it was at best irrelevant and at worst a dangerous illusion.

DISAGGREGATING THE LAW-WAR RELATIONSHIP: AN INDIRECT ROLE FOR LAW?

Regardless of the merits of this realist claim, however, it hardly seems satisfactory to examine the correlation between war and lawmaking only in global, generalised terms. There are at least two reasons for this. First, as was pointed out in Chapter 2, it is highly likely that different dyads have different *a priori* probabilities of going to war: in these

TABLE 3.4 *Summary statistics (gammas) derived from 3-way cross-tabulations between (1) war occurs after 1920/no war between 1921 and 1942 and (2) each of the treaty types identified in Table 2.2: controls applied for (a) cultural similarity/difference, (b) geographical proximity and (c) differentials in power status*

		War occurs after 1920/ not			*War occurs after 1920/ not*
Financial	no cultural difference	0.41 (N=593)	Transport/ comm.	no cultural difference	0.31
	cultural difference	−0.36 (N=423)		cultural difference	−0.03
	near	0.33 (N=246)		near	0.35
	not near	0.09 (N=770)		not near	0.03
	no power differential	0.59 (N=664)		no power differential	0.41
	power differential	−0.30 (N=352)		power differential	−0.08
General Economic	no cultural difference	0.09	General political	no cultural difference	0.50
	cultural difference	−0.47		cultural difference	0.26
	near	0.45		near	0.41
	not near	−0.40		not near	0.42
	no power differential	−0.08		no power differential	0.60
	power differential	−0.36		power differential	0.12
Specific Economic	no cultural difference	0.25	Friendship and co-operation	no cultural difference	0.48
	cultural difference	−0.20		cultural difference	−0.57
	near	0.40		near	0.46
	not near	−0.13		not near	−0.32
	no power differential	0.48		no power differential	0.41
	power differential	−0.33		power differential	−0.19
Most favoured nation	no cultural difference	0.12	Territory/ boundaries	no cultural difference	0.55
	cultural difference	−0.33		cultural difference	−0.22
	near	0.25		near	068
	not near	−0.21		not near	−0.06
	no power differential	−0.25		no power differential	0.68
	power differential	−0.05		power differential	0.06
Short run economic	no cultural difference	−0.07	Diplomatic	no cultural difference	0.14
	cultural difference	0.12		cultural difference	−0.19
	near	−0.45		near	−0.05
	not near	0.18		not near	−0.31
	no power differential	0.24		no power differential	0.07
	power differential	−0.27		power differential	−0.23

circumstances it becomes necessary to attempt to establish how far the effects of the treaty-making process might vary according to the different *contexts* in which it occurs. Second, as has been documented elsewhere,[5] apparently simple and conclusive global correlations frequently conceal a rich and complex pattern of variation which a thorough-going empirical analysis should attempt to identify and take into account. Indeed, when such an effort at disaggregation is undertaken in the context of the global correlations described in Table 3.3, a very different picture of the relationship between war and law emerges.

TABLE 3.4 *Continued*

		War occurs after 1920/ not			*War occurs after 1920/ not*
Aliens' rights/ limits	no cultural difference	0.09	General military	no cultural difference	0.39
	cultural difference	0.02		cultural difference	0.18
	near	0.18		near	0.24
	not near	− 0.05		not near	0.37
	no power differential	0.11		no power differential	0.68
	power differential	−0.14		power differential	−0.12
Arbitration/ conciliation	no cultural difference	0.21	Military short of alliance	no cultural difference	0.35
	cultural difference	0.10		cultural difference	−0.44
	near	0.46		near	0.08
	not near	−0.07		not near	0
	no power differential	0.18		no power differential	0.60
	power differential	0.08		power differential	−0.48
Cultural/ medical/ scientific	no cultural difference	0.19	Non-aggression/ anti-war pact	no cultural difference	0.50
	cultural difference			no cultural difference	−0.26
	near	0.05		near	0.53
	not near	0		not near	−0.02
	no power differential	0.21		no power differential	0.61
	power differential	−0.17		power differential	0.37
Administrative co-operation	no cultual difference	0.23	Mutual assistance	no cultural difference	−1
	cultural difference	−0.03		cultural difference	−1
	near	0.31		near	−1
	not near	−0.04		not near	−1
	no power differential	0.42		no power differential	−1
	power differential	−0.18		power differential	−1
Specific political	no cultural difference	0.12	Reciprocal Neutrality	no cultural difference	0.04
	cultural difference	−0.60		cultural difference	−0.17
	near	0.37		near	−0.22
	not near	0.04		not near	0.16
	no power differential	0.44		no power differential	0.38
	power differential	−0.55		power differential	−0.43

Table 3.4 describes the effect on the law-war relationship of controlling for three different variables, each of which was defined in Chapter 2: geographical proximity, power status differential and cultural difference.[6] Although the magnitudes of the coefficients are not particularly large, a close inspection of Table 3.4 reveals a remarkably consistent pattern of empirical relationships which indicates that in certain identifiable contexts treaty-making does appear to correlate negatively with the occurrence of war. In order to observe this effect initially, it is necessary to recognise that the coefficients in Table 3.4 are

grouped in pairs according to each of the two alternative values of the geographical proximity (not near/near), cultural difference (cultural difference/no cultural difference) and power status differential (power differential/no power differential) variables. Viewed on this basis, with very few exceptions[7] Table 3.4 indicates two very clear tendencies:

1 the 'near', 'no power differential' and 'no cultural difference' categories continue to furnish *positive* coefficients for the law-war relationship;
2 if there *are* cultural differences between nations or if they are not particularly close geographically or if the power status differential between them is significant, then war and treaty-making are *negatively* related.

As with the results reported in Table 3.3, the realist who wishes to reject the thesis that international lawmaking can have a reductive effect on nations' propensities to engage in warfare has a ready-made explanation for the positive coefficients reported in Table 3.4: those coefficients occur in contexts where a high level of 'contact' between countries might be expected; where cultures and power status are similar and territorial borders are adjacent or close. Again, the realist can argue, contact (since it both encourages treaty-making and increases the chances of a vital clash of interest if the available channels for peaceful conflict resolution are inadequate), explains both lawmaking and war, thereby producing a positive empirical correlation between the two. While there may be some validity in this argument with regard to the positive coefficients in Table 3.4, it is less easy to see how *lack* of contact could produce a pattern of *negative* correlation between law and war in the 'not near', 'cultural difference' and 'power status differential' categories of Table 3.4. Indeed if the realist reasoning about 'contact' were correct, positive coefficients should also be observable in these very categories: low contact should mean minimal treaty-making activity and a minimal risk of war; which in turn also implies a positive correlation between law and war. In these circumstances it is clear that the simple notion of 'contact' cannot adequately account for the negative law-war coefficients in Table 3.4.

What needs to be emphasised, however, is that there is a very consistent empirical tendency here which does require both explanation and further examination. Regardless of treaty type (general political treaties excepted), the more treaties that pairs of nations signed in the interwar period, provided that the countries involved were not too close geographically or were dissimilar in culture or power status, the less likely they were subsequently to engage in warfare with one another. An obvious question immediately needs to be addressed: if 'varying levels of contact' is an inadequate explanation for the negative correlation between law and war when there are significant differences in geography, culture and power status, how can this negative correlation be explained? The most likely explanation is probably to be found in the lower intensity of mutual security concerns in those dyads which exhibit differences in geography, culture or power status. It seems reasonable to suppose, for example, that when countries are either geographically remote or in different geocultural regions,[8] any differences over sovereignty or vital interest are less likely to be in need of the sort of immediate resolution that sometimes only war can provide than might be the case if the states involved were direct neighbours. Similarly, when a significant power status differential exists within any given dyad, the stronger nation of the two is less likely to feel seriously threatened should a divergence of vital interest occur than would be the case if both of the parties in the dyad were of a similar power status. Security problems, in short, tend to be perceived as less severe (1) when there is no direct, immediate threat from a neighbouring state and/or (2) when a potential antagonist is relatively weak. It is perhaps in these circumstances that politics, in the form of the treaty-making process, can be substituted for force; a substitution which is not so easy to effect when the disputing nations are either geographically close or evenly matched in terms of their power capabilities.

In essence, therefore, it is being suggested that the general pattern of negative law-war coefficients in Table 3.4 is derived from those situations where the divergence of security interests between the parties involved was neither particularly pressing nor particularly intense. There is, however, a potentially damaging implication of this interpretation. It could be concluded that it in effect means that lawmaking only exerted a reductive influence upon the recourse to war in 'unimportant situations', where there were no 'serious' conflicts of interest. Such a conclusion, however, would certainly be a misrepresentation of the argument that is being advanced. It is not being suggested that lawmaking had an effect only in 'unimportant situations'. Neither is it being claimed that those conflicts where the parties involved were either geographically remote or culturally different or significantly different in power status were not 'serious' conflicts: on the contrary, of the 770 geographically remote dyads, for example, some 83 actually engaged in overt warfare, which presumably means that for those dyads at least there *were* serious conflicts of national interest. Rather it is being suggested that although law and diplomacy failed to have an effect in the *most* important and most visible conflicts in the interwar period, it does appear to have had an effect in those situations where the conflicts of national interest were perhaps not so *sharply focused*. Given that it was not until after 1920 that there was a widespread acceleration in both treaty-making activity and the commitment (at least in notional terms) to pacific forms of settlement, this conclusion is not as unimpressive as it might first appear. What it suggests is that after a period of only 20 years, and despite the onset of a major global war involving all the Great Powers of the state system, international lawmaking does seem to have had an inhibiting effect on nations' recourse to war in those situations which were to some degree peripheral to the major conflict of the period. That these situations were peripheral in this sense, however, does not alter the possibility that the treaty-making process was indeed beginning to have an effect on interwar international relations, if only at the margin. If this appears a somewhat restricted conclusion, then so be it. What it indicates, crucially, is that contrary to existing accounts, there were a number of contexts in the interwar period when international lawmaking *did* make a positive contribution to the cause of peace. The remainder of this chapter – and Chapter 4 – seeks to offer further empirical corroboration for this proposition. Specifically, it attempts to demonstrate that the negative correlations thus far observed between lawmaking and war describe a causal, rather than a spurious, relationship between the two.

CONTROLLING FOR FRIENDSHIP/ANTAGONISM: THE SPURIOUS CORRELATION PROBLEM CONSIDERED

In Chapter 2 it was pointed out that if any negative correlation between treaty-making and war were to be observed (as it has been in the preceding section), it would be possible for the critic of the general 'idealist hypothesis' to argue that the correlation is essentially theoretically spurious, on the grounds that pairs of nations would (1) sign lots of treaties and avoid war if they were already, for whatever other reasons, relatively friendly, or (2) sign few if any treaties and engage in warfare if they were already, again for whatever other reasons, relatively antagonistic. Fortunately this spurious correlation interpretation of the findings presented in the preceding section can be tested empirically by employing statistical controls for pre-existing 'friendship/antagonism'.

Specifically, if pre-existing 'friendship/antagonism' does explain the negative law-war correlations identified in Table 3.4, then it is to be expected that for those dyads which can be defined as either 'not already friendly' or 'already antagonistic' the negative correlations between the occurrence of war and treaty-making activity should disappear.

The logic behind the need for these correlations to disappear when appropriate statistical controls are made is well established in quantitative social science and extremely simple. If the negative correlation between law and war is the result of prior antagonism among the 'no law–war occurs' dyads and of prior friendship among the 'law occurs–no war' dyads, then among the 'previously antagonistic' dyads there should be little or no lawmaking activity at all. Thus, even if war subsequently occurs within the 'previously antagonistic' group, it must be uncorrelated with the treaty-making activities of those dyads because none of them has engaged in treaty-making to any significant degree: they are part of the 'no law–war occurs' grouping. As a result, if it can be shown that the negative law-war correlations *continue* even for those dyads defined as being 'previously antagonistic' or as having 'no pre-existing friendship', then the claim that the law-war correlations are spurious can sensibly be rejected.

Employing the measures of 'friendship-antagonism' outlined in Chapter 2, Tables 3.5, 3.6 and 3.7 show that in general the negative law-war correlations uncovered initially in Table 3.4 *are* sufficiently robust to withstand the accusation that they are theoretically spurious. The tables only report the coefficients for those dyads defined as 'previously antagonistic' or as having 'no pre-existing friendship' according to each of the 'friendship/antagonism' variables. This is partly for reasons of parsimony but also because these are the categories, as was discussed immediately above, which are of greatest theoretical relevance given the spurious correlation accusation. What the tables demonstrate is that whichever definition of 'friendship/antagonism' is used, where there was no pre-existing friendship or even where there was some clear pre-existing antagonism, the dyads which participated more fully in the treaty-making process were less likely subsequently to go to war than similarly placed dyads which signed few treaties or none at all.[9]

Table 3.5 reports the summary statistics from a series of cross-tabulations between the occurrence of war/not and each treaty type, controlling for cultural difference/similarity and each of the five 'friendship/antagonism' variables introduced in the last chapter. It would be possible to speculate almost endlessly as to why certain of the coefficients reported in Table 3.5 take on the values that they do; or why

TABLE 3.5 *Summary statistics (gammas) derived from 4-way cross-tabulations between (1) war occurs after 1920/no war between 1921 and 1942 and (2) each of the treaty types identified in Table 2.2; controlling for (a) cultural difference/no cultural difference and (b) five alternative definitions of 'friendship/antagonism' outlined in Table 2.5. (COEFFICIENTS ARE ONLY REPORTED FOR THE 'NOT FRIENDS' = 'ANTAGONISTIC' DYADS FROM EACH 'FRIENDSHIP/ANTAGONISM' VARIABLE)*

Treaty type		*Friendship/ Antagonism I: 'friends' had not been at war with one another since 1900; 'antagonists' had been at war with one another sometime between 1900 and 1920*	*Friendship/ Antagonism II: 'friends' had signed either a general military or a non-aggression treaty and had not been at war with one another since 1900; 'antagonists' had not*	*Friendship/ Antagonism III: 'friends' shared the same language; 'antagonists' did not*	*Friendship/ Antagonism IV: 'friends had signed at least five treaties of whatever type since 1920; 'antagonists' had signed less than five such treaties*	*Friendship/ Antagonism V: 'friends' had been allies in war at least once and never enemies in the period since 1815; 'antagonists' had not*
Financial	no cultural difference	0.18 (N=40)	0.48 (N=480)	0.34 (N=465)	−1 (N=309)	0.49 (N=513)
	cultural difference	−0.38 (N=25)	−0.31 (N=405)	−0.35 (N=421)	0.14 (N=333)	−0.30 (N=394)
General Economic	no cultural difference	0.41	0.04	0.02	−0.55	0.11
	cultural difference	−0.94	−0.51	−0.47	−0.39	−0.46
Specific Economic	no cultural difference	0.37	0.19	0.22	−0.58	0.31
	cultural difference	−0.45	−0.33	−0.21	−0.20	−0.17
Most Fav. Nation	no cultural difference	0.30	0.01	0.06	−0.74	0.11
	cultural difference	0.14	−0.30	−0.33	−0.39	−0.28
Short-run Economic	no cultural difference	−0.63	−0.09	−0.06	−1	0.04
	cultural difference	−0.71	0.13	0.11	0.67	0.14
Transport/ comm.	no cultural difference	0.62	0.27	0.35	−0.41	0.34
	cultural difference	−0.45	0.28	−0.03	−0.28	−0.09
General political	no cultural difference	0.73	0.65	0.55	−1	0.56
	cultural difference	−0.71	0.22	0.25	0.74	0.24
Friendship/ Co-op.	no cultural difference	0.84	0.52	0.43	−0.15	0.51
	cultural difference	−0.71	−0.53	−0.57	−0.63	−0.54

Territory/ boundaries	no cultural difference	0.67	0.63	0.52	−0.18	0.59
	cultural difference	−0.82	−0.70	−0.21	−1	−0.34
Diplomatic	no cultural difference	0.01	−0.09	0.13	0	0.18
	cultural difference	−0.55	−0.16	−0.18	−0.14	−0.18
Aliens' rights	no cultural difference	0.08	0.10	0.09	−0.26	0.07
	cultural difference	−0.45	0	0.02	0.12	0.04
Arbitration/ conciliation	no cultural difference	0.81	0.15	0.17	−0.64	0.21
	cultural difference	−1	−0.01	0.09	0.09	0.11
Cultural/ admin.	no cultural difference	0.60	0.22	0.20	−1	0.20
	cultural difference	−0.16	−0.35	−0.40	−0.37	−0.38
	no cultural difference	0.51	0.27	0.17	−0.37	0.26
operation	cultural difference	−0.71	−0.71	−0.03	−0.10	−0.06
Specific political	no cultural difference	0.17	0.12	0.22	−1	0.19
	cultural difference	−1	−0.1	−0.60	−1	−0.56
General military	no cultural difference	0.25	*	0.37	−1	0.44
	cultural difference	−0.71	*	0.18	0.53	0.24
Military	no cultural difference	0.05	0.58	0.38	−1[a]	0.58
	cultural difference	−0.86	−0.63	−0.44	−1	−0.41
Non-agression	no cultural difference	0.73	*	0.59	−1	0.48
	cultural difference	−1	*	−0.26	−1[a]	−1
Mutual assistance	no cultural difference	−1	−1	−1	−1	−1
	cultural difference	−1	−1	−1	n	−1
Reciprocal neutrality	no cultural difference	0.16	0.28	0.01	−1[a]	0.07
	cultural difference	−0.71	−0.10	−0.17	n	−0.17

* These coefficients were not computed in order to avoid tautological double counting since the treaty types involved are also included in the definition of the Friendship/Antagonism control variable.

[a] This denotes that a coefficient has been artificially inflated by an extreme imbalance in the row or column marginals. The sign of the coefficient is nonetheless of interest.

n indicates that one of the rows or columns in the appropriate table was empty: gamma could not therefore be calculated.

[b] Armistice/peace treaties are excluded from the remaining tables in this chapter because such treaties, since they by definition serve essentially to terminate war between enemy states, cannot plausibly be regarded as contributing to any subsequent build-up of mutual trust between them.

the coefficients for some treaty types are not consistently negative; or why some of the friendship/antagonism control variables seem to produce more consistent results than others. Such speculation, however, would be extremely time consuming and would miss the whole point behind the evidence that is presented in the table: what is of central importance to the case that is being made here is not the specific signs or magnitudes of particular coefficients but the overall *pattern* which the coefficients taken together produce.

Viewed in this light, three main features of Table 3.5 are worth emphasising. First, the pattern of positive (for 'no cultural difference') and negative (for 'cultural difference') coefficients observed in Table 3.4 is clearly in evidence throughout the table, but especially in the column for 'Friendship/Antagonism I'. This is particularly satisfactory as far as what might be termed the 'circumscribed' ('circumscribed' in the sense that it is now being restricted to those contexts where the pairs of nations involved are geographically remote, culturally different or dissimilar in power status) 'reconstructed idealist hypothesis' that is now being advanced is concerned. This is because all of the 65 pairs of nations to which this column refers had actually been at war with one another in the years immediately prior to the time period under analysis. All of these dyads, in short, had just previously been bitter enemies yet the pairs which subsequently participated extensively in the treaty-making process were significantly less likely to find themselves at war at the end of the period under investigation than pairs which did not participate in that process. This, essentially, is what the negative coefficients in the first column of Table 3.5 mean: they strongly support the view that the negative correlation between treaty-making and the occurrence of war is not theoretically spurious.[10]

A second feature of Table 3.5 is that among the pairs of nations defined as culturally dissimilar there is a consistent tendency for negative law-war correlations to be found *across virtually all treaty types* (in fact there is not a single treaty type which does not produce a negative law-war correlation under the effects of at least one of the friendship/antagonism control variables). Indeed, the extent of this pattern is reflected in the fact that of the 96 (calculable) coefficients in the 'cultural difference' categories in Table 3.5, 75 – over three-quarters – are negative as the 'circumscribed reconstructed idealist hypothesis' would predict. Though this by no means constitutes conclusive proof that international lawmaking inhibited the recourse to war, it does represent an additional piece of evidence which makes it a little more difficult for the self-proclaimed realist to reject outright the notion that lawmaking could have played a positive role in international politics in the interwar years.

The third observation which needs to be made about Table 3.5 concerns the 'friendship/antagonism' control variables. The importance of these variables lies in the *variety* of ways in which they seek to operationalise the notions of pre-existing friendship and/or pre-existing antagonism; as is evidenced by the very different numbers of dyads which the different definitions assign as 'antagonists'. ('Friendship/Antagonism I', for example, defines only 40+25=65 dyads as 'antagonistic', whereas 'Friendship/Antagonism V' so defines some 513+394=907 dyads.) Despite these wide differences in definition and scope, each of the five 'antagonistic' groupings of dyads furnishes a large number of negative law-war correlations in the cultural difference category consistent with the modified general idealist hypothesis. This again serves to reinforce the notion that pre-existing friendship/enmity cannot explain why, for certain groupings of dyads, treaty-making consistently correlates negatively with the occurrence of war; which in turn supports the hypothesis that there may be an indirect causal, rather than a spurious, relationship between the two.

Table 3.6 (which controls for geographical proximity/remoteness rather than cultural similarity/difference) and Table 3.7 (which controls for power status differential/not) present findings which yield very similar conclusions to those derived from Table 3.5. In both tables, there is generally the same pattern of paired positive and negative coefficients which was initially described in Table 3.4; and the same tendency for negative coefficients to be observed in certain contexts (the 'not near' dyads in Table 3.6 and the 'power differential' dyads in Table 3.7) both across all treaty types and across all the different definitions of 'Friendship/Antagonism'. Once again, the remarkable consistency of these patterns – despite the relatively low levels of intercorrelation among the near/not near, culturally different/similar and power status differential/not variables[11] – reinforces the main thesis of this study; that in certain limited contexts in the interwar period, perhaps in situations where disputes between nation-states were less intense and less in immediate need of resolution by force than they were at the (European) core of the international system, the employment of the treaty-making process did indirectly reduce nation-states' tendency to use force as a means of settling the conflicts of interest between them.

TABLE 3.6 *Summary statistics (gammas) derived from 4-way cross-tabulations between (1) war occurs after 1920/no war between 1921 and 1942 and (2) each of the treaty types identified in Table 2.2; controlling for (a) geographical proximity (near/not near) and (b) five alternative definitions of 'friendship/antagonism' outlined in Table 2.5 (COEFIICIENTS ARE ONLY REPORTED FOR THE 'NOT FRIENDS' = 'ANTAGONISTIC' DYADS FROM EACH 'FRIENDSHIP/ANTAGONISM' VARIABLE)*

Treaty type		*Friendship/ Angagonism I: 'friends' had not been at war with one another since 1900; 'antagonists' had been at war with one another sometime between 1900 and 1920*	*Friendship/ Antagonism II: 'friends' had signed either a general military or a non-aggression treaty and had not been at war with one another since 1900; 'antagonists' had not*	*Friendship/ Antagonism III: 'friends' shared the same language; 'antagonists' did not*	*Friendship/ Antagonism IV: 'friends' had signed at least five treaties of whatever type since 1920; 'antagonists' had signed less than five such treaties*	*Friendship/ Antagonism V: 'friends' had been allies in war at least once and never enemies in the period since 1815; 'antagonists' had not*
Financial	near	0.36 (N=33)	0.54 (N=171)	0.22 (N=168)	−1 (N=83)	0.42 (N=217)
	not near	−0.32 (N=32)	0.04 (N=716)	0.07 (N=718)	−0.12 (N=559)	0.19 (N=690)
General economic	near	−0.17	0.49	0.54	0.02	0.47
	not near	−0.75	−0.46	−0.43	−0.49	−0.38
Specific economic	near	0.47	0.44	0.42	−1	0.42
	not near	−0.33	−0.27	−0.15	−0.35	−0.05
Most Fav. Nation	near	0.05	0.12	0.23	−1	0.25
	not near	0.43	−0.20	−0.25	−0.47	−0.18
Short-run economic	near	−0.64	−0.24	−0.45	n	−0.39
	not near	−0.69	0.10	0.16	0.41	0.25
Transport and communications	near	0.46	0.43	0.43	−1	0.37
	not near	0.10	−0.15	0.06	−0.31	0.05
General political	near	0.62	0.55	0.48	−1	0.46
	not near	−0.32	0.44	0.40	0.52	0.47

Friendship and co-operation	near not near	0.48 −0.08	0.44 −0.33	0.36 −0.35	0.43 −0.58	0.48 −0.30
Territory/ boundaries	near not near	0.66 −0.69	0.71 −0.33	0.66 −0.08	0.25 −1	0.69 −0.06
Diplomatic	near not near	0.01 −0.52	0.32 −0.27	0.36 −0.32	0.50 −0.17	0.37 −0.28
Aliens' rights	near not near	0.47 −0.64	0.34 −0.11	0.16 −0.04	−0.09 −0.03	0.19 −0.06
Arbitration/ conciliation	near not near	0.78 −0.41	0.54 −0.22	0.45 −0.07	0.02 −0.29	0.49 −0.07
Cultural/ medical	near not near	0.47 0.40	0.15 −0.05	−0.06 0.05	−1 −0.61	0.06 0.03
Administrative Co-operation	near not near	0.72 −0.70	0.46 −0.14	0.23 −0.06	0.50 −0.39	0.32 −0.01
Specific political	near not near	0.18 −1	0.22 −1	0.13 −0.28	– −1	0.10 −0.23
General Military	near not near	0.31 0.01	* *	0.18 0.35	−1 0.45	0.27 0.46
Military short of alliance	near not near	−0.07 −0.79	0.34 −0.11	0.07 −0.02	−1 −1	0.19 0.14
Non-aggression/ anti-war	near not near	0.54 −0.38	* *	0.53 0.21	−1 −1	0.53 −0.22
Mutual assistance	near not near	−1 −1	−1 −1	−1 −1	−1 n	−1 −1
Reciprocal neutrality	near not near	−0.46 −0.17	−0.03 0.16	−0.30 0.12	−1 n	−0.21 0.12

* These coefficients were not computed in order to avoid tautological double counting since the treaty types involved are also included in the definition of the friendship/antagonism control variable.
n indicates that one of the rows or columns in the appropriate table was empty: gamma could not therefore be calculated.

TABLE 3.7 *Summary statistics (gammas) derived from 4-way cross-tabulations between (1) war occurs after 1920/no war between 1921 and 1942 and (2) each of the treaty types identified in Table 2.2; controlling for (a) power status differential/no power status differential and (b) five alternative definitions of 'friendship/antagonism' outlined in Table 2.5 (coefficients are only reported for the 'not friends' = 'antagonistic' dyads from each 'friendship/antagonism' variable)*

Treaty type		*Friendship Antagonism I: 'friends' had not been at war with one another since 1900; 'antagonists' had been at war with one another sometime between 1900 and 1920*	*Friendship/ Antagonism II: 'friends' had signed either a general military or a non-aggression treaty and had not been at war with one another since 1900; 'antagonists' had not*	*Friendship/ Antagonism III: 'friends' shared the same language; 'antagonists' did not*	*Friendship/ Antagonism IV: 'friends' had signed at least five treaties of whatever type since 1920; 'antagonists' had signed less than five such treaties*	*Friendship/ Antagonism V: 'friends' had been allies in war at least once and never enemies in the period since 1815; 'antagonists' had not*
Financial	no power differential	0.78 (N=26)	0.64 (N=582)	0.61 (N=553)	−1 (N=472)	0.64 (N=607)
	power differential	−0.50 (N=39)	−0.26 (N=305)	−0.32 (N=333)	−0.39 (N=170)	−0.22 (N=300)
General economic	no power differential	0.26	−0.20	−0.04	−1	−0.04
	power differential	−0.85	−0.36	−0.38	−0.24	−0.32
Specific economic	no power differential	0.80	0.35	0.55	−1	0.53
	power differential	−0.29	−0.36	−0.35	−0.30	−0.29
Most Fav. nation	no power differential	0.16	−0.30	−0.27	−1	−0.23
	power differential	0.33	−0.03	0.06	−0.35	0.09
Short-run Economic	no power differential	−0.69	0.06	0.26	−1	0.30
	power differential	−0.60	−0.21	−0.22	0.27	−0.20
Transport/ comm.	no power differential	0.69	0.29	0.54	−1	0.44
	power differential	0.13	−0.14	−0.08	−0.27	−0.02
General political	no power differential	0.48	0.74	0.7	−1	0.66
	power differential	0.12	0.16	0.13	0.39	0.15
Friendship and co-op.	no power differential	0.83	0.35	0.31	−0.46	0.43
	power differential	−0.27	−0.25	−0.18	−0.46	−0.18

Territory/ boundaries	no power differential	0.59	0.68	0.65	−0.02	0.71
	power differential	−0.01	0.02	0.08	−1	0.10
Diplomatic	no power differential	0.18	0.29	0.04	−1	0.09
	power differential	−0.44	−0.40	−0.22	−0.22	−0.21
Aliens' rights	no power differential	0.16	0.07	0.22	−1	0.13
	power differential	−0.17	−0.15	−0.16	0	−0.14
Arbitration/ conciliation	no power differential	0.38	0.04	0.20	−1	0.20
	power differential	0.23	0.01	0.08	−0.03	0.15
Cultural/ Medical/ Scientific	no power differential	0.23	0.13	0.27	−1	0.23
	power differential	0.58	−0.20	−0.16	−0.65	−0.11
Admin. co-operation	no power differential	0.42	0.50	0.44	−0.09	0.47
	power differential	−0.08	−0.23	−0.20	−0.22	−0.11
Specific political	no power differential	0.14	0.25	0.57	−1	0.48
	power differential	−0.60	−0.57	−0.56	−1	−0.48
General military	no power differential	0.18	*	0.71	−1[a]	0.72
	power differential	−0.23	*	−0.10	0.06	−0.07
Military short of alliance	no power differential	−0.16	0.67	0.65	−1[a]	0.69
	power differential	−0.60	−0.41	−0.48	−1[a]	−0.41
Non-agression	no power differential	0.73	*	0.69	−1	0.62
	power differential	−0.04	*	0.45	−1[a]	0.39
Mutual assistance	no power differential	−1	−1	−1	n	−1
	power differential	−1	−1	−1	−1	−1
Reciprocal neutrality	no power differential	0.14	−1	0.38	−1[a]	0.44
	power differential	−0.68	−1[a]	−0.39	n	−0.50

* These coefficients were not computed in order to avoid tautological double counting since the treaty types are also included in the definition of the Friendship/Antagonism control variable.

n indicates that one of the rows or columns in the appropriate table was empty: gamma could not therefore be calculated.

[a] This denotes a coefficient that has been artificially inflated by an extreme imbalance in the row or column marginals. The sign of the coefficient is nonetheless of interest.

SUMMARY AND CONCLUSIONS

For over a generation, both practitioners and students of international politics have been highly sceptical as to whether international law and lawmaking can perform any useful function, either direct or indirect, in the cause of world peace. Any attempt to assert the view that law might, however indirectly, play a positive role invariably invokes a stern response from the realist establishment: 'Look what happened in the 1930s; paper treaties didn't stop Hitler and Mussolini; national security interests and ambitions always override express treaty commitments'. While not wishing to deny the main thrust of this response, particularly in the context of Great Power interrelations, this chapter has attempted to show that the experience of the 1930s, in terms of the indirect effects of law and the lawmaking process, was not as uniformly disastrous as is often assumed. To be sure, the global correlations between treaty-making activities and the incidence of war generally seem to confirm the pessimistic realist view. Indeed it could be argued that from 1940 onwards the realist orthodoxy in effect took implicit cognisance of those global correlations, inferred accordingly that international law was largely irrelevant as a vehicle for sustaining peace and consequently set itself the task of attempting to preserve national and bloc security without recourse to the clearly fallible machinations of the international legal process.

The disaggregation of the global correlations, however, suggests that there were certain contexts – admittedly at the periphery of the international system, where the conflicts between the parties involved, though serious, were not as intense or as pressing as the conflicts at the core of the system – in which treaty-making clearly correlated negatively with the occurrence of war. While this finding does little to contradict the orthodox realist view of the most visible world events of the 1930s, it does suggest that the realists' wholesale rejection of law as a vehicle for peace in all situations where potentially there is a conflict of vital interests may not be entirely warranted: the negative correlations indicate that there were contexts in which what differentiates the pairs of nations that subsequently went to war with one another from those which did not is the fact that the latter engaged in more extensive treaty-making than the former.

The problem with this empirical observation, however, is that it may conceal the fact that none of the pairs of nations thus identified as participating fully in the treaty-making process were ever likely (for whatever other reason) to go to war with one another anyway. Similarly it might also have been the case that those pairs of nations which signed no treaties at all were highly likely (again, for other reasons) to find themselves at war. Under these circumstances, there would clearly be no *causal* link underlying the observed empirical correlation between treaty-making and war-avoidance: the correlation would be essentially *spurious*. In fact in this chapter a systematic effort has been made to test this spurious correlation possibility by applying statistical controls for a series of variables which attempt to categorise dyads according to their pre-existing patterns of 'friendship/antagonism'. If dyads have a clear record of strong prior antagonism (which is certainly true in the context of 'Friendship/Antagonism I' where antagonistic dyads had actually been at war only a few years previously), then the claim that any negative law-war correlation is the result of the fact that the dyads which avoided war did so 'because they were never likely to go to war anyway' looks extremely implausible. The conclusion that emerges strongly from these tests is that the spurious correlation interpretation is not vindicated: the negative correlations between treaty-making and the occurrence of war are still in evidence even when only dyads with a clear prior record of strong mutual antagonism are considered.

All of these findings lend support to what has been termed the 'circumscribed idealist hypothesis'; that in a limited number of general contexts which have now been clearly specified, international lawmaking appears to have been a critical variable in affecting the subsequent chances for international peace. In the next chapter, yet more rigorous tests are undertaken in order to see if this conclusion can be sustained, first, in the face of evidence concerning the *economic* dimension of international relations, and second, under the more stringent conditions of alternative statistical techniques.

4 Treaty-making, War and Peace: Further Empirical Evidence

The results which were reported in the previous chapter demonstrated a complex but consistent pattern of correlation between international lawmaking and war-avoidance that is clearly supportive of what has for the sake of brevity somewhat unattractively been described as the 'circumscribed idealist hypothesis'. While in no sense wishing to deny that in many contexts – arguably the most important ones in terms of the broad sweep of world events – law signally failed to assist in the maintenance of peace in the 1920s and 1930s, a set of empirical findings has been outlined which suggests that in certain limited contexts international lawmaking may indeed have begun to play an indirect but positive role in the international politics of the period; a role which most previous observers have either completely ignored or summarily dismissed as ineffectual. Since the empirical findings which have been presented suggest the need for a small but significant revision in the orthodox realist interpretation of the 1930s (and perhaps, therefore, in the realist position generally), this chapter is devoted to an attempt to reinforce their plausibility.

The chapter is divided into five main sections: the first attempts to synthesise the findings reported in Chapter 3 in order to reduce them to more manageable proportions for further investigation. The second introduces an economic dimension into the analysis, in the form of bilateral trade data and colonial dependency status, in order to establish how far the tentative conclusions drawn thus far about the role of treaty-making might be confounded by influences from the international economy. The next section indicates the effect on the law-war correlations of controlling for economic and political 'friendship/antagonism' factors simultaneously. The fourth section subjects the empirical findings presented to the statistical technique of log-linear modelling in order to ascertain whether or not those findings are sufficiently robust to meet the more searching standards which that technique demands. In the final section, somewhat grandiosely perhaps, a predictive model of the occurrence of war in the interwar period is developed. This is not in any sense posited as an 'explanation' of war in this context (given the low level of explained variance in the model this is just as well), but rather is intended to offer an additional means of ascertaining how far treaty-making activity is capable of predicting the occurrence of war when a number of other relevant variables are controlled for.

REDUCING THE COMPLEXITY OF THE EMPIRICAL RESULTS

In Chapter 3 it was indicated that across all treaty types, when controls were applied for (1) cultural dissimilarity, geographical remoteness and power status differential and (2) various definitions of pre-existing 'friendship/antagonism', treaty-making activity consistently correlated with war-avoidance. The pattern observed, however, took the form of rather a large number of coefficients which for the sake both of intuitive comprehension and of further statistical manipulation certainly requires simplification. I propose to effect this simplication in three ways.

The most obvious means of simplifying the findings is to combine the different treaty types on some basis in order to construct composite indices of treaty-making activity. While a multidimensional scaling algorithm could be used for this purpose, the method of aggregation chosen (on the grounds that it produces indices which are both unambiguous and easily understood) was to add together the number of treaties signed by each dyad under three separate headings: political, economic and military. Three separate indices were thus constructed – Aggregate of Political Agreements, Aggregate of Economic Agreements and Aggregate of Military Agreements – according to the groupings of treaty types identified in Table 4.1. Each index was then recoded to give four possible values: 0, 1, 2 and 3 or more. Quite apart from performing a simplifying function, however, these indices have the additional and desirable attribute of corresponding rather more closely than the individual treaty variables to the idea of a *network* of treaty commitments which was mentioned in Chapter 2. This is simply because for a dyad to score relatively highly on, say, the 'aggregate of political agreements index' the pairs of countries involved must have signed several different sorts of political agreement: a relatively low score, on the other hand, will result when pairs of nations have confined their treaty-making to one or two narrowly defined areas or if they have engaged in no treaty-making at all. Moreover, if one of the ideas advanced in Chapter 1 is correct, namely that the treaty-making process is more likely to facilitate the build-up of inter-nation trust if it proceeds on a relatively broad front encompassing several different types of treaty-making activity, then it is to be expected that this 'network' characteristic of the aggregated indices may serve to strengthen the observed correlations between lawmaking and war-avoidance.

A second means of simplifying the empirical findings reported in the previous chapter is to combine the three existing control variables which define the contexts in which treaty-making and war correlate negatively – cultural similarity/difference, geographical proximity/remoteness and power differential/not – into a single composite index. This was achieved by creating a dummy variable, DIFF3, which divides the pairs of nations under analysis into two groups: (1) those which were

TABLE 4.1 *Groupings of treaty types employed to produce aggregated indices*

Treaty type	
General political Specific political Friendship and co-operation Territory/boundaries Diplomatic Aliens' rights/duties/limitations Arbitration/conciliation Administrative co-operation	Additively aggregated to produce an 'Aggregate of Political Agreements' index[a]
Financial General economic Specific economic Most Favoured Nation Short-run economic Transport and communications	Additively aggregated to produce an 'Aggregate of Economic Agreement' index[a]
General military Military agreements short of alliance Non-aggression/anti-war pact Mutual assistance Reciprocal neutrality	Additively aggregated to produce an 'Agreement of Military Agreements' index[a]

[a] Prior to aggregation, each treaty type variable was first coded as a dummy variable so that each dyad either scored 1 (meaning that either one or more treaties of the particular type were signed after 1920 by the pair of nations concerned) or zero (meaning that no such treaties were signed).

culturally dissimilar *and* geographically remote *and* of differential power status and (2) those which did not exhibit all three of these characteristics.

Finally, some degree of simplification can be achieved by considering only those 'friendship/antagonism' control variables which in theoretical terms most clearly and most plausibly distinguish 'pre-existing friendship' and 'pre-existing antagonism'. As was intimated in Chapter 2, the two variables which perform this task most effectively are 'Friendship/Antagonism V' and 'Friendship/Antagonism I' respectively. 'Friendship/Antagonism V', since it categorises as 'friends' those dyads which had been allies in war at least once and never enemies in any war since 1815, clearly identifies pairs of nations which had enjoyed relatively good relations over a long period. 'Friendship/Antagonism I', in contrast, since it classes as 'antagonists' those dyads which had been on opposite sides in war in the period immediately prior to 1920, clearly identifies pairs of nations whose relations can fairly be characterised as highly antagonistic at the beginning of the time period under analysis. The two variables, in short, provide a sound basis for evaluating the 'spurious correlation' claim that any negative law-war correlations which might be observed are the result of pre-existing friendship among the 'treaty-making–no war' dyads and/or pre-existing enmity among the 'no treaty-making–war occurs' dyads.

Table 4.2 shows the results of these efforts to reduce the complexity of the findings presented earlier. For completeness, the war-law coefficients are now reported for the 'friends' = 'not antagonists' dyads (see columns 2 and 4 of Table 4.2) though these coefficients are not directly relevant to the arguments that are being advanced here. Since there is now less detail to report, the appropriate tau_b coefficients from the various tables are also shown. Although these coefficients are generally lower than the gamma summary statistics, they follow the same broad pattern of positive coefficients (where there are no significant differences in geography, culture or power status) and negative coefficients (where such differences do exist) that was observed in Chapter 3. Indeed, the consistency of these positive-negative pairings is the most marked feature of columns 1 and 3 of the table. Moreover the fact that most of the negative coefficients are noticeably larger than those reported in Tables 3.5, 3.6 and 3.7 supports the notion that it is when there is a well-established *network* of treaty commitments that the indirect effects of international lawmaking on war-avoidance are greatest.

The major conclusion suggested by the findings shown in Table 4.2, however, is that once again the 'circumscribed idealist hypothesis' derives

TABLE 4.2 *Summary statistics (gammas and – in brackets – tau_b) derived from 4-way cross-tabulations between (1) war occurs after 1920/no war between 1921 and 1942 and (2) each of the aggregate treaty indices defined in Table 4.1; controlling for (a) cultural similarity/difference, geographical proximity/remoteness, power status differential/not and DIFF 3 and (b) 'Friendship/Antagonism I' and 'Friendship/Antagonism V'*

Treaty index		*'Friendship/Antagonism I': 'friends' had not been at war with one another since 1900; 'antagonists' had been at war with one another sometime between 1900 and 1920*		*'Friendship Antagonism V': 'friends' had been allies in war at least once and never enemies in the period since 1815; 'antagonists' had not*	
		Column 1 *'Antagonists'*	*Column 2* *'Friends'*	*Column 3* *'Antagonists'*	*Column 4* *'Friends'*
Aggregate of Economic Agreements	no cultural difference	0.63 (0.29) N = 40	−0.05 (0) N = 553	0.19 (0.07) N = 513	/ N = 80
	cultural difference	−0.66 (−0.43) N = 25	−0.44 (−0.16) N = 398	−0.33 (−0.13) N = 394	−0.50 (−0.23) N = 29
	near	0.57 (0.27) N = 33	0.21 (0.07) N = 213	0.44 (0.18) N = 217	/ N = 29
	not near	−0.38 (−0.23) N = 32	−0.38 (−0.14) N = 738	−0.26 (−0.10) N = 690	−0.62 (−0.16) N = 80
	no power differential	0.64 (0.26) N = 26	−0.40 (−0.10) N = 638	0.01 (0) N = 607	−1 (−0.17) N = 57
	power differential	−0.24 (−0.13) N = 39	−0.36 (−0.18) N = 313	−0.24 (−0.13) N = 300	−0.63 (−0.18) N = 52
	not different on all 3	0.54 (0.25) N = 49	0.01 (−0.38) N = 781	0.26 (0.09) N = 736	−1 (−0.16) N = 94
	different on all 3[a]	−0.66 (−0.46) N = 16	−0.61 (−0.31) N = 170	−0.53 (−0.29) N = 171	−0.41 (−0.22) N = 15
Aggregate of Political Agreements	no cultural difference	0.87 (0.44)	−0.02 (0)	0.21 (0.08)	/
	cultural difference	−0.93 (−0.68)	−0.29 (−0.10)	−0.30 (−0.11)	−0.12 (−0.04)
	near	1 (0.46)	0.30 (0.09)	0.56 (0.20)	/
	not near	−0.75 (−0.48)	−0.29 (−0.10)	−0.25 (−0.09)	0 (0)
	no power differential	0.43 (0.15)	−0.08 (0)	0.22 (0.06)	−1 (−0.13)
	power differential	−0.23 (−0.13)	−0.33 (−0.17)	−0.24 (−0.13)	0 (0)
	not different on all 3	0.83 (0.35)	0.09 (0.02)	0.33 (0.11)	−1 (−0.11)
	different on all 3	−0.96 (−0.74)	−0.50 (−0.26)	−0.53 (−0.29)	−0.12 (−0.04)

Aggregate of Military Agreements	no cultural difference	0.65 (0.30)	0.14 (0.03)	0.43 (0.15)	
	cultural difference	−0.88 (−0.59)	−0.21 (−0.03)	−0.23 (−0.04)	0.15 (0.04)
	near	0.55 (0.19)	0.06 (0)	0.38 (0.14)	
	not near	−0.51 (−0.26)	0.01 (0)	0.11 (0.02)	−0.27 (0.05)
	no power differential	1 (0.44)	0.39 (0.07)	0.67 (0.19)	−1 (−0.06)
	power differential	−0.60 (−0.32)	−0.34 (−0.10)	−0.20 (−0.07)	0.20 (0.03)
	not different on all 3	0.58	0.33	0.56	−1
	different on all 3	−0.90 (−0.61)	−0.77 (−0.17)	−0.81 (−0.20)	0.23 (0.08)

/ indicates that no coefficient could be computed because of an empty row or column in the corresponding crosstabulation.
[a] 'different on all 3' refers to those dyads which were culturally different, *and* geographically remote *and* different in power status; 'not different on all 3' refers to all other dyads.

significant support from the evidence (see all the negative coefficients in columns 1 and 3 of Table 4.2). This is particularly the case for that small group of dyads which are culturally dissimilar, geographically remote and of differential power status. In column 1 of Table 4.2, for example, this group furnished law-war coefficients of $\gamma = -0.66$ ($\tau_b = -0.46$) for economic agreements, $\gamma = -0.96$ ($\tau_b = -0.74$) for political agreements and $\gamma = -0.90$ ($\tau_b = -0.61$) for military agreements; all among dyads which could reasonably be described as enemies in the early interwar years. Even though there are only a small number of cases involved (N = 16), these are strong statistical relationships by any standards and they accordingly lend considerable weight to the notion that treaty-making activity could have had an effect on nations' propensities to wage war in the interwar period. That these results are not confined to a small number of cases, however, is evidenced by the coefficients shown in column 3 of Table 4.2. On the basis of a much larger number of cases (N = 177), the corresponding 'different on all 3' category of dyads produces law-war coefficients of $\gamma = -0.53$ ($\tau_b = -0.29$) for both economic and political agreements and $\gamma = -0.81$ ($\tau_b = -0.20$) for military agreements. Yet again, then, the case for an indirect link, in limited contexts, between treaty-making and war-avoidance is reinforced.

THE LAW-WAR CORRELATIONS AND INTERNATIONAL ECONOMIC FACTORS

An obvious potentially confounding influence upon any political mechanisms which might operate in the relations between nation-states is that of international economics. Patterns of bilateral international trade particularly are a good indicator of the extent to which the mutual economic interests of different nation-states coincide and it might well be expected that where economic interests strongly converge there could also be a convergence of security interests. In these circumstances we might anticipate that dyads which enjoyed a strong trading relationship in the interwar period would be less inclined to engage in mutual hostilities than those whose trading relationship was relatively weak. Bilateral trade patterns, therefore, in effect constitute another set of control factors, the effects of which must be taken into account if the 'circumscribed idealist hypothesis' is to be sustained.

These trade patterns are perhaps best conceptualised in the first instance as a set of *economic* 'friendship/antagonism' variables analogous to the five (political) 'friendship/antagonism' variables which were examined in Chapter 3. Table 4.3 identifies five such economic 'friendship/antagonism' variables. As was pointed out in Chapter 2, the employment of VOLUME28 and VOLUME38 is largely self-explanatory. In providing information about the trading position of dyads in 1928 and 1938, the two variables provide a summary indication of the state of bilateral relations both before and after the depression and trade war of the 1930s. In using both variables it is assumed that economic relations are relatively good if trade is high and relatively bad if trade is low. A slightly different way of examining the possibly confounding impact of patterns of trade is to assess the degree to which bilateral trade is *imbalanced.* IMBALANCE28 and IMBALANCE38, for 1928 and 1938 respectively, distinguish between pairs of nations whose exports to each other were roughly equivalent and those in which one 'partner' exported much less to the other than it imported from it. Again a relatively even balance is assumed to denote 'good' economic relations and an uneven balance, 'bad' relations. Finally, VOLCHANGE distinguishes between those dyads whose bilateral trade *declined* significantly between 1928 and 1938 and those whose trade remained at broadly the same level (or even increased) in the face of the growing economic nationalism which characterised the international political economy of the 1930s. Again a broadly constant volume of trade is assumed to denote 'good' economic relations, and a significant decrease, 'bad' relations.

As Table 4.3 indicates, when controls are applied for the 'economic' 'friendship/antagonism' variables, the robustness of the negative correlations between treaty-making and the recourse to war which were reported earlier is strongly confirmed. Specific comment on the magnitudes of the particular coefficients, however, is again unnecessary for our present purposes: what matters is that within the categories of *all* of the trade variables, the same pattern of positive-negative pairings of coefficients that has been repeatedly observed is clearly in evidence. In essence, Table 4.3 demonstrates that trade patterns make virtually no difference to the relationship between treaty-making and war-avoidance. Again, therefore, the broad pattern of law-war correlations serves to corroborate the 'circumscribed idealist hypothesis' which has been advanced in the course of the last two chapters.

Table 4.4 illustrates the effect on the pattern of war-law correlations of controlling for colonial and quasi-colonial status. While the issues which this variable raises are in some important respects 'political' – realists have always argued, for example, that long-term security motives were at the root of European imperialism in the nineteenth and

TABLE 4.3 *Summary statistics (gammas and – in brackets – tau$_b$) derived from 4-way cross-tabulations between (1) war occurs after 1920/no war between and 1942 and (2) each of the aggregate treaty indices defined in Table 4.1, controlling for (a) cultural similarity/difference, geographical proximity/remoteness, p status differential/not and DIFF3 and (b) five bilateral trade variables which define groups of dyads which have 'relatively poor' bilateral economic relat*

		VOLUME 28 (*volume of bilateral trade 1928*)		*VOLUME 38* (*volume of bilateral trade 1938*)	
		trade low (economic relations relatively poor)	*trade high* (economic relations relatively good)	*trade low* (economic relations relatively poor)	*trade high* (economic relations relatively good)
Aggregate of Economic Agreements	no cultural difference	−0.11 (−0.2) N = 483	0.02 (0) N = 110	0.31 (−0.05) N = 216	0.14 (0.04) N = 37
	cultural difference	−0.32 (−0.07) N = 362	−0.41 (−0.16) N = 61	−0.35 (−0.05) N = 150	−0.31 (−0.10) N = 27
	near	0.13 (0.03) N = 178	0.34 (0.07) N = 68	−0.04 (0) N = 90	0.29 (0.07) N = 15
	not near	−0.37 (−0.09) N = 667	−0.28 (−0.11) N = 143	−0.43 (−0.07) N = 276	−0.26 (−0.08) N = 49
	no power differential	−0.20 (−0.03) N = 614	1 (0.23) N = 50	−0.013 (−0.02) N = 290	0.38 (0.08) N = 36
	power differential	−0.45 (−0.19) N = 231	−0.27 (−0.11) N = 121	−0.58 (−0.15) N = 70	−0.38 (−0.16) N = 28
	not different on all 3	0.04 (0.01) N = 704	0.08 (0.02) N = 126	−0.28 (−0.04) N = 316	0.40 (0.11) N = 51
	different on all 3	−0.52 (−0.22) N = 141	−0.55 (−0.23) N = 45	−0.42 (−0.11) N = 50	−0.64 (−0.29) N = 13
Aggregate of Political Agreements	no cultural difference	−0.06 (−0.01)	0.03 (0.01)	−0.06 (−0.01)	0.17 (0.05)
	cultural difference	−0.08 (−0.02)	−0.59 (−0.24)	0.09 (0.02)	−0.29 (−0.09)
	near	0.21 (0.05)	0.43 (0.10)	0.39 (0.10)	0.21 (0.05)
	not near	−0.22 (−0.05)	−0.39 (−0.16)	−0.15 (−0.03)	−0.22 (−0.06)
	no power differential	0 (0)	1 (0.291)	0.05 (0.01)	0.49 (0.11)
	power differential	−0.33 (−0.13)	−0.38 (−0.17)	−0.23 (−0.09)	−.35 (−0.15)
	not different on all 3	0.10 (0.02)	0.10 (0.03)	0 (0)	0.39 (0.11)
	different on all 3	−0.35 (−0.14)	−0.82 (−0.35)	−0.10 (−0.03)	−0.61 (−0.26)
Aggregate of Military Agreements	no cultural difference	0.30 (0.07)	0.25 (0.11)	0 (0)	0.46 (0.17)
	cultural difference	−0.12 (−0.02)	−0.47 (−0.16)	−0.06 (−0.01)	−0.25 (−0.05)
	near	0.36 (0.10)	0.19 (0.08)	0.20 (0.04)	0.27 (0.10)
	not near	0 (0)	−0.10 (−0.03)	−0.13 (−0.02)	0.13 (0.03)
	no power differential	0.35 (0.06)	1 (0.44)	0.04 (0)	0.82 (0.29)
	power differential	−0.24 (−0.08)	−0.25	−0.28 (−0.08)	−0.23 (−0.08)
	not different on all 3	0.44 (0.10)	0.26 (0.11)	0.09 (0.01)	0.59 (0.21)
	different on all 3	−0.52 (−0.29)	−0.34 (−0.09)	−0.80 (−0.22)	

The original data for all the trade variables in this table were measured at interval level in US$ equivalents. In order to use trade variables for cross-tabula purposes, each was recoded into a 2-category variable with the cut-off at the original interval level global mean. The 'trade low' category of VOLUME28, example, refers to all those dyads whose volume of bilateral trade in 1928 was less than or equal to the average volume of trade for all dyads in that year, the 'tr high' category refers to those dyads whose volume of trade was greater than the global average.

VOLCHANGE indirectly measures the extent to which there was a significant decline in the volume of bilateral trade between 1928 and 1938 in percent terms. A 'relatively large reduction in trade' is defined as more than a 50 per cent reduction in the volume of bilateral trade. 'Trade constant' includes all th dyads which experience less than a 50 per cent reduction in trade.

early twentieth centuries – there is also no doubt that *economic* domination and exploitation were a central feature of the hegemony which European imperialism exercised over its colonial dependencies in the period before 1945. The need to apply statistical controls for colonial status at all derives from the following possibility: it could be argued that in all the previous analysis law and war only correlated negatively for dyads which were culturally dissimilar, geographically remote or of differential power status because the presence of these characteristics indicates the existence of a series of colonial or quasi-colonial relationships in which the dominant partner in each dyad was in a position to determine the course of relations between the two states involved. In

IMBALANCE28 (*imbalance in bilateral trade 1928*)		*IMBALANCE38* (*imbalance in bilateral trade 1938*)		*VOL-CHANGE* (*change in volume of trade 1928–38*)	
Imbalance significant (economic relations relatively poor)	*No significant imbalance* (economic relations relatively good)	*Imbalance significant* (economic relations relatively poor)	*No significant imbalance* (economic relations relatively good)	*Relatively large reduction in trade* (economic relations relatively poor)	*Trade constant or increase* (economic relations relatively good)
0.19 (0.06) N = 436	0.26 (0.06) N = 157	0.18 (0.05) N = 426	0.14 (0.04) N = 167	0.17 (0.06) N = 248	0 (0) N = 345
0.35 (−0.09) N = 329	0.12 (0.03) N = 94	−0.42 (−0.10) N = 303	0 (0) N = 120	−0.28 (−0.09) N = 180	−0.35 (−0.07) N = 248
0.53 (0.21) N = 180	1 (0.10) N = 66	0.45 (0.16) N = 78	0.35 (0.08) N = 68	0.11 (0.03) N = 121	0.42 (0.11) N = 125
0.39 (−0.10) N = 585	0.22 (0.06) N = 185	−0.30 (−0.08) N = 551	−0.09 (−0.03) N = 219	−0.18 (−0.06) N = 307	−0.31 (−0.07) N = 463
0.24 (0.05) N = 522	0.45 (0.07) N = 142	0.06 (0.01) N = 503	0.59 (0.14) N = 161	0.54 (0.15) N = 251	−0.69 (−0.09) N = 412
0.37 (−0.016) N = 243	−0.08 (−0.02) N = 109	−0.33 (−0.14) N = 226	−0.35 (−0.15) N = 126	−0.43 (−0.17) N = 177	−0.29 (−0.12) N = 175
0.34 (0.10) N = 633	0.44 (0.10) N = 197	0.28 (0.08) N = 606	0.45 (0.12) N = 224	0.35 (0.11) N = 338	0.13 (0.02) N = 492
0.62 (−0.23) N = 132	−0.30 (−0.11) N = 54	−0.65 (−0.26) N = 123	−0.48 (−0.21) N = 63	−0.64 (−0.31) N = 90	−0.50 (−0.17) N = 96
0.30 (0.10)	−0.21 (−0.06)	0.18 (0.05)	0.16 (0.04)	0.29 (0.09)	−0.10 (−0.02)
0.08 (−0.02)	−0.40 (−0.10)	−0.21 (−0.05)	−0.10 (−0.03)	−0.46 (−0.14)	0.11 (0.03)
0.50 (0.16)	1 (0.09)	0.47 (0.13)	0.30 (0.06)	0.41 (0.10)	0.09 (0.02)
0.13 (−0.03)	−0.27 (−0.07)	−0.21 (−0.05)	−0.12 (−0.03)	−0.32 (−0.10)	−0.05 (−0.01)
0.36 (0.09)	0.46 (0.07)	0.20 (0.04)	0.64 (0.16)	0.66 (0.19)	0.46 (−0.06)
0.24 (−0.10)	−0.50 (−0.20)	−0.28 (−0.12)	−0.38 (−0.16)	−0.45 (−0.21)	−0.17 (−0.07)
0.43 (0.13)	0 (0)	0.30 (0.09)	0.42 (0.12)	0.43 (0.14)	0.03 (0)
040 (−0.16)	−0.75 (−0.26)	−0.47 (−0.18)	−0.55 (−0.23)	−0.82 (−0.37)	−0.10 (−0.01)
0.51 (0.18)	0 (0)	0.31 (0.09)	0.61 (0.23)	0.49 (20)	0.08 (0.01)
0.15 (−0.03)	−0.26 (−0.05)	−0.21 (−0.03)	−0.15 (−0.03)	−0.23 (−0.06)	−0.29 (−0.03)
0.43 (0.17)	0.26 (0.05)	0.32 (0.11)	0.52 (0.17)	0.30 (0.11)	0.07 (0.01)
0.14 (0.02)	0.02 (0)	−0.06 (−0.01)	0.29 (0.08)	0.11 (0.03)	−0.04 (0)
0.65 (0.19)	0.81 (0.19)	0.54 (0.13)	0.86 (0.31)	0.85 (0.34)	−1 (−0.06)
0.16 (−0.06)	−0.54 (−0.15)	−0.32 (−0.11)	−0.06 (−0.02)	−0.26 (−0.10)	−0.22 (−0.07)
0.61 (0.21)	0.19 (0.04)	0.41 (0.11)	0.73 (0.28)	0.58 (0.22)	0.23 (0.04)
0.65 (−0.19)	−1 (−0.18)	−0.53 (−0.14)	−1 (−0.26)	−0.78 (−0.24)	−0.55 (−0.12)

these circumstances, the colonial power would be able to persuade, or if necessary coerce, the subordinate dependent state to enter into whatever treaty commitments suited the former's own national interest. The subordinate state, by the same token, would be in too weak a position to contemplate engaging in overt warfare against the colonial power, even if its own vital interests seemed to be at variance with those of that colonial power. Indeed, so the argument runs, it is perhaps the very existence of an imperialist-colony set of relationships that produces a group of dyads which engage extensively in treaty-making and which do not engage in war; a group of 'high-law-no-war' dyads. Moreover, when these dyads are included in a (controlled) cross-tabulation between

TABLE 4.4 *Summary statistics (gammas and – in brackets – tau_b) derived from 4-way cross-tabulations between war occurs after 1920/no war between 1921 and (2) each of the aggregate treaty indices defined in Table 4.1; controlling for (a) cultural similarity/difference, geographical proximity/remoteness, power status differential/not and DIFF 3 and (b) Friendship/Antagonism I and Friendship/Antagonism V. (ALL COLONIAL AND QUASI-COLONIAL DYADS REMOVED FROM THE ANALYSIS.)*[a]

		'Friendship/Antagonism I': 'friends' had not been at war with one another since 1900; 'antagonists' had been at war with one another sometime between 1900 and 1920		*'Friendship/Antagonism V': 'friends' had been allies in war at least once and never enemies in the period since 1815; 'antagonists' had not*	
Treaty index		*'Antagonists'*	*'Friends'*	*'Antagonists'*	*'Friends'*
Aggregate of Economic Agreements	no cultural difference	0.63 (0.21) N=40	−0.04 (−0.01) N=549	0.21 (0.07) N=510	N=79
	cultural difference	−0.61 (−0.33) N=22	−0.25 (−0.06) N=374	−0.16 (−0.04) N=369	0.09 (0.02) N=27
	near	0.41 (0.13) N=33	0.25 (0.07) N=206	0.46 (0.16) N=210	N=29
	not near	−0.26 (−0.12) N=29	−0.2 (−0.07) N=717	−0.14 (−0.04) N=669	−0.35 (−0.06) N=77
	no power differential	1 (0.26) N=26	−0.15 (−0.02 N=638	0.26 (0.06) N=607	−1 (−0.11) N=57
	power differential	−0.20 (−0.09) N=36	−0.37 (−0.16) N=285	−0.23 (−0.10) N=272	−0.36 (−0.07) N=49
	not different on all 3	0.60 (0.19) N=49	0.15 (0.03) N=771	0.39 (0.12) N=727	−1 (−0.12) N=93
	different on all 3[b]	−0.42 (−0.21) N=13	−0.58 (−0.22) N=152	−0.52 (−0.21) N=152	0.27 (0.13) N=13
Aggregate of Political Agreements	no cultural difference	1 (0.36)	−0.08 (−0.02)	0.19 (0.06)	
	cultural difference	−0.97 (−0.81)	0 (0)	−0.10 (−0.02)	−0.25 (−0.07)
	near	1 (0.36)	0.17 (0.04)	0.49 (0.15)	
	not near	−0.87 (−0.56)	−0.17 (−0.04)	−0.14 (−0.04)	−0.20 (−0.03)
	no power differential	1 (0.14)	0.03 (0)	0.36 (0.08)	−1 (−0.10
	power differential	−0.31 (−0.15)	−0.34 (−0.14)	−0.23 (−0.10)	−0.36 (−0.07)
	not different on all 3	1 (0.31)	0.12 (0.03)	0.39 (0.12)	−1 (−0.10
	different on all 3	−1 (−1)	−0.32 (−0.12)	−0.46 (−0.18)	−0.27 (−0.10)

Aggregate of Military Agreements	no cultural difference	0.65 (0.30)	0.14 (−0.03)	0.43 (0.10)	/
	cultural difference	−0.92 (−0.64)	0.01 (0)	−0.17 (−0.02)	0.31 (0.05)
	near	0.55 (0.19	0.08 (0.01	0.40 (0.15)	/
	not near	−0.54 (−0.27)	0.08 (0.01)	0.14 (0.03)	0.32 (0.06)
	no power differential	1 (0.44)	0.39 (0.07)	0.67 (0.19)	−1 (−0.06
	power differential	−0.60 (−0.32)	−0.24 (−0.05)	−0.12 (−0.04)	0.23 (0.01)
	not different on all 3	0.58 (0.23)	0.34 (0.08)	0.57 (0.19)	−1 (−0.06
	different on all 3	−1 (−0.69)	−0.62 (−0.12)	−1 (−0.18)	0.45 (0.17)

[a] colonial dyads were defined as all those pairs of nations which had experienced a formal-legal metropolitian–colonial relationship at some stage between 1850 and 1942.

[b] 'different on all 3' referes to those dyads which were culturally different *and* geographically remote *and* different in power status; 'not different on all 3' referes to all other dyads.

Quasi-colonial dyads were defined to include the relations between the US and each of the countries of Latin America. Leaving these dyads in the analysis yields results very similar to those reported in this table.

indicates that no coefficients could be computed because of an empty row or column in the corresponding cross-tabulation.

treaty-making activity and the occurrence of war/not, their possible presence in the 'high-law-no-war' cell could be sufficient to produce a negative correlation overall between law and war. Thus it is the unequal nature of imperialist-colony relations which (indirectly) produces the negative treaty-making – war correlations, not the fact that the treaty-making process itself in some indirect way encourages peaceful internation relations. Though this argument seems intuitively plausible, the results reported in Table 4.4 indicate that it is simply not consistent with the available empirical evidence. Table 4.4 clearly shows that when all colonial and quasi-colonial relations are removed from the analysis, the pattern of negative law-war coefficients remains (and if anything the magnitudes of the negative coefficients are actually increased). In these circumstances it can obviously not be the case that it is the 'weight' of colonial or quasi-colonial dyads which has in some way artificially generated the negative law-war correlations previously observed: the 'circumscribed idealist hypothesis', therefore, again derives support from the data.

CONTROLLING FOR ECONOMIC AND POLITICAL 'FRIENDSHIP/ANTAGONISM' FACTORS SIMULTANEOUSLY

It is clear from the preceding analysis that the negative law-war correlations predicted by the 'circumscribed idealist hypothesis' continue to be in evidence when separate statistical controls are applied for pre-existing political and economic 'friendship/antagonism'. In this section, controls for these two sets of variables are applied simultaneously in order to discover if the interaction of political and economic factors could have had some confounding influence upon those war-law correlations. Table 4.5 reports the results of a set of 5-way cross-tabulations which seek to establish if this is indeed the case.

As the table indicates, if anything simultaneous controls for political and economic 'friendship/antagonism' actually strengthen the pattern of war–law correlations which has previously been encountered. (See, for example, the series of $\gamma = +1$ and $\gamma = -1$ coefficients shown in the aggregate political agreements segment of the first column of Table 4.5). Indeed, although the number of cases in some of the categories is (inevitably, with so many controls) extremely small, the overall pattern of coefficients lends strong support to the 'circumscribed idealist hypothesis': even when there is both a prior record of political antagonism *and* a prior record of poor bilateral economic relations (see, for example, the coefficients which have been underlined in Table 4.5), the relationship between treaty-making and the occurrence of war continues to furnish large negative coefficients. Yet again, therefore, the notion that treaty-making activity, in certain limited contexts, serves to reduce the probability of war is reinforced by the evidence.

AN APPLICATION OF LOG-LINEAR MODELLING TECHNIQUES

The findings which have so far been reported have indicated that in the interwar period the pursuit of co-operative strategies at the dyadic level does seem to have reduced the probability of war: in statistical terms, the negative law-war correlations first observed in Chapter 3 have proved remarkably robust. The 4- and 5-way cross-tabulations which have been presented, however, have on occasion necessarily involved cells which contain relatively few cases. This was particularly evident for those tables which included 'Friendship/Antagonism I' in which only 65 pairs of countries (those that had been at war with another between 1900 and 1910) fell into the 'prior record of antagonism' category. It could be argued that because of this small number of cases, the results reported are not particularly convincing from a statistical point of view and that had a more rigorous form of analysis been applied, the empirical results might not so consistently have supported the 'circumscribed idealist hypothesis'. It is in this context that the log-linear modelling technique assumes particular relevance in the sense that it enables the analyst to assess the relative importance of any given interaction effect among a group of variables whilst simultaneously considering all the other possible interaction effects among those variables. Thus, for any given multi-way table, log-linear techniques can be employed to discover whether or not a particular observed effect based on a relatively small number of cases continues to be in evidence when all other interactions among all (combinations of) variables and across all cases are considered.[1] The essential reason for using log-linear procedures in this analysis, therefore, is most emphatically not a matter of employing the most fashionable or sophisticated technique available. Rather it is that log-linear models offer an additional means of *confirming* (or refuting as the case may be) the findings which have already been presented.

It would be unnecessarily cumbersome to report on the results of all the log-linear models which could be tested against each of the multi-way tables that have been presented in this and the previous chapter. However, Tables 4.6 to 4.9 inclusive provide an illustration of the

TABLE 4.5 *Summary statistics (gammas and – in brackets – tau_b) derived from 5-way cross-tabulations between (1) war occurs after 1920/not and (2) aggregate of political agreements and aggregate of economic agreements; controlling for (a) DIFF3, (b) Friendship/Antagonism I and V; and (c) five bilateral trade variables which define groups of dyads which have 'relatively good' vs 'relatively poor' bilateral economic relations*

Treaty type	Bilateral trade control variable		Cultural similarity, geographical proximity power status differential (DIFF3)	'Friendship/Antagonism I': 'Friends' had not been at war with one another since 1900; 'antagonists' had been at war with one another some time between 1900 and 1920				'Friendship/Antagonism V': 'Friends' had been allies in war at least once and never enemies in the period since 1815; 'antagonists' had not			
				'Antagonists'		'Friends'		'Antagonists'		'Friends'	
Aggregate of Political Agreements	Volume of trade 1928	trade low = poor economic relations	not different on all 3	1 (0.33)	N = 28	−0.21 (−0.04)	N = 676	0.12 (0.02)	N = 642	−1 (−0.10)	N = 62
			different on all 3[a]	−1 (−0.85)	N = 13	−0.23 (−0.08)	N = 128	−0.38 (−0.15)	N = 133	1 (.29)	N = 8
		trade high = good economic relations	not different on all 3	1 (0.21)	N = 21	−0.08 (−0.02)	N = 105	0.06 (0.02)	N = 94	/	N = 32
			different on all 3	−1 (−1)	N = 3	−0.75 (−0.29)	N = 42	−0.75 (−0.31)	N = 38	−1 (=0.64)	N = 7
	Volume of trade 1938	trade low = poor economic relations	not different on all 3	1 (0.44)	N = 8	−0.23 (−0.04)	N = 308	0.05 (0.01)	N = 300	−1 (−0.17)	N = 16
			different on all 3	/	N = 2	−0.25 (−0.08)	N = 48	−0.01 (0)	N = 47	/	N = 3
		trade high = good economic relations	not different on all 3	1 (0.26)	N = 41	0.16 (0.04)	N = 473	0.40 (0.13)	N = 436	/	N = 78
			different on all 3	−1 (−1)	N = 14	−0.45 (−0.17)	N = 122	−0.62 (−0.26)	N = 124	−0.40 (−0.15)	N = 12
	Trade imbalance 1928	imbalance high = poor economic relations	not different on all 3	1 (0.44)	N = 30	0.19 (0.04)	N = 603	0.48 (0.15)	N = 567	−1 (−0.12)	N = 66
			different on all 3	−1 (−0.84)	N = 12	−0.30 (−0.11)	N = 120	−0.38 (−0.15)	N = 121	−0.33 (−0.17)	N = 11
		imbalance low = good economic relations	not different on all 3	1 (0.14	N = 19	−0.16 (−0.04)	N = 178	−0.01 (0)	N = 169		N = 28
			different on all 3	−1 (−1)	N = 4	−0.58 (−0.17)	N = 50	−0.72 (−0.26)	N = 50	/	N = 4
	Trade imbalance 1938	imbalance high = poor economic relations	not different on all 3	1 (0.43)	N = 32	0 (0)	N = 574	0.35 (0.10)	N = 546	−1	N = 60
			different on all 3	−1 (−0.85)	N = 13	−0.36 (−0.13)	N = 110	−0.47 (−0.18)	N = 113	−0. 5 (−0.21)	N = 10
		imbalance low = good economic relations	not different on all 3	/	N = 17	0.30 (0.08)	N = 207	0.44 (0.14)	N = 190	/	N = 34
			different on all 3	=1 (=1)	N = 3	−0.47 (−0.19)	N = 60	−0.52 (−0.22)	N = 58	/	N = 5
	Change in volume of trade 1928–38	reduction in trade = poor economic relations	not different on all 3	−0.03 (0)	N = 33	0.12 (0.03)	N = 305	0.38 (0.13)	N = 297	/	N = 41
			different on all 3	−0.71 (−0.40)	N = 10	−0.72 (−0.32)	N = 80	−0.70 (−0.35)	N = 81	−0.14 (−0.05)	N = 9
		trade increase or constant = good economic relations	not different on all 3	1 (0.25)	N = 16	0.05 (0.01)	N = 476	0.20 (0.04)	N = 439	−1 (−0.13)	N = 53
			different on all 3	−0.50 (−0.25)	N = 6	−0.58 (−0.19)	N = 90	−0.50 (−0.17)	N = 90	/	N = 6

Aggregate of economic Agreements	Volume of trade 1928	trade low = poor economic relations	not different on all 3	0.5 (0.18)	−0.21 (−0.04)	0.07 (0.01)	−1 (−0.10)
			different on all 3	−0.93 (−0.69)	−0.53 (−0.19)	−0.65 (−0.25)	1 (0.48)
		trade high = good economic relations	not different on all 3	/	−0.06 (−0.02)	0.17 (0.06)	/
			different on all 3	1 (1)	−0.83 (−0.38)	−0.47 (−0.19)	−1 (−0.47)
	Volume of trade 1938	trade low = poor economic relations	not different on all 3	0.33 (0.14)	−0.53 (+0.06)	−0.28 (−0.04	/
			different on all 3	/	−0.40 (−0.11)	−0.38 (−0.10	/
		trade high = good economic relations	not different on all 3	1 (0.18)	0.21 (0.05)	0.43 (0.13)	/
			different on all 3	−0.78 (−0.45)	−0.71 (−0.30)	−0.68 (−0.31)	0 (0)
	Trade imbalance 1928	imbalance high = poor economic relations	not different on all 3	0.67 (0.20)	0.09 (0.02)	0.40 (0.12)	−1 (−0.14)
			different on all 3	−0.81 (−0.50)	−0.63 (−0.32)	−0.70 (−0.26)	0.33 (0.12)
		imbalance low = good economic relations	not different on all 3	1 (0.14)	0.35 (0.08)	0.43 (0.10)	/
			different on all 3	−1 (−0.33)	−0.46 (−0.15)	−0.28 (−0.10)	/
	Trade imbalance 1938	imbalance high = poor economic relations	not different on all 3	0.52 (0.18	0.04 (0)	0.34 (0.10)	−1 (−0.14)
			different on all 3	−0.84 (−0.53)	−0.64 (−0.23)	−0.72 (−0.28)	0.33 (0.12)
		imbalance low = good economic relations	not different on all 3	1 (0.23)	0.32 (0.08	0.48 (0.14)	/
			different all 3	/	−0.69 (−0.28)	−0.46 (−0.20)	/
	Change in volume of trade 1928–38	reduction in trade = poor economic relations	not different on all 3	1 (0.24)	0.16 (0.04)	0.45 (0.16)	0.09 (0.02)
			different on all 3	−1 (−1)	−0.74 (−0.29)	−0.89 (−0.37)	−0.06 (−0.02)
		trade increases or constant = good economic relations	not different on all 3	1 (0.25)	−0.05 (−0.01)		−1 (−0.12)
			different on all 3	−1 (−0.70)	−0.04 (−0.01)	−0.71 (−0.35)	/

/ indicates that no coefficient could be computed because of an empty row or column in the corresponding crosstabulation.
[a] 'different on all 3' refers to those dyads which were culturally different *and* geographically remote *and* different in power status, 'not different on all 3' refers to all other dyads.

TABLE 4.6 (*a*) *Cell frequencies for the 4-way cross-tabulation between war occurs after* 1920/*not and aggregate political agreements, controlling for* (1) *geographically remote and culturally dissimilar and different in power status vs not; and* (2) *'Friendship/Antagonism I' ('antagonists' had been at war with one another between* 1900 *and* 1920), *and* (*b*) *effect parameters* (λ) *for the saturated log-linear model defined by the table*[a]

	'Friendship/Antagonism I' ('antagonists' had been at war with one another between 1900 and 1920)							
	'antagonists'				*not 'antagonists'*			
	not different on all three		different on all three[b]		not different on all three		different on all three[b]	
	treaty-making limited[c]	treaty-making relatively extensive	treaty-making limited	treaty-making relatively extensive	treaty-making limited	treaty-making relatively extensive	treaty-making limited	treaty-making relatively extensive
No war occurs 1920–42	7	24	0[d]	7	432	297	81	51
War occurs after 1920	0[d]	18	8	1	28	24	30	8

(b) Effect parameters for the above table were estimated for the model Ln (fijkm) $= \theta + \lambda_i^W + \lambda_j^L + \lambda_K^D + \lambda_M^A + \lambda_{ij}^{WL} + \lambda_{ik}^{WD} + \lambda_{im}^{WA} + \lambda_{jk}^{LD} + \lambda_{jm}^{LA} + \lambda_{km}^{DA} + \lambda_{ijk}^{WLD} + \lambda_{ijm}^{WLA} + \lambda_{jkm}^{LDA} + \lambda_{ikm}^{WDA} + \lambda_{ijkm}^{WLDA}$

Interaction effect	*λ effect parameter*	*Interaction effect*	*λ effect parameter*	*Interaction effect*	*λ effect parameter*	*Key to notation*
(W)	0.610	(WD)	0.415	(WLD)	0.494	W = war occurs/not
(L)	−0.219	(WA)	−0.390	(WLA)	−0.089	L = treaty-making relatively extensive/not
(D)	0.499	(LD)	−0.315	(WDA)	0.111	D = different on all three/not[b]
(A)	−1.307	(LA)	−0.502	(LDA)	−0.163	A = antagonistic/not
(WL)	−0.163	(DA)	−0.053	(WLDA)	0.364	

[a] The grand mean effect for this table is $\theta = 2.720$; standard error for all parameters = 0.145. All parameters estimated by ECTA Version 4, University of Essex; implementation by Graham Upton.

[b] 'different on all three' refers to those dyads which were culturally dissimilar *and* geographically remote *and* different in power status; 'not different on all three' refers to all other dyads.

[c] 'treaty-making limited' refers to those dyads which scored 0 or 1 on the aggregate of *political* agreements index; 'treaty-making relatively extensive' refers to dyads which scored two or more on this index.

[d] A constant of 0.5 was added to each observed cell frequency prior to the computation of the effect parameters. This device avoids the problem of generating expected odds ratios of infinity and is known not to confound the resultant parameter estimates. See R. C. Plackett, *The Analysis of Categorical Data*, 2nd Edn (London: Griffin, 1982) ch. 1.

TABLE 4.7 (*a*) *Cell frequencies for the 4-way cross-tabulation between war occurs after* 1920/*not and aggregate economic agreements, controlling for* (1) *geographically remote and culturally dissimilar and different in power status vs not; and* (2) *'Friendship/Antagonism I'* (*'antagonists' had been at war with one another between* 1900 *and* 1920), *and* (*b*) *effect parameters* (λ) *for the saturated log-linear model defined by the table*[a]

	'Friendship/Antagonism I': ('antagonists' had been at war with one another between 1900 and 1920) 'antagonists'				not 'antagonists'			
	not different on all three		different on all three[b]		not different on all three		different on all three[b]	
	treaty-making limited[c]	treaty-making relatively extensive	treaty-making limited	treaty-making relatively extensive	treaty-making limited	treaty-making relatively extensive	treaty-making limited	treaty-making relatively extensive
No war occurs 1920–42	6	25	2	5	429	300	76	56
War occurs after 1920	1	17	6	3	27	25	33	5

(b) Effect parameters for the above table were estimated for the model Ln (fijkm) $= \theta + \lambda_i^W + \lambda_j^L + \lambda_k^D + \lambda_m^A + \lambda_{ij}^{WL} + \lambda_{ik}^{WD} + \lambda_{im}^{WA} + \lambda_{jk}^{LD} + \lambda_{jm}^{LA} + \lambda_{km}^{DA} + \lambda_{ijk}^{WLD} + \lambda_{ijm}^{WLA} + \lambda_{jkm}^{LDA} + \lambda_{ikm}^{WDA} + \lambda_{ijkm}^{WLDA}$

Interaction effect	*λ effect parameter*	*Interaction effect*	*λ effect parameter*	*Interaction effect*	*λ effect parameter*	*Key to notation*
(W)	0.631	(WD)	0.289	(WLD)	0.305	W = war occurs/not
(L)	−0.116	(WA)	−0.432	(WLA)	0.069	L = treaty-making relatively extensive/not
(D)	0.467	(LD)	−0.362	(WDA)	0.048	D = different on all three/not[b]
(A)	−1.169	(LA)	−0.444	(LDA)	−0.142	A = antagonistic/not
(WL)	−0.094	(DA)	−0.135	(WLDA)	0.072	

[a] The grand mean effect for this table is $\theta = 2.799$; standard error for all parameters = 0.105. All parameters estimated by ECTA Version 4, University of Essex; implementation by Graham Upton.

[b] 'different on all three' refers to those dyads which were culturally dissimilar *and* geographically remote *and* different in power status; 'not different on all three' refers to all other dyads.

[c] 'treaty-making limited' refers to those dyads which scored 0 or 1 on the aggregate of *economic* treaties index; 'treaty-making relatively extensive' refers to dyads which scored 2 or more on this index.

TABLE 4.8 (*a*) *Cell frequencies for 5-way cross-tabulation between war occurs after* 1920/*not and aggregate political agreements, controlling for* (1) *geographically remote and culturally dissimilar and different in power status vs not;* (2) '*Friendship/Antagonism I*' ('*antagonists*' *had been at war with one another between* 1900 *and* 1920 *VOLUME*28 (*volume of bilateral trade* 1928), *and* (*b*) *effect parameters* (λ) *for the saturated log-linear model defined by the table*[a]

	VOLUME28[b] *Volume of bilateral trade* 1928 *Trade relatively low* (*economic relations relatively poor*)							
	'antagonists' on 'Friendship/Antagonism I'				not 'antagonists' on 'Friendship/Antagonism I'			
	not different on all 3[c]		different on all 3		not different on all 3		different on all 3	
	treaty-making limited[d]	treaty-making relatively extensive	treaty-making limited	treaty-making relatively extensive	treaty-making limited	treaty-making relatively extensive	treaty-making limited	treaty-making relatively extensive
No war occurs 1920–40	6	14	0	6	412	234	66	30
War occurs after 1920	0[e]	8	6	1	22	8	25	7

(b) Effect parameters for the above table were estimated for the model

$$\text{Ln}\,(\text{fijkmn}) = 0 + \lambda_i^{W} + \lambda_j^{L} + \lambda_k^{D} + \lambda_m^{A} + \lambda_n^{T} + \lambda_{ij}^{WL} + \lambda_{ik}^{WD} + \lambda_{im}^{WA} + \lambda_{in}^{WT} + \lambda_{jk}^{LD} + \lambda_{jm}^{LA} + \lambda_{jn}^{LT} + \lambda_{km}^{DA} + \lambda_{kn}^{DT} + \lambda_{mn}^{AT} + \lambda_{ijk}^{WLD} + \lambda_{ijm}^{WLA} + \lambda_{ijn}^{WLT} + \lambda_{ikm}^{WDA} + \lambda_{ikn}^{WDT} + \lambda_{imn}^{WAT} + \lambda_{jkm}^{LDA} + \lambda_{jkn}^{LDT} + \lambda_{jmn}^{LAT} + \lambda_{kmn}^{DAT} + \lambda_{ijkm}^{WLDA} + \lambda_{ijkn}^{WLDT} + \lambda_{ikmn}^{WLAT} + \lambda_{jkmn}^{LDAT} + \lambda_{ijkmn}^{WLDAT}$$

Interaction effect	*λ effect parameter*	*Interaction effect*	*λ effect parameter*	*Interaction effect*	*λ effect parameter*
(W)	0.391	(LT)	0.118	(LDA)	−0.265
(L)	−0.338	(DA)	−0.082	(LDT)	0.206
(D)	0.458	(DT)	0.088	(LAT)	0.005
(A)	−1.016	(AT)	−0.098	(DAT)	−0.146
(T)	0.480	(WLD)	0.279	(WLDA)	−0.075
(WL)	−0.108	(WLA)	0.146	(WLDT)	0.247
(WD)	0.266	(WLT)	−0.216	(WLAT)	−0.072
WA	−0.292	(WDA)	0.034	(WDAT)	−0.158
(WT)	0.125	(WDT)	0.383	(LDAT)	−0.010
(LD)	−0.248	(WAT)	0.026	(WLDAT)	0.307
(LA)	−0.376				

VOLUME28[b]
Volume of bilateral trade 1928
Trade relatively high
(economic relations relatively good)

'antagonists' on 'Friendship/Antagonism I'				not 'antagonists' on 'Friendship/Antagonism I'			
not different on all 3		different on all 3		not different on all 3		different on all 3	
treaty-making limited	treaty-making relatively extensive	treaty-making limited	treaty-making relatively extensive	treaty-making limited	treaty-making relatively extensive	treaty-making limited	treaty-making relatively extensive
1	10	0	1	20	63	15	21
0	10	2	0	6	16	5	1

Key to notation

W = war occurs/not
L = treaty-making relatively extensive/not
D = different on all 3/not[c]
A = prior record of antagonism/not
T = trade relatively high/low

[a] The grand mean effect for this table is $\theta = 1.815$; standard error for all λ parameters = 0.127. All parameters estimated by ECTA, version 4, University of Essex.
[b] The 'trade relatively low' category of VOLUME28 refers to all those dyads whose volume of bilateral trade in 1928 was less the average volume of trade for all dyads in that year; the 'trade relatively high' category refers to those dyads whose volume of trade was greater than the global average.
[c] 'different on all 3' refers to those dyads which were culturally dissimilar *and* geographically remote *and* different in power status; 'not different on all 3' refers to all other dyads.
[d] 'treaty-making limited' refers to those dyads which scored 0 or 1 on the aggregate of *political* agreements index; 'treaty-making relatively extensive' refers to dyads which scored 2 or more on this index.
[e] A constant of 0.5 was added to each observed cell frequency prior to the computation of the effect parameters. This device avoids the problem of generating expected odds ratios of infinity and is known not to confound the resultant parameter estimates. See Table 4.6.

TABLE 4.9 *(a) Cell frequencies for the 5-way cross-tabulation between war occurs after 1920/not and aggregate economic agreements, controlling for (1) geographically remote and culturally dissimilar and different in power status vs not; (2) 'Friendship/Antagonism I' ('antagonists' had been at war with one another between 1900 and 1920) VOLUME28 (volume of bilateral trade 1928), and (b) effect parameters (λ) for the saturated log-linear model defined by the table*[a]

	VOLUME28[b] *Volume of bilateral trade 1928* *Trade relatively low* *(economic relations relatively poor)*							
	'antagonists' on 'Friendship/Antagonism I'				not 'antagonists' on 'Friendship/Antagonism I'			
	not different on all 3[c]		different on all 3		not different on all 3		different on all 3	
	treaty-making limited[d]	treaty-making relatively extensive	treaty-making limited	treaty-making relatively extensive	treaty-making limited	treaty-making relatively extensive	treay-making limited	treaty-making relatively extensive
No war occurs 1920–42	6	14	1	5	412	234	65	31
War occurs after 1920	1	7	6	1	22	8	28	4

(b) Effect parameters for the above table were estimated for the model $\text{Ln}\,(\text{fijkmn}) = 0 + \lambda_i^{W} + \lambda_k^{L} + \lambda_k^{D} + \lambda_m^{A} + \lambda_n^{T} + \lambda_{ij}^{WL} + \lambda_{ik}^{WD} + \lambda_{im}^{WA} + \lambda_{in}^{WT} + \lambda_{jk}^{LD} + \lambda_{jm}^{LA} + \lambda_{jn}^{LT} + \lambda_{km}^{DA} + \lambda_{kn}^{DT} + \lambda_{mn}^{AT} + \lambda_{ijk}^{WLD} + \lambda_{ijm}^{WLA} + \lambda_{ijn}^{WLT} + \lambda_{ikm}^{WDA} + \lambda_{ikn}^{WDT} + \lambda_{imn}^{WAT} + \lambda_{jkm}^{LDA} + \lambda_{jkn}^{LDT} + \lambda_{jmn}^{LAT} + \lambda_{kmn}^{DAT} + \lambda_{ijkm}^{WLDA} + \lambda_{ijkn}^{WLDT} + \lambda_{ikmn}^{WLAT} + \lambda_{jkmn}^{LDAT} + \lambda_{ijkmn}^{WLDAT}$

Interaction effect	*λ effect parameter*	*Interaction effect*	*λ effect parameter*	*Interaction effect*	*λ effect parameter*
(W)	0.475	(LA)	−0.389	(WAT)	−0.061
(L)	−0.169	(LT)	0.286	(LDA)	−0.175
(D)	0.398	(DA)	−0.020	(LDT)	0.114
(A)	−1.017	(DT)	0.029	(LAT)	−0.008
(T)	0.600	(AT)	−0.100	(DAT)	−0.084
(WL)	−0.054	(WLD)	0.150	(WLDA)	−0.101
(WD)	0.121	(WLA)	0.096	(WLDT)	0.118
(WA)	−0.379	(WLT)	−0.163	(WLAT)	−0.123
(WT)	0.210	(WDA)	0.060	(WDAT)	−0.132
(LD)	−0.340	(WDT)	0.238	(LDAT)	0.079
				(WLDAT)	0.281

VOLUME28[b]
Volume of bilateral trade 1928
Trade relatively high
(economic relations relatively good)

'antagonists' on 'Friendship/Antagonism I'				not 'antagonists' on 'Friendship/Antagonism I'			
not different on all 3		different on all 3		not different on all 3		different on all 3	
treaty-making limited	treaty-making relatively extensive	treaty-making limited	treaty-making relatively extensive	treaty-making limited	treaty-making relatively extensive	treaty-making limited	treaty-making relatively extensive
0[e]	11	1	0	17	16	11	25
0	10	0	2	5	17	5	1

Key to notation

W = war occurs/not
L = treaty-making relatively extensive/not
D = different on all 3/not[c]
A = prior record of antagonism/not
T = trade relatively high/low

[a] The grand mean effect for this table is $\theta = 1.936$; standard error for all λ parameters = 0.116. All parameters estimated by ECTA, version 4, University of Essex.
[b] The 'trade relatively low' category of VOLUME28 refers to all those dyads whose volume of bilateral trade in 1928 was less than the average volume of trade for all dyads in that year; the 'trade relatively high' category refers to those dyads whose volume of trade was greater than the global average.
[c] 'different on all 3' refers to those dyads which were culturally dissimilar *and* geographically remote *and* different in power status; 'not different on all 3' refers to all other dyads.
[d] 'treaty-making limited' refers to those dyads which scored 0 or 1 on the aggregate of *economic* agreements index; 'treaty-making relatively extensive' refers to dyads which scored 2 or more on this index.
[e] A constant of 0.5 was added to each observed cell frequency prior to the computation of the effect parameters. This device avoids the problem of generating expected odds ratios of infinity and is known not to confound the resultant parameter estimates. See Table 4.6.

consequences of applying such techniques to four of the most critical multi-way cross-tabulations that have been analysed: those pertaining to the relationship between war, treaty-making, 'differences' (in geography, culture and power status) and 'Friendship/Antagonism I'. The tables report only the full *saturated* models since the object of the exercise is not to obtain the most parsimonious fit to the observed data but to establish if certain of the lambda (λ) effect parameters figure significantly in each of the models.

For each table, the specific parameter which is of importance in this context is the λ^{WLD}, which measures the 3-way interaction effect among the 'war/not', 'lawmaking' and 'different on all three' variables. This parameter is important because in terms of the overall pattern described by the multi-way cross-tabulation, it reflects the strength of the empirical relationship which has been identified above as supportive of the 'circumscribed idealist hypothesis', that is to say, the tendency for war and treaty-making to be (negatively) correlated in those contexts where dyads are culturally dissimilar, geographically remote and of differential power status.

As Tables 4.6 to 4.9 inclusive indicate, the λ^{WLD} parameters are indeed relatively large. Although they are obviously not as important as the one-way (for example, λ^{W}) and two-way (for example, λ^{LT}) interactions, in Tables 4.6 and 4.7 they represent the only significant 3-way interaction ($\lambda^{WLD} = 0.494$ and 0.305 respectively), in Table 4.9 λ^{WLD} is the largest ($= 0.279$) of the 3-way interaction parameters, and in Table 4.8, one of the largest ($\lambda^{WLD} = 0.15$). While these results considered on their own do little more than hint at some sort of statistical interaction between war, lawmaking and the three contextual 'difference' variables, taken in combination with the rest of the cross-tabulation evidence presented in this chapter they serve to reinforce the claim embodied in the 'circumscribed idealist hypothesis' that even where there is a prior record of enmity in certain contexts treaty-making does appear to inhibit the recourse to war. In short, the results of the log-linear modelling procedure reinforce the view that at the dyadic level the pursuit of co-operative foreign policy strategies can enhance the prospects for subsequently peaceful bilateral relations.

A PREDICTIVE MODEL OF THE OCCURRENCE OF WAR IN THE 1921–42 PERIOD

As was indicated earlier, the predictive model which is advanced here is not intended in any sense to 'explain' the incidence of warfare during the period after 1920. Rather its primary purpose is to ascertain how far the statistical effects which have so far been reported, and in particular those which relate to the role of the treaty-making process as an inhibiting influence upon nations' recourse to war, continue to be in evidence when interval-level (regression) techniques of statistical analysis are employed. Given the nature of the data available, the use of the regression model makes extremely good sense. First, all the independent variables that have been identified are either already measured at interval level (this certainly applies to the bilateral trade data and to the set of variables used to operationalise treaty-making activity) or else can easily be converted into dummy variables suitable for use with regression techniques. (The latter category includes both the 'friendship/antagonism' variables and the contextual variables – cultural similarity/difference, geographical proximity/remoteness and power status differential – which have been analysed in this chapter.) Second, the dependent variable itself – whether or not war occurred between 1921 and 1942 – can also be operationalised as a dummy variable (war occurs = 1; not = 0). The standard objection to the use of a dummy dependent variable in a multiple regression model, of course, is that strictly speaking there can be no 'real' condition, at least in terms of what the data actually measure, between the two observed values of the dependent variable dichotomy; in this case between war and peace. However, it can be argued that this ceases to be a problem if the predicted values from the relevant equations are regarded as reflecting the different case-by-case *probabilities* that the dependent characteristic (in this context, war) will occur.[2] This indeed is the sense in which the regression model is employed here. In these circumstances it is a relatively simple matter to set up a multiple regression model in which occurrence of war/not is dependent and all the other variables identified in this and in the previous chapter are regarded as independent variables.

Table 4.10 describes each of the variables included in the regression analysis undertaken and indicates the predicted effects (positive or negative) of each variable, together with a brief statement of the rationale underlying its inclusion in the modelling procedure. All of these variables were included in a stepwise regression model with war occurs/not as the dependent variable. Table 4.11 reports the results of the stepwise procedure, showing the best fitting model after all nonsignificant and co-linear independent variables had been removed.[3] It should be recognised that each of the standardised regression coefficients reported in Table 4.11 measures the direction and relative

TABLE 4.10 *Independent variables included in regression analysis (dependent variable: war occurs between 1921 and 1942/not)*

Variable name/description	Rationale	Predicted Relationship
I *Individual treaty-making variables* 1. Financial 2. General economic 3. Specific economic 4. Most Favoured Nation 5. Short-run economic 6. Transport and communications 7. General political 8. Friendship and co-operation 9. Territory/boundaries 10. Diplomatic 11. Aliens' rights/duties 12. Arbitration conciliation 13. Cultural/Medical/Scientific 14. Administrative co-operation 15. Specific politics 16. General military 17. Military short of alliance 18. Non-aggression/anti-war 19. Mutual assistance 20. Reciprocal neutrality	The treaty-making process, *ceteris paribus*, encourages the breakdown of mistrust and mutual suspicion between nations. It also broadens the opportunities for the peaceful resolution of conflicts in later crises. Both of these mechanisms serve to reduce the probability of war	Negative
II *Aggregated treaty-making variables* 21. Aggregate of Economic Treaties 22. Aggregate of Political Treaties 23. Aggregate of Military Treaties	As above. These variables also measure the extent to which pairs of countries have developed a ***network*** of treaty commitments. The treaty-making process is more likely to reduce the probability of war occuring if it is conducted across a broad range of policy areas	Negative
III *Contextual variables* 24. Cultural similarity = 0/difference = 1 25. Geographical proximity = 0/remoteness = 1 26. Power status differential = 1/not = 0 27. DIFF3: different on all of 24, 25, 26 = 1/not = 0 28. DIFF1: different on any of 24, 25, 26 = 1/not = 0	The previous results reported show that these variables identify the contexts in which the treaty-making process appears to have an effect on the probability of (avoiding) war. They define situations in which vital conflicts of interest, though they may occur, do not necessarily require immediate resolution. In these situations it is more likely that a strong record of treaty-making activity will enable peaceful means of conflict resolution rather than force to be employed.	Possibility negative

Variable	Rationale	Expected effect
29. Both powers were Great Powers = 1/not = 0 (Great Powers = Britain, France, Germany, Italy, USA, Japan, USSR)	Since the security and economic interests of the Great Powers extended beyond their own immediate boundaries to all or several parts of the international system, they are more likely to experience a mutual clash of vital interest than are minor powers. This in turn makes war between them more likely, *ceteris paribus*.	Positive
IV *'Friendship/antagonism' variables*		
30. 'Friendship/Antagonism I' antagonists had been at war between 1900 and 1921 = 0/not = 1	Pairs of nations which had been enemies before 1920 (especially in the First World War), given the nature of the postwar peace settlements, were more likely to be enemies again in the event of any future global war. Non-antagonists were less likely subsequently to go to war	Negative
31. 'Friendship/Antagonism III': friends shared the same language = 1/not = 0	A shared language fosters a sense of mutual identity and understanding and accordingly reduces the chances of violent confrontation	Negative
32. 'Friendship/Antagonism V': friends had been allies in war once and never enemies in war since 1815 = 1/not = 0	A long experience of being on the same side in war (s) suggests a convergence of longterm security interests and therefore a reduced probability of war	Negative
V *Bilateral trade variables: economic relations*		
33. VOLUME28: volume of trade for 1928 ($ equivalents) 34. VOLUME38; volume of trade for 1938 ($ equivalents)	A higher level of trade implies greater economic interdependence which perhaps acts as a brake on the recourse to war	Negative
35. IMBALANCE28: imbalance in trade 1928 36. IMBALANCE38: imbalance in trade 1938	A high trade imbalance, since it works to the considerable disadvantage of one 'partner', represents a continuing source of inter-nation tension and therefore increases the chances of war	Positive
37. VOLCHANGE: change in the volume of bilateral trade between 1928 and 1938	The larger the decrease in the volume of trade, the greater the deterioration in the state of bilateral economic relations and therefore the greater the chance of war	Negative

TABLE 4.11 *Predictive model of war occurs between 1921 and 1942/not*[a]
Dependent variable: war occurs between 1921 and 1942 = 1; no war occurs between 1921 and 1942 = 0

Independent variable	*Standardised regression coefficient*[b]
One of the nations in the dyad was a Great Power (= 1; not = 0)	0.31
'Friendship/Antagonism I' (antagonists had been at war between 1900 and 1920 = 0; not antagonists = 1)	−0.21
Both of the nations in the dyad were Great Powers (= 1; not = 0)	0.17
Aggregate political agreements	−0.15
Mutual assistance treaties	−0.11
Volume of trade 1928 (in $ equivalents)	0.10
'Friendship/Antagonism V' (friends had been allies in war but never enemies since 1815 = 1; not = 0)	−0.10
Cultural dissimilarity (= 1; similarity = 0)	−0.12
'Friendship/Antagonism III' (friends shared the same language = 1; not = 0)	−0.07
Aggregate economic agreements	−0.07

N = 1016
$R^2 = 0.208$ Standard error of estimate = 0.28
f = 26.49

[a] The predictive model reported represents the 'best' combination of the independent variables defined in Table 4.10 where best is defined as that model which maximises R^2 while ensuring (a) that all coefficients are more than twice their own standard errors and (b) that there is no co-linearity among predictor variables greater than r = 0.7. For a discussion of these criteria see David Sanders, *Patterns of Political Instability* (London: Macmillan, 1981), ch. 8.

[b] All coefficients are more than twice their own standard errors.

magnitude of effect of each independent variable while the effects of all the other independent variables are being simultaneously estimated, that is to say, while their effects are being held constant. (Table A.1 in the Appendix, *inter alia*, identifies those dyads which, on the basis of the model defined in Table 4.11, were correctly predicted as going to war in the period under analysis.)

Although the level of explained variance is relatively low (R^2 =0.208), the results provided in Table 4.11 not only support a number of the implicit hypotheses advanced in Table 4.10 but also make good intuitive sense. Specifically, four main conclusions may be drawn.

(1) The negative coefficients for 'Friendship/Antagonism I' ($\beta = -0.10$), for 'Friendship/Antagonism III' ($\beta = -0.07$) and for Friendship/Antagonism V' ($\beta = -0.21$) indicate that a prior long-term record of either friendly or nonantagonistic bilateral relations reduces the chances of war occurring. It would have been curious, of course, had these three independent variables furnished anything other than negative coefficients. Nonetheless, given that empirical data in the social sciences can so frequently confound common-sense expectations, the fact that the three coefficients *are* negative reinforces the plausibility of the model as a whole.

(2) The coefficients for 'both powers were Great Powers' and for 'power status differential' are both positive ($\beta = 0.17$ and $\beta = 0.31$ respectively). The former is entirely consistent with the notion briefly advanced in Table 4.10 that the more widely spread global interests of the Great Powers increase the chances, *ceteris paribus*, of their experiencing a vital conflict of interest. The positive coefficient for 'power status differential', however (unlike the negative coefficient for cultural differences), at first sight seems to contradict both the prediction of Table 4.10 and the previous findings which have been reported concerning the impact of this variable on the probability of war occurring between pairs of nations. In fact the contradiction is more apparent than real. What has been said so far about the role of power status differentials, cultural differences and geographical remoteness is not that the presence of these characteristics necessarily of itself reduces the probability of war, but that in situations where such differences exist *a greater commitment to the treaty-making process reduces the chances of war occurring*, while a lesser (or no) commitment to that process increases those chances. The relationship between war, treaty-making and each of these three contextual variables, therefore, is essentially an interactive one in which lawmaking and war correlate negatively when geographical distances are great or when cultures or power status are significantly different. This does not necessarily mean that when statistical controls are applied for a number of other variables (as, implicitly, they are in the model reported in Table 4.11) or even when no such controls are applied, the three contextual variables will of themselves serve to reduce the probability of war. Rather the positive cofficient for power status differential simply indicates that controlling for all the other variables in the model, dyads where one of the nations is a Great Power were more

likely to engage in warfare than those in which both the parties involved are minor powers.[4] This is entirely consistent with the observation which has repeatedly been made: where there is a power status differential, more treaty-making implies a reduced probability of war. The positive coefficient merely indicates that dyads containing only one Great Power had a higher *a priori* probability of going to war regardless of the extent of their treaty-making activity. As with the positive coefficient for the 'both powers were Great Powers' variable, this is perhaps a consequence of the fact that, other things being equal, the more widely dispersed security interests of the Great Powers rendered them rather more likely to experience serious conflicts of interest with other states than was the case when both powers were minor ones.

(3) Only three of the 23 treaty-making variables in Table 4.10 figure significantly in the 'best model' identified in Table 4.11: Aggregate of Economic Agreements ($\beta = -0.15$), Aggregate of Political Agreements ($\beta = -0.07$) and mutual assistance treaties ($\beta = -0.11$). The negative coefficients for each of these variables again make good intuitive sense. It would have been very surprising, for example, if dyads that had signed mutual assistance treaties had *not* been less likely to engage in warfare than those which did not sign such treaties. Mutual assistance treaties, after all, represent a form of military *alliance*: they presumably only come into existence when the security interests of different states strongly converge; and in these circumstances war seems relatively unlikely anyway. It is entirely reasonable on common-sense grounds, therefore, to find that when the effects of a number of other variables are held constant, the signing of mutual assistance treaties is associated with a reduced probability of war.

The significant negative coefficients for aggregate economic and political agreements, however, are perhaps of greater substantive importance. It should be noted that over and above the effects of these aggregate measures, none of the other treaty-making variables had a significant impact upon the probability of war occurring. This finding serves to underline the importance of the development of a *network* of several different types of treaty commitment, since (as was pointed out earlier) both of these aggregate measures indicate the extent to which dyads were engaged in a variety of different kinds of treaty-making activity during the interwar period. The negative coefficients for the aggregate agreement variables, therefore, serve indirectly to reinforce the claim that a generalised commitment to the treaty-making process across a broad range of treaty types is more likely (than a heavily proscribed one) to foster that greater sense of mutual trust and understanding which is central to the conduct of peaceful bilateral international relations.

(4) It is worth noting, finally, that of the five bilateral trade variables identified in Table 4.10 only VOLUME 28 appears as a significant predictor of war occurs/not in Table 4.11: controlling for the effects of the other variables in the model, pairs of countries which enjoyed a relatively strong bilateral trading relationship in the period before the Great Depression of the 1930s were (somewhat counterintuitively) *more* likely subsequently to go to war with one another than dyads which experienced a relatively weak trading relationship.[5] It is in the context of the trade variables, however, that the omissions from Table 4.11 are perhaps more important than what is included in it. The fact that IMBALANCE 28, IMBALANCE 38 and the change in the volume of trade 1928–38 fail to appear in the 'best model' represents the rejection of two of the implicit hypotheses advanced in Table 4.10. Neither trade imbalances nor the decline in the volume of trade during the 1930s were directly associated with either an increased or a decreased probability of going to war. There is certainly no evidence in terms of bilateral patterns of trade to support the view that the trade 'war' of the 1930s significantly worsened international relations, thereby encouraging warfare at a later date: dyads which encountered either a significant decline in trade or which experienced a considerable imbalance in the pattern of bilateral trade were no more likely subsequently to go to war than those dyads which continued to enjoy a relatively good trading relationship throughout the 1920s and 1930s.[6] Changing patterns of trade, in short, appear to have exerted only a negligible influence upon the political relations between nation-states in the interwar period.

SUMMARY AND CONCLUSIONS

It has not been the intention in this chapter to offer an explanation of why wars occurred, or failed to occur, in the period after 1920. The fact that even the 'best model' for predicting war occurs/not produced an R^2 of only 0.208 attests to the pointlessness of such an exercise given the sort of data currently available: almost 80 per cent of the variance in the dependent variable is 'explained' by 'unmeasured' variables omitted from the model. Rather the primary purpose of the empirical analysis conducted in this and in the previous chapter has been to establish whether or not a particular set of treaty-making variables can plausibly be regarded as having had a causal effect on the probability of pairs of nations going to war with one another in the interwar years. What needs to be reemphasised, moreover, is that the specific findings reported are less important than the overall pattern of interrelationship that they *collectively* portray. Taken as a single finding, for example, the fact that the aggregate treaty-making variables furnish significant negative coefficients in the regression model could be deemed to demonstrate very little; particularly in view of the methodological objections which can easily be raised against both the estimates and the interpretation of the coefficients produced by such a dummy dependent variable model. Similarly, considered in isolation, the fact that the saturated log-linear models reported provide significant parameters for the appropriate 'treatymaking-war-difference' interaction terms could be regarded as being of rather limited theoretical interest. Such criticisms, however, misunderstand the purpose of the log-linear and regression models that have been presented. The results outlined in these models essentially need to be considered in combination with the negative law-war correlations observed in the various multiway tables reported in this and in the previous chapter. Considered *together*–following the principle of 'convergent validity'–these findings reveal a general and consistent empirical pattern which strongly supports the notion of a connection between treaty-making and war-avoidance. The broad conclusion suggested by the foregoing quantitative analysis is that treaty-making did indeed have a limited but consistently reductive effect on dyads' propensities to go to war in a number of specifiable contexts during the interwar period.

Most importantly, however, the empirical results presented suggest that this reductive effect cannot be explained away (on the grounds that treaty-making either only occurs when bilateral relations are *already* good or else is simply an *indicator* of harmonious relations) as an empirical correlation that is theoretically spurious. The negative correlation between lawmaking and war has persisted despite numerous statistical tests which, had the correlation indeed been spurious, should have resulted in its disappearance. It has been shown that the negative correlation cannot be explained by reference to prior patterns of political antagonism; or by reference to worsening bilateral economic relations; or by reference to colonial or quasi-colonial patterns of political authority. It has also been shown, moreover, that the interaction effect between lawmaking, differences (in geography, culture and power-status) and war-avoidance is broadly corroborated by log-linear forms of statistical analysis. Even in the regression model, where the effects of a large number of exogenous variables can be explicitly controlled for, treaty-making still figures significantly in the appropriate 'best' equation.

In these circumstances it is reasonable to conclude that even in the interwar period, at the dyadic level international lawmaking seems to have exerted a limited (reductive) *causal* influence on the propensity to engage in war. To be sure, the effect is not a large one, as the relatively small magnitudes of the standardised regression coefficients for the two aggregate treaty-making variables in Table 4.11 attest. Nonetheless, that effect suggests that in certain contexts – most notably where differences in geography or power status rendered conflicts of vital interest less in need of immediate resolution by force – lawmaking was capable of shifting the balance of probability, however marginally, in favour of peace.

Of course, what is still unclear are the precise mechanisms which might link participation in treaty-making activity to a lower probability of war occurring. It has been speculated, first, that the diplomatic contact, negotiation and compromise associated with the treaty-making process itself encourages two tendencies – the build-up of trust and mutual understanding and the breakdown of the barriers of Hobbesian fear and suspicion characteristic of any anarchical society –which are crucial to the long-term development of a stable pattern of international relations. Second, it has been suggested that by increasing the sense of mutual trust, participation in the treaty-making process can broaden the range of options available for the peaceful resolution of conflicts. This may not be of immediate short-term relevance, but in the event of some later crisis of national security – when 'realist' security concerns become the dominant influence upon all nation-states' foreign policy strategies – that greater range of peaceful options may be critical in enabling states to avoid outright violent confrontation with one another.

While it has obviously not been established that these mechanisms did operate during the interwar period, it can fairly be concluded – in the phrase much loved by quantitative social researchers – that the data are at least 'consistent with' their operation. It is also clear that the precise nature of the connections between the pursuit of co-operative treaty-making strategies and the subsequent avoidance of war – connections which have thus far only been examined in general statistical terms – could only be determined by a detailed analysis of the specific historical contexts in which lawmaking appears to have been a significant factor in the maintenance of international peace. This task is in fact begun in the next chapter, where the case of Anglo-Turkish relations in the 1920s and 1930s is examined in order to ascertain how far the broad theoretical and empirical themes that have been advanced here have any relevance when applied to a particular historical example.

5 A Case-study: Anglo-Turkish Relations during the Interwar Years

In the preceding chapters it has been suggested that in certain limited but specifiable circumstances, the pursuit of strategies of co-operation – operationalised in this context as participation in the bilateral treaty-making process – appears to have a reductive impact upon (pairs of) nations' propensities to engage in warfare; even when pre-existing patterns of antagonism are taken into account. A major problem associated with this conclusion, however, is that given the nature of the data-analytic approach adopted, it has not been possible to specify the precise mechanisms that might have generated the statistical relationships which have been repeatedly observed.

This chapter adopts an historical case study approach in order to discover how plausible the supposed linkage between treaty-making and the subsequent avoidance of war appears when it is subjected to a more detailed and precise form of empirical evidence. The problem that immediately needs to be confronted, however, is the question as to which case is appropriate for this purpose. In this context the data analysis undertaken in previous chapters constitutes a useful instrument for identifying 'critical' cases worthy of further investigation. Table 5.1 provides a listing of all interwar dyads which exhibited a record of pre-existing antagonism on 'Friendship Antagonism I', a variable which defines 'antagonists' as those pairs of nations which had been at war with one another sometime between 1900 and 1920. Given the empirical findings reported in Chapters 3 and 4, the crucial segment of Table 5.1 is 'CELL A'. This cell identifies six dyads which: (1) exhibit cultural, geographical and power status differentials; (2) had been at war between 1900 and 1920; (3) participated relatively extensively in the treaty-making process during the interwar period; and (4) subsequently avoided war. As both Turkey and Britain feature prominently in the list of dyads thus defined, the isolation of Anglo-Turkish relations for the purposes of a more detailed study seems particularly appropriate. The choice of the Anglo-Turkish dyad, moreover, has two added attractions. Not only was Turkish foreign policy in the 1930s something of a contemporary *cause célèbre* both for advocates and for opponents of treaty revision – one of the important and difficult issues of the interwar period – but in addition, the Anglo-Turkish accord over the Straits question achieved at Montreux in 1936 has frequently, though contentiously, been cited by diplomatic historians as a classic example of the successful use of negotiation and compromise in international politics.[1]

From a number of perspectives, therefore, the relationship between Britain and Turkey in the interwar period was a crucial one. Turkey was transformed from a disgraced and dismembered enemy at Sèvres in 1920 to a valued friend and collaborator at Montreux in 1936. The central question which this chapter seeks to analyse is how such a transformation came about. *In particular, did participation in the process of bilateral treaty-making play any significant part in that transformation and, if so, how*? Contrary to the prevailing orthodox historiography of the period – which stresses the importance of the shifting realities of global and regional power politics – it will be argued here (1) that participation in lawmaking *was* a critical factor in transforming Anglo-Turkish relations from a condition of intense enmity and hatred to one of extreme cordiality and even alliance; and (2) that the primary means by which that participation in lawmaking contributed to the transformation in relations was through the increased sense of mutual trust and understanding which it fostered between leading British and Turkish diplomats and foreign policy decision-makers of the time. The chapter begins with a summary of the conventional *realpolitik* view of the development of Anglo-Turkish relations in the interwar period.

THE EXISTING ORTHODOXY: AN OVERVIEW OF ANGLO-TURKISH RELATIONS 1920–45

In the same way that most general historical accounts of the interwar years tend to focus on the 'great events' of the period,[2] so most political and diplomatic historians of Anglo-Turkish relations in the interwar period have tended to restrict their attention to the major landmarks in the development of those relations: the armistice of Mudroson in 1918; the abortive Treaty of Sèvres in 1920; the Treaty of Lausanne and its annexed Straits Convention in 1923; the Mosul settlement of 1926; Turkey's accession to the League in 1932 and its acquisition of a semi-

TABLE 5.1 *Listing of cases from 4-way cross-tabulation between war occurs after 1921/not and aggregate political agreements; controlling for (1) DIFF 3 (dyads are dissimilar in culture and power status and are geographically remote* vs *those which are not dissimilar on all those three characteristics) and (2) 'Friendship/Antagonism I' ('antagonists' were at war between 1900 and 1920); ANTAGONISTIC DYADS ONLY*

	Not dissimilar on all three characteristics Political agreements				*Dissimilar on all three characteristics Political agreements*			
	none	*one*	*two*	*three or more*	*none*	*one*	*two*	*three or more*
No war occurs 1921–42	(no cases)	Bulg–Ital Bulg–France Bulg–USSR China–USSR Lith–USSR Ukra–USSR Austria–Pana	Austria–Lux Austria–Rum Portug–Ger Czech–USSR Pole–Ukra	Austria–Belg GB–Austria GB–USSR GB–Spain Austria–France USSR–France Finl–Ger Ital–Ger Japan–Ger Rum–Ger Hung–Rum Pole–Lith Austr–USSR Turk–USSR Greek – Turk Rum–Turk USSR–USA Austria–Yugo Turk–Yugo	(no cases)	(no cases)	Haiti–US	GB–Afgha GB–Iraq GB–Turk Turk–France Thai–Ger Ital–Turk CELL A

War occurs between 1921 and 1942	(no cases)	(no cases)	Ital–USSR	GB–Bulg GB–Ger Bulg–Greek Czech–Hung Ger–France Belg–Ger Greek–Ger Latv–Ger Pole–Ger USSR–Ger Yugo–Ger Fin–USSR Jap–USSR Pole–USSR Rum–USSR Ger–US Hung–Yugo	China–Ger Cuba–Ger Haiti–Ger Pana–Ger	Braz–Ger Cost–Ger Hond–Ger Nica–Ger	(no cases)	Syria–France

permanent seat on the Council in 1934; the Montreux Convention revising the regime of the Straits in 1936; the British-French-Turkish Mutual Assistance Pact of October 1939; the Turco-German Friendship treaty of 1941; Turkey's tightrope diplomacy during the war years which maintained its continued neutrality despite extensive cajoling from both Axis and Allied Powers to enter the war on their side; and Turkey's final declaration of war against Germany in February 1945 in the face of American threats to the effect that without such a declaration full participation in the UN would not be possible. Almost without exception, analyses of these developments concentrate primarily on the endless search for security or territorial advantage pursued by the various nation-state actors involved; a focus which of itself tends to preclude a proper evaluation of the possible role of the treaty-making process as a vehicle for transforming bilateral relations. Before such an evaluation can be undertaken, however, a brief review of existing secondary accounts of the changing relationship between Britain and Turkey during the interwar period is necessary.

Throughout the nineteenth century Anglo-Turkish relations were generally marked by an atmosphere of extreme cordiality. In an era in which the Great Powers consistently sought to maintain global and regional balances of power, Britain and Turkey invariably found a common cause in opposing Russia's westward expansion.[3] While Turkey was simply seeking a protector who might assist in preserving its territorial integrity,[4] Britain for its part sought both to maintain its own predominant position in the Mediterranean (by ensuring that a friendly and non-Russian power remained in control of the Straits) and to guarantee the continued existence of the Ottoman Empire as a strategic buffer between Europe and India.[5]

The tacit alliance between Britain and Turkey came to an abrupt end in 1914, however, when the Turks entered the war on the side of the Central Powers.[6] While there had been a substantial increase in Turco-German trade in the period since 1870,[7] particularly in terms of German purchases of raw materials from Turkey,[8] the fact that Britain and Russia – in virtue of their separate alliances with France – were now collaborating in a major European war was probably the main factor in Turkey's decision to side with Germany.[9]

The defeat of the Central Powers, however, was disastrous for the Turks. In a separate armistice negotiated at Mudroson in October 1918, with British, French and Italian occupation forces entrenched in Southern Anatolia,[10] the final stage of the dismantling of the Ottoman Empire began. By August 1920, the dissolution – formalised in the

Treaty of Sèvres – was complete: the Greeks had wrested control of Eastern Thrace (Rumeli); plans for an independent Armenian state were well advanced; Kurdistan was to be given autonomy; the Arab Provinces in Iraq and Palestine were mandated to the British, those in Syria and the Lebanon to the French; and the Straits were to be demilitarised.[11] In short, 'Turkey in Europe' had ceased to exist, 'Turkey in Asia' had been radically compressed and the Turkish Government was not fully sovereign over militarily crucial parts of the territory that remained.

The provisions of the unratified Treaty of Sèvres, however, were never put into effect. The Turkish nationalist movement under Mustapha Kemal Pasha, renouncing any international engagements entered into by the Sultan, embarked on a four-year 'war of independence' (1920–3),[12] and under Kemal's generalship, the Greeks were driven out of Rumeli, the Italians removed from Southern Anatolia and the Armenian Republic destroyed.[13] The British and French, facing strong domestic pressures for demobilisation, were obliged to recognise that although the Ottoman Empire no longer existed, Turkey itself could not be wholly dismembered. The Treaty of Lausanne, signed in July 1923, gave formal expression to the new politico-military realities which Mustapha Kemal's campaign had produced: Eastern Thrace was formally returned to Turkey and Turkish sovereignty over the whole of Anatolia re-established.

Despite the fact that the British Government, formerly a staunch supporter of pan-Hellenism, made important concessions at Lausanne, the treaty did little to improve Anglo-Turkish relations. To the Turkish leadership, Britain's 'real' intentions *vis-à-vis* Turkey were revealed in the conditions imposed upon the discredited Sultanate at Sèvres: that Turkish Nationalist military superiority had forced the Allies to shift their position did nothing to vitiate the immense resentment towards the British and French which was widespread in Turkey at the time; particularly in view of the continued Allied instance on the demilitarisation of the Straits,[14] representing as it did a continuing affront to Turkish sovereignty. Writing in the mid-1950s one Nationalist leader noted that in the aftermath of the First World War Britain had attempted to 'destroy all Turkish social bonds, to kill the progressive spirit, to foment religious reaction, and to make of the Turks individual slaves chained to the past . . . [the British were] . . . the merciless enemies of the very existence of Turkey'.[15]

The hatred of the British, moreover, was by no means confined to the Nationalist leadership:

> No single country at the end of the [1914–18] war was hated more than England, regarded as the chief of the Imperialist Powers which sought to destroy Turkey. Armenian, Kurdish and Greek nationalist movements were ascribed to her machinations. Mr. Lloyd George was held directly responsible for the Greek invasion . . . The leading newspaper in Ankara expressed Turkish feeling thus: 'We Turks have an implacable hate for this accursed race. We will never forget the evil it has done us . . . The hate of a people, the disgust of a nation, are stronger than the utilitarian concept of politics.'[16]

The postwar anti-British campaign in Turkey continued well into the 1920s and, as late as July 1925, British Foreign Secretary Austen Chamberlain, on the basis of reports from Mr Hoare, the British representative in Constantinople, noted the intensity of anti-British sentiment in the Turkish Press.[17]

Anglo-Turkish relations were further strained by the Mosul affair, one of the disputes left unresolved by the Treaty of Lausanne. Under the provisions of the treaty, Britain and Turkey had agreed to settle their differences over the possession of the supposedly oil-rich territory (which the British believed should become part of Iraq) within nine months. After this time, if no such resolution had been achieved, the matter was to be referred to the League Council.[18] On 16 December 1925 the Council awarded the territory to Iraq and the Turkish Government promptly rejected both the award and the Council's competence to make it.[19] On 17 December Anglo-Turkish relations were further strained when the Turks signed a Non-aggression and Security Pact with the Soviet Union, a country which HMG firmly believed was encouraging the Turks to go to war with Britain.[20] The Turks subsequently rejected an Advisory Opinion from the Permanent Court which ruled that the Council's decision had been valid[21] and threatened to initiate a guerrilla war in the Mosul region if a satisfactory outcome to the dispute was not forthcoming.[22]

After five months of intense diplomatic negotiation in London and Constantinople outside the framework of the League, '[by] . . . a triumph of diplomacy . . . Turkey was persuaded to conclude a treaty with Great Britain and Iraq [5 June 1926] adopting the League's decision.'[23]

Although the Turks could console themselves with the thought that the ceding of Mosul to Iraq effectively put an end to Kurdish hopes of national autonomy,[24] the loss of Mosul was nonetheless a bitter blow which could only be 'rationalised . . . (by the Turkish government) . . . as a necessary step . . . to normalise relations with Great Britain'.[25] In essence, however, the Turkish government had been forced to recognise the simple political reality that 'a decision confirming the will of the Great Powers, approved by the Council as a whole, and reinforced by the Permanent Court's assertion of the Council's authority, could not be profitably resisted'.[26]

In July 1932, following delicate negotiations with Britain over a period of two years as to how far London would support Ankara's request for a seat on the Council,[27] Turkey acceded to the League of Nations. Two years later, though Britain had expressly refused to make any promises in this regard, Turkey was awarded a semi-permanent seat on the Council.

The Turks' real reward for the co-operative stance which they had adopted towards the Western Powers since the early 1930s, however, was the Montreux Convention of July 1936 which, *inter alia*, abolished the International Commission of the Straits established at the time of Lausanne and permitted the Turks to remilitarise the Straits.[28] To some contemporary observers, the Turks' successful use of the principle of treaty revision at Montreux demonstrated the enormous contribution that international law and diplomacy could make to peaceful conflict resolution; it showed that

> there was at least one 'ex-enemy' power with a dictator at the head of its government which . . . [unlike Germany in April in the Rhineland and Italy in May in Abyssinia] . . . had not succumbed to the fascination of the *fait accompli* . . . and still retained a proper respect for its international engagements.[29]

In what is still perhaps the definitive study of Montreux, however, Routh strongly challenges this interpretation both of Turkey's motivation and of the underlying reasons for the success of the conference; and a more recent detailed study by MacFie confirms Routh's view.[30] In Routh's opinion, Turkey's decision to opt for a negotiated settlement was not the result of any 'genuine respect for international engagements', but rather was 'dictated by more favourable circumstances'.[31] Through patient diplomatic enquiries, the Turkish government had established that with the exception of Italy (which, as a pariah since the invasion of Abyssinia, could be safely ignored anyway), all the original signatories to the 1923 Straits Convention were prepared to accept its substantial revision.[32] The 'favourable circumstances' to which Routh refers were that the realities of balance of power politics had changed significantly since 1923. As far as Britain was concerned, the Italian adventure in Abyssinia, coming on top of Mussolini's longstanding (though unspecified) interest in colonial expansion in Asia – usually presumed to be in Anatolia[33] – represented enough of a potential Italian threat to both British and Turkish security interests in the Eastern Mediterranean as to warrant an unequivocal signal that London was broadly committed to Turkey's territorial integrity.[34] The Turks, for their part, were only too happy, in view of the informal 'gentlemen's agreement' with Britain reached at Montreux, to indicate clearly to Mussolini that Turkey would not face Italy alone in the event of any future Italian aggression in Asia Minor.[35]

However, perhaps more significant as a motive behind Montreux than Britain and Turkey's fears of Italian intentions was their mutual fear of Soviet Russia.[36] In the early days of the war of independence, the Nationalist government in Ankara had signed a Friendship Treaty with the Soviet Union, and at the height of the Mosul dispute, as noted earlier, Turkey and Russia had entered into a non-aggression and security pact (December 1925). Turkey's friendship with the Soviet Union, however, was always decidedly double-edged. As a British diplomat perceptively observed in 1929, shortly after the 1925 Turco-Soviet Treaty had been renewed for a further three years:

> When the Turks say . . . how much they love the Russians what they really mean is that potentially they fear them so much that they are delighted to be friends with them. The bullying of the Tsars is not forgotten. It is an enormous relief to be on such friendly terms with Russia. The Turks have no fear of her at present. They merely dread the day when *internal consolidation will allow her to resume her old pushfulness in the South*. In the meantime they regard it as of paramount importance to keep Russia well disposed.[37]

By the mid-1930s, the Soviet Union had achieved a sufficient degree of 'internal consolidation' to trouble the Turkish leadership: Turkey was no longer in a position to do without a 'protector against Russian ambitions'[38] and accordingly attempted to bolster her security position by strengthening her informal ties with Britain. London, in turn,

> calculated . . . that, providing her relations with her new friend could be rendered sufficiently intimate, Turkey could be weaned from the dominating influence of the USSR, the fear of which had in past years been one of the British Government's main reasons for refusing the Turkish request . . . [for the revision of Lausanne].[39]

On Routh's account, then – and it is not an account with which I wish to disagree – the revision of Lausanne that was achieved at Montreux was the result not of a commitment to legal principle or diplomatic compromise but of the signatories' changing perceptions of their own security interests. Turkey eschewed the use of the *fait accompli* not because she was devoted to the ideal of peaceful change but because objective circumstances fortunately made it possible to achieve her immediate goals (the remilitarisation of the Straits and a reassurance that Turkey would not be isolated if the presumed Italian threat turned into overt aggression) without resort to force.

It is worth noting at this stage that Routh's conclusions about the motivations of the Montreux signatories are typical of virtually all analyses of crisis decision-making.[40] It has been repeatedly observed that in crisis situations, the decision calculus of any nation-state invariably focuses upon the realities of power politics and the need for security maximisation, to the exclusion of considerations of legal rectitude or even moral obligation.[41] Not surprisingly, perhaps, this emphasis on *realpolitik* continues in most accounts of Anglo-Turkish relations in the period after 1936; a period which is undoubtedly best conceived as one of continuing crisis, as the League's collective security system collapsed and the Great Powers manoeuvred their way towards war.

Turkish foreign policy after 1936 was primarily concerned with preventing any foreign incursion into Turkish territory; an objective which was to be achieved from a position of formal neutrality broadly sympathetic towards, and (it was hoped) deriving support from, the West. The outcome of the Munich crisis of 1938, however, raised grave doubts within the Turkish leadership that the Western Powers – and Britain in particular – could be relied upon to act positively on Turkey's behalf in the event of any subsequent Axis threat of aggression.[42] Nonetheless, as the European security situation deteriorated during late 1938 and early 1939, the Turks were obliged to move closer to Britain simply because 'no defence in the Mediterranean against Italy was conceivable without British help'.[43] The German occupation of Czechoslovakia in March 1939 triggered an exchange of notes between the British and Turkish Governments which resulted in a joint Declaration on 12 May 1939 announcing that the two countries would conclude a 'long-term' mutual assistance agreement (universally recognised as a deterrent against Italian aggression) in the near future.[44]

In October 1939, Britain and Turkey, together with France, duly signed a Mutual Assistance treaty in Ankara (a compact which Churchill consistently sought to use after 1940 in order to bring Turkey into the war on the Allied side), though the Turks were careful not to incur Soviet displeasure at the agreement by insisting on the inclusion of a protocol excluding the USSR from its provisions.[45] It seems likely, however, that the Ankara Pact was

> hardly more than an anti-German gesture ... it was ... inconceivable that Turkey could obtain adequate military support from her British protector if Germany and/or Russia should descend upon her ... Military realities thus forced Turkey to adopt a policy of ... [in] formal neutrality throughout the war. Only in the case of an actual German invasion would Turkey join her British ally in active warfare.[46]

Despite the formal abandonment of neutrality, therefore, and despite the fact that both Britain and France were at war with the Axis Powers, Turkey managed to remain effectively neutral until the last months of the war; even signing a Friendship Treaty with Germany on 18 June 1941.[47]

With regard to the question of motivation, it would appear that prior to the German invasion of Russia on 22 June 1941, Turkey's main reason for refusing actively to support Britain and France was its fear of some sort of adverse Soviet response:[48] the Molotov-Ribbentrop non-aggression pact of August 1939 had caused considerable uncertainty in Ankara as to Soviet intentions towards Turkey.[49] Thereafter Turkey's neutral posture was in part a response to its continued mistrust of the USSR and its fear that Britain and the US might secretly have agreed to concede parts of Turkish territory to the Soviet Union in the postwar settlement.[50]

Whatever specific factors entered into the Turkish decision calculus, however, Inönü's wartime diplomacy was singularly successful in its strategy of insulating Turkish sovereign territory from attack. If this meant breaching an international engagement which Turkey had recently made with Britain and France – once again illustrating the irrelevance of legal constraints and obligations in vital matters of war and peace – then this was a price the Turks were willing to pay in order to maintain their own security. What is abundantly clear is that from 1936 onwards, the course of Anglo-Turkish relations was on both sides entirely determined by considerations of *realpolitik*; by hard calculation as to whether a particular manoeuvre at a particular time would enhance or detract from the security interests of the nation-state. Pre-existing treaty commitments were of no direct relevance whatsoever.

'REALPOLITIK' AND ANGLO-TURKISH RELATIONS: A SPECULATIVE QUALIFICATION

The conclusion that international law and lawmaking were irrelevant to decisions taken in the threatening situation after 1936 is essentially unsurprising: common sense, as well as a wealth of documentary evidence, clearly suggests that in the tense international conditions of the late 1930s, *realpolitik* security motives and objectives would inevitably predominate over formal legal obligations, mutual understandings or emotional attachments. However, before this observation is taken as a direct contradiction of the main thesis of the present study – that the pursuit of co-operative strategies of treaty-making can assist significantly in the promotion of peaceful relations between states – it needs to be re-emphasised that the arguments advanced in previous chapters focus on the long-term, latent, political role of the lawmaking process rather than on the immediate manifest role of law as a means of 'legislating peace'. That *realpolitik* overrode considerations of legal rectitude after 1936 is in fact irrelevant to the question as to the possible effects of the treaty-making process on the long-term development of good relations between Britain and Turkey. In this latter context, the question of central importance is how the *initial* transformation came about that made it possible for Britain and Turkey to enjoy such cordial relations by 1936, so that after that date, Turkey was able to use her friendship with Britain as a political resource with which to withstand subsequent German blandishments, incentives and threats aimed at shifting the Turkish position to one more favourably disposed towards the Axis.

It is not a matter of either idle or wild speculation to suggest that if Anglo-Turkish relations had not been so cordial in 1936, the international position of Turkey in the late 1930s might have been very different. In the first place, without such good relations, it is conceivable that the peaceful treaty revision enacted at Montreux might never have occurred. In planning their campaign to achieve a revision of Lausanne, the Turks had intended to avoid a formal approach to either the League or to the Lausanne signatories, and instead to '[simultaneously notify] . . . the signatories of Turkey's intention to raise the issue and . . . [to] . . . dispatch . . . Turkish troops into the Straits zone.'[51] Without the strong sense of mutual confidence between the British Embassy in Turkey and the Turkish Foreign Ministry, which had been built up during the earlier ambassadorship of Sir George Clerk,[52] it is possible that British Ambassador Lorraine might not have had the opportunity to dissuade the Turkish Government – as he subsequently did[53] – from such a dangerous unilateral occupation of the Straits zone. In these circumstances, the Turks might well have resorted to the very *fait accompli*, strongly advocated by the powerful Turkish General Staff,[54] which they were subsequently lauded for avoiding. Turkey would thus undoubtedly have joined the two other revisionist Powers (Germany and Italy) as a third international moral reprobate – with obvious implications for her relations with Britain – rather than acquiring the status of the 'good girl of Europe' which she subsequently achieved.[55]

A second reason for supposing that the cordiality of Anglo-Turkish relations in the mid-1930s was crucial in determining Turkey's later international stance concerns Turkey's relations with Germany. In the economic sphere, Turco-German trade had expanded rapidly from 0.3 per cent of Turkish imports in 1878 to 11.2 per cent in 1913.[56] During the First World War Germany took advantage of her alliance with Turkey to increase trade further, to the considerable detriment of Britain which had earlier been Turkey's greatest trading partner.[57] The British policy of imperial preference in the interwar years rendered Turkish exports to Britain even more uncompetitive with the result that

> during the world economic depression beginning in 1930, and especially . . . [after] . . . the establishment of the Nazi regime in Germany, Great Britain lost both absolutely and relatively in the foreign trade of Turkey . . . [There was] . . . a definite correlation between the progress of . . . [German] . . . foreign economic policy in . . . [Turkey] . . . and the decline in the percentage share of Great Britain in . . . Turkish foreign trade.[58]

During the 1930s, therefore, there was a strong convergence of material interest between Germany and Turkey, particularly as the Germans relied heavily on the Turks for their supply of certain strategic minerals, notably chrome ore.[59]

If this convergence of material interest is combined, first, with the argument that German Ambassador von Papen advanced (unsuccessfully as it turned out) to Turkish Foreign Minister Saracoglu in May 1939 – that as the senior partner in the Axis Coalition, Germany was willing and able to prevent any Italian incursion against Turkish sovereignty[60] – and second, with the possible neutralisation of the Soviet threat to Turkey which the Molotov-Ribbentrop pact of August 1939 could at the time have been interpreted as representing, then the possibility of a *realpolitik*-motivated tacit alliance between Turkey and Germany could conceivably have emerged. In short, there was no ineluctable logic to the *realpolitik* situation that existed in 1939 which necessarily led to the strategy that Turkey did in fact adopt; that of an informal neutrality broadly sympathetic towards the Western Powers.

It is by no means fanciful to hypothesise that a critical factor in determining the Turkish position both in 1936 and in 1939 was the extremely good relations enjoyed between London and Ankara. In both situations there was a high degree of free and frank discussion between the British and Turkish Governments prior to any decision being taken,[61] and of crucial importance in this regard was the reservoir of trust and the spirit of compromise which had been a key feature of Anglo-Turkish relations since the early 1930s. As a British diplomat observed in a confidential memorandum to the Foreign Secretary as early as 1929: 'Turkey would sooner have our help than that of any other Power[62] . . . [she] . . . has of late become increasingly conviced of our desire to maintain existing frontiers and of the fact that we have no territorial ambitions in Turkey.'[63]

What is being suggested, then, is not that *realpolitik* was anything other than crucially important in the foreign policy decisions taken by the British and Turkish Governments from 1936 onwards, but that without the high degree of mutual confidence and trust which had been established between those governments in the period *before* 1936, the *realpolitik* decisions taken subsequently might have been very different from those which actually obtained. Given this perspective, it becomes clear why it is necessary to focus on the transformation of Anglo-Turkish relations *prior* to 1936 in order to establish if the treaty-making process played any significant part in the promotion and maintenance of peaceful relations between London and Ankara in the interwar period. In particular this involves the examination of a period of Anglo-Turkish relations which has hitherto been somewhat under-researched: between 1926, when the Turks resentfully conceded Mosul to Iraq (and when, as noted earlier, the Turks were threatening war against Britain if Mosul was lost), and July 1932 when Turkey acceded to the League of Nations, by which time relations with Britain had achieved a pronounced degree of cordiality. How, then, did the transformation in Anglo-Turkish relations come about? In what sense, if any, can the treaty-making process be construed as having contributed to that transformation?

THE TRANSFORMATION OF ANGLO-TURKISH RELATIONS 1926–32

As noted earlier, while relations between London and Ankara had recovered slightly from their low point at Sèvres in virtue of the concessions made by Britain at Lausanne, those relations were still extremely strained well into the mid-1920s. The large-scale nationalisation by Mustapha Kemal's government of the 'foreign companies that had been directing the economy' not surprisingly caused immense resentment in the West.[64] The dispute over Mosul, 'which had almost ended in war'[65] between Britain and Turkey, 'so exacerbated Anglo-Turkish relations . . . [that it] . . . led in 1925 to a Russo-Turkish treaty of friendship',[66] thus fuelling British concern that Turkey and the Soviet Union, both feeling threatened by Western imperialism,[67] would draw even closer together in the future.

In reviewing the December 1925 Russo-Turkish pact, the British Ambassador to Constantinople informed the Foreign Secretary: 'The Turk means his signature of the treaty to serve as a warning to the west that circumstances may force him to leave his position of equilibrium and come down on the Russian side of the fence'.[68] Anglo-Turkish relations were further strained by the campaign of harrassment against foreign – especially British – institutions in Turkey in February and March of 1926.[69] Ambassador Lindsay observed, 'Good relations are not possible if British commerce and institutions are harrassed in this manner'.[70]

The resolution of the Mosul dispute in June 1926 did little in the short term to improve relations, which was only to be expected in view of the Turks' resentment at having to concede the territory in the face of intense British diplomatic pressure. Ankara's flirtation with Moscow continued and in October Mr R. H. Hoare in Constantinople notified Chamberlain that the Russians were encouraging the Turks

> to feel surrounded by a ring of enemies, who are only prevented from falling upon Turkey by their own dissensions . . . the modest ambition of the Kemal regime is to divide its foreign enemies in the hope that it may thereby survive . . . [for Turkey] . . . it would be delightful if England and Italy were on bad terms.[71]

The immediate injury to Turkish nationalist pride invoked by the Mosul settlement, however, rapidly began to dissipate. Within five months of the signature of the Mosul treaty, a distinct thawing in Anglo-

Turkish relations was clearly in evidence; as Turkish Foreign Minister Tevfik Rüstü was subsequently to confirm in a press interview in February 1927.[72] In November 1926 the new ambassador to Constantinople, Sir George Clerk, reported to Chamberlain on a leading article in *Echo de Turquie* which was

> under the signature of Agha Oglou Ahmed, who is one of the principal leader writers in the *Hakimiet-i-Millie*, the official organ of the Turkish Government... The general tone of the article is in favour of closer relations between Britain and Turkey . . . there are signs that this more friendly spirit . . . is bearing fruit in a more helpful attitude on the part of the authorities where British interests are concerned in this country.[73]

The timing of this shift in the Turkish position – for as Clerk correctly judged, this is essentially what it was – is highly significant. Britain had been consistently vilified in the Government-sponsored Turkish press since 1919, a pattern which was necessarily maintained in the immediate wake of the adverse (to Turkey) settlement over Mosul. Once this initial resentment had died down, however, the dual opportunity for an improvement in relations created by the treaty and by the appointment of a new ambassador to Constantinople was seized upon by both sides. In December, Clerk again reported to Chamberlain on a prominent item in the Turkish press, this time by Younous Nady, a well-known Anglophobe whose articles in the past had, according to Clerk, been 'bitterly and wilfully hostile to Great Britain'. Nady's report was so favourable that Clerk felt that it could 'only do good, coming, as it does, at a time when the Turks are mending their ways in many respects'.[74] On 29 December, Clerk provided further confirmation of the softening of the Turkish position:

> Not only was my own reception at Angora [in November 1926] distinctly friendly, but the attitude of the Turkish authorities on a number of occasions . . . (on) . . . questions of minor importance has been more helpful of late. The press also has reflected this change of tone. We are now far from the days when His Majesty's Government was held up to the Turkish public as the disturber of the peace, as the jealous Imperialist who could not forgive the new Turkey for bursting her swathing bonds and trying to *take her place as an equal among the European nations*. There was no journalist in Turkey who did more to

> misrepresent the policy of His Majesty's Government during the Mosul crisis than Younous Nady, the editor of the *Republique* and *there is no journalist here today who is going so far in the opposite direction* ... [Nady's] aim is to reflect the opinion of those in power in Angora and . . . he never strays far from the path which the Government would consider strictly orthodox. For this reason I am disposed to attach some importance . . . to the articles which he is sending to his paper from abroad.
>
> In his article which appeared in the *Republique* on the 27th December, Younous Nady adopts a distinctly friendly attitude towards the League of Nations . . . he emphasises the predominant role played by England at Geneva and . . . the predominant role played by England in Europe ... [As] ... regards the smaller powers in the League, Younous Nady maintains – and *this seems to me of importance*, for Turkey recognises that she is a small power – that *in spite of the predominance of England, they, too are treated on an equality with the others.*[75]

In Clerk's reference to Turkey 'trying to take her place as an equal among the European nations' and in Nady's reference to small Powers being 'treated on an equality with the others', an important insight can be gained both into the psychology of the Turkish leadership of the time and, more significantly, into why the Mosul negotiations – despite their adverse *outcome,* as far as Turkey was concerned – were crucial to the restoration of good Anglo-Turkish relations. Throughout the Mosul negotiations, even during the abortive attempt at resolution undertaken under the auspices of the League Council, Turkey – though not a member of the League – was treated as a party of equal status to Britain.[76] To a nation struggling to achieve a sense of national identity and searching for a new international role in its difficult initial phase of post-imperialism, this was a vitally important psychological and symbolic concession. Especially in view of the demilitarisation clauses imposed at Lausanne, Mustapha Kemal, if only to bolster his own domestic position, desperately needed a public demonstration of Turkey's formal equality of sovereign status with one of the Great Powers. In the Mosul negotiations this was essentially what Britain provided. In an indirect but very important sense, therefore, the treaty-making process which preceded the Mosul settlement made a concrete contribution to the subsequent improvement in Anglo-Turkish relations by engineering a subtle but significant change in the Turkish Government's perception of its own status in world politics; a new image which it could display both at home and abroad as one which was shared by HMG.[77]

Relations between London and Ankara continued to improve throughout 1927. In January, the Foreign Secretary notified Ambassador Clerk of a conversation he had recently had with the Turkish Ambassador to London who had expressed how delighted the Turks were both with Clerk himself and with the improved relations that he had established with them.[78] The improvement in relations, however, was not confined solely to the person of Ambassador Clerk. While Clerk was on leave in March 1927 his temporary replacement, Mr R. H. Hoare, a rather more cynical – even acidic – analyst of Turkish affairs than Clerk,[79] reported to Chamberlain on a reception given for Mustapha Kemal at which Mr Haddow, a junior diplomat at the British Embassy, was regaled by a possibly drunken Ghazi for some 90 minutes. During this time Haddow was repeatedly informed that Britain was 'the greatest of all nations in the world; the world's greatest coloniser; the nation which, by its valour and perseverance, had succeeded in building up the greatest of all empires; the people in whose fairness he trusted'. Hoare concluded:

> It would be quite unwise to attach any special importance to the Ghazi's utterances, but they are a clear indication that the present tendency of the Turkish Government to cultivate better relations with HMG has the approval of the director of Turkey's destinies.[80]

Confirmation that the Turkish Government was increasingly inclined to put its trust in Britain's good intentions towards Turkey was provided in July 1927 in a report from Ambassador Clerk on a conversation between Mr Alex V. Helm, second secretary at the British consulate in Ankara, and Col. Edib Bey, an 'influential deputy to the Grand National Assembly'. Edib Bey is reported to have commented: 'Before the war, we regarded Great Britain . . . as our deadly foe. Now we know we have nothing to fear from Britain, whose policy we know is open . . . We want to advance along the road with England'.[81]

The increasing cordiality of relations was emphasised once more in February 1928. Clerk again reported on Mustapha Kemal's outspokenness in praise of Britain and the Ghazi's statement as to his 'belief in the honesty of our policy and its accordance with that of Turkey'.[82] Clerk also summarised a conversation with Foreign Minister Tevfik Rüstü and Prime Minister Ismet Pasha which was

> chiefly remarkable for the friendliness shown towards Great Britain. Both Tevfik Rüstü and Ismet Pasha expressed much pleasure . . . at the amicable development of our relations, and neither of them coupled their statements with a request for, or even hint at, some tangible recognition on our part of this happy state of affairs. I think, therefore, that *one may take their satisfaction as, at all events for the moment, genuine.*[83]

A similar meeting with a similar outcome was to occur in October 1928 at which both Tevfik Rüstü and Ismet Pasha 'genuinely . . . voice[d] their pleasure at the satisfactory development of the relations between the two countries . . . there was no hint of what they said being gratitude for possible favours to come'.[84]

The critical link between the Mosul treaty and the improvement in relations was reasserted in April 1928 in a report by Mr Knox on the 'Final Report of Military Attaché Major Harenc'. Knox observed that 'Normal diplomatic relations were not resumed till 1925 and until the summer of 1926 the Mosul question made anything like friendly relations with the Turks impossible'.[85] Politely rejecting Harenc's view that 'thinking and educated Turks dislike England intensely', Knox contended that

> what surprises . . . at the present day is not so much the suspicion with which we are viewed as the rapidity of its decrease. There is now happily no doubt that, with the governing classes at least, *the position that we occupy in this country since the Mosul Agreement has improved and is daily improving out of all recognition.* Individually we are already often liked and even respected. Collectively, we are no longer held in the same esteem as before the occupation, but I notice signs that a new respect for us, material rather than ethical, is growing up.[86]

In spite of a brief wave of xenophobia in the Turkish press in February 1929 – targeted tangentially at Britain as a result of a delay in a fire-brigade reaching a fire owing to the failure of a British-supplied telephone system[87] – Anglo-Turkish relations continued to develop amicably. In the same month, in a 'Memorandum on the Present Position in Turkey', A. K. Helm reported that

> In the space of five years British prestige in Turkey has recovered to an extent which could never have been imagined, and with it, thanks to some extent to leading Turks having become better acquainted with

> the outside world, has developed a sincere admiration for Anglo-Saxon methods and culture.[88]

In June, Clerk again wrote to Chamberlain following a meeting with Foreign Minister Tevfik Rüstü: 'Throughout the interview His Excellency was so *profuse in expressions of gratification at the growth of . . . friendliness* that I was in momentary expectation of some concrete request, but nothing materialised, and *I think that His Excellency's observations were genuine*'.[89] In October, following the highly successful goodwill visit of Admiral Field's naval squadron to Turkey, Clerk commented 'Whether the effect of the visit is to be lasting depends on the future, but for the moment British stock stands higher in Turkey than it has done than at any time since the armistice',[90] though he did also make the reservation that

> I should be conveying a false impression if I led you to believe that the visit of the fleet has at one stroke renewed the traditional . . . [pre-1914] . . . friendship between Great Britain and Turkey . . . The visit . . . [nonetheless] . . . makes a definite advance along the path of friendship, but complete trust in our sincerity has still to be achieved.[91]

In January 1930 a series of informal negotiations began in London and Ankara, concerning Turkey's possible entry to the League of Nations, which gave British diplomacy its opportunity to move closer to gaining the 'complete trust' of the Turkish Government. In conversation with Sir George Clerk, Tevfik Rüstü reiterated Turkey's favoured conditions of entry (to be *invited* to join the League and to be 'rewarded' with either a permanent or a semi-permanent seat on Council) which had first been articulated to the British Foreign Secretary in November 1926.[92] Clerk avoided making a direct response to Tevfik Rüstü's implied request and in turn requested advice from London as to the line he should take in any future conversations.[93] Foreign Secretary Henderson replied, confirming Clerk's expectations, indicating that while Britain would welcome Turkish entry to the League, no definite promises of support for a semi-permanent Turkish seat on Council could be made. Nonetheless, His Majesty's Government 'would hope to be able to support her candidature for Council at the first favourable opportunity which would, no doubt, occur during the early years of her membership'.[94] In February 1931, as a result of a meeting with the Turkish Ambassador to London, Henderson was able to inform Clerk that Turkey would no longer insist on a permanent seat on Council as a condition of their entry to the League, though the Turks obviously hoped they could count on the support of HMG for a semi-permanent seat.

The developing Anglo-Turkish understanding that accompanied these protracted negotiations was given symbolic expression in the rapturous welcome accorded to the Earl of Athlone and Princess Alice on their visit to Turkey in April 1931. Clerk observed

> 'it would be foolish to suppose that the Ghazi's attitude was merely a rather effusive welcome to illustrious guests. That is contrary to the man's whole nature. The Ghazi and the Turkish Government . . . feel that the only European Great Power that is genuinely working for lasting peace is Great Britain, and they are honestly anxious to work together with us to that end.[95]

In April 1932, the final stage of the negotiations was reached. Following a conversation with Ismet Pasha and Tevfik Rüstü, Clerk informed London that Turkey would now be prepared to join the League if she were invited to do so by the Great Powers.[96] Two months later Clerk was able to report to Sir John Simon that there was 'abundant evidence of the friendly relations now prevailing between Britain and Turkey'.[97] On 6 July 1932, the League of Nations passed a resolution inviting Turkey to join the League and on 9 July the Turkish Government accepted the invitation. Within two years, Turkey had obtained its coveted semi-permanent seat on Council. His Majesty's Government, though it had made no specific promises, had kept good faith with the Turks. Crucially, it had demonstrated that a genuine transformation in Anglo-Turkish relations, founded upon the treaty-making efforts of the British and Turkish Governments in 1925 and 1926, had been effected. A reserve of trust and goodwill had been thus established which would prove to be of critical importance in the difficult period of crisis ahead.

SUMMARY AND CONCLUSIONS

The primary objective of this chapter has been to ascertain whether the conclusions arrived at in Chapters 3 and 4 – that in certain contexts participation in the treaty-making process can serve to reduce the probability of war occurring between nations – are supported by a detailed examination of a particular historical case. In the context of the particular case-study selected – Anglo-Turkish relations in the interwar period – there is abundant evidence that at the beginning of the period under investigation, relations between the two countries involved were extremely hostile. Given that war did not subsequently occur between Britain and Turkey, the main substantive question that needed to be addressed was how this transformation in relations came about and, in particular, how far, and in what way, participation in the treaty-making process might have been involved.

The first task of this chapter was to show that existing secondary accounts of Anglo-Turkish relations between the two wars have in their various expositions tended, first, to focus on events either before 1926 or after 1936, and second, to explain these developments primarily in terms of *realpolitik*. It has not been my intention here to challenge the conclusions concerning the role of *realpolitik* – particularly from 1936 onwards – thus reached. What I have tried to suggest, however, is that this focus on 'milestone' events and *realpolitik* motives has meant that existing analyses have virtually ignored the critical period in the transformation of Anglo-Turkish relations between 1926 and 1932. Those analyses have also tended to underestimate the extent to which the extreme cordiality which marked relations between London and Ankara during the mid-1930s was an important part of the subsequent *realpolitik* equation, and that without that cordiality, the ensuing *realpolitik* outcome could have been very different. (In economic terms, Turkey's trading interests were far more closely connected with Berlin than with London; in military-strategic terms, the Turks could easily have concluded that Germany was much better placed than Britain to offer effective protection against Italian and Soviet ambitions towards Turkish sovereign territory; either or both of these considerations could have motivated a *realpolitik* decision to side with the Axis powers.) In these circumstances, it is essential to establish how the dramatic improvement in Anglo-Turkish relations came about and what factors might have been responsible for it.

This is not to suggest, of course, that matters of *realpolitik* were irrelevant between 1926 and 1932. There is no doubt that during the early part of this period at least, the Turks consistently tried to play off Britain and the Soviet Union against each other; that Turkey sought to use her burgeoning friendship with Britain as protection against her fears of Italian intentions; and that HMG attempted to weaken the relatively close relations which Turkey had developed with the Soviet Union during the 1920s. What is being contended, however, is that in addition to these considerations of power politics, two other factors were significant in the transformation of Anglo-Turkish relations. The first of these was good old-fashioned diplomacy: Sir George Clerk performed superbly in gaining the trust and confidence of the Turkish Government and in convincing Ankara of Britain's benign intentions *vis-à-vis* Turkish interests. Given the depth of Turkish hatred of all things British in the early 1920s, this was an extraordinary achievement. *Realpolitik* alone may be sufficient to generate hostility between nations, but patient and intelligent diplomacy – which Clerk was able to supply in abundance – is a necessary adjunct to the logic of *realpolitik* if cordiality and friendship are to be developed.

The second additional factor in the transformation of relations was the treaty-making process itself; in this case, the negotiations which preceded the Mosul settlement in June 1926. The equality of status accorded to the Turks and the intimations of British good intent provided at those negotiations were sufficient to produce a thaw in Anglo-Turkish relations despite an outcome which the Turkish Government clearly regarded as highly unsatisfactory. It was this initial thawing that made Clerk's subsequent diplomacy, together with the build-up of mutual trust which it engendered, possible. While not denying the importance of diplomacy and *realpolitik*, therefore, it is being suggested that the treaty-making process represented a crucial first stage in the transformation of relations between London and Ankara in the interwar period. In this respect, it is not unreasonable to conclude that by providing a basis for subsequent diplomacy, international lawmaking assisted in the creation of an important political resource that could be drawn upon in later *realpolitik* power plays. In short, participation in the treaty-making process in the 1920s performed a seminal role in the subsequent avoidance of hostilities between Britain and Turkey.

Conclusion: Reconstructed Idealism and Revised Realism

This study has attempted to demonstrate empirically that in certain limited contexts in the interwar years, the pursuit of co-operative treaty-making strategies by nation-states significantly reduced the probability that the parties involved would subsequently go to war. It has also tried to show that the empirical relationship thus described is not simply a spurious statistical coincidence. Both the detailed quantitative analysis developed in Chapter 3 and 4 and the case-study examined in Chapter 5 lend strong support to the idea that co-operation – in the form of a commitment to the bilateral treaty-making process – constituted a significant *causal* factor in the complex balance of forces which enabled certain dyads to maintain peaceful relations even in the face of the general conflagration of 1939–45.

These findings potentially have two important implications. First, they suggest a possible need for a partial revision in the orthodox historiography of the 1920s and 1930s. To be sure, as most analyses of the period have rightly maintained, at the core of the international system – particularly in the relations between the Great Powers – international law and gestures of co-operation were at best useless and at worst dangerously illusory. However, in terms of the relations between the Powers at the core of the system and those at its periphery – such as the relationship between Britain and Turkey discussed in Chapter 5 – it is less clear that co-operation and lawmaking were always and everywhere without beneficial effects. On the contrary, it has been shown that in these contexts, the pursuit of lawmaking and co-operation *did* have a positive payoff in terms of increasing the chances for the maintenance of bilateral peace. It is perhaps the case that these findings as to the positive role of international lawmaking could provide a new perspective on the mechanisms underlying the changing relations between a number of other states during the 1930s; though inevitably, this must be a matter for further research.

A second, and more significant, implication of the results presented in the present study is concerned with the possible need for a revision in the orthodox, 'power politics' perspective on international relations; the realist view which sees power maximisation as the fundamental foreign policy strategy that nation-states pursue, and which regards all outcomes in international politics as the essential result of the exercise of power.[1]

Strictly speaking, this implied revision is only of relevance if the power politics approach is conceptualised in terms of what has been described as 'concessional', as opposed to 'traditional', realism.[2] While both realisms start from the same assumption, that 'the world is divided into independent sovereign states among which there can be established at most an unstable and uncertain balance of power',[3] 'traditional realism' is grounded in the principles of normative political theory: its adherents take the view that as a result of direct experience, introspection and insight, they have arrived at a broadly satisfactory understanding of 'the way things really are in international politics'; and no amount of supposedly systematic empirical evidence will alter their perceptions in this regard. Concessional realism, on the the other hand, makes a crucial epistemological 'concession' to 'positivist empiricism'.[4] It acknowledges that if realism is to achieve the status of an explanatory empirical theory – which is what it should be aiming for – it must not only couch its theoretical propositions in terms that are in principle capable of falsification, but it must also seek to assemble systematic, as opposed to illustrative, empirical evidence in order to demonstrate that those propositions are indeed sustainable.

It would not be appropriate here to attempt to specify all of the falsifiable propositions which a 'concessional' version of realism might develop. Rather it is sufficient in the context of the present study to note that for any realist – concessional or traditional – a gesture or a strategy of co-operation in international politics possesses no autonomy of its own. Although co-operation is possible, it is always *motivated* by considerations of power maximisation, while its *consequences* are invariably governed by and subordinated to the needs of national security. If the logic of the *realpolitik* situation points towards inter-state violence, then no amount of co-operation can lead to peace. Co-operation, in essence, can have no effect on the relations between nation-states independently of the given imperatives of power politics.

If this interpretation of the extent of the role of co-operation in international politics is, in the concessional realist sense, regarded as a falsifiable empirical proposition, then the results reported in this study suggest that that proposition is by no means entirely consistent with the available empirical evidence. While not denying the central importance of power politics as a determinant of both strategies and outcomes in international relations, the results indicate that co-operation *does* have an autonomy of its own; it can have an effect independent of the logic of *realpolitik*. In the case-study examined in Chapter 5, this was precisely what was meant by the argument that the sense of mutual trust developed by Britain and Turkey after 1926 not only was critical in the transformation of Anglo-Turkish relations from a position of intense antagonism to one of extreme cordiality, but also became part of the subsequent *realpolitik* equation in the period after 1936: the earlier pursuit of a co-operative treaty-making strategy actually changed the *realpolitik* position. In a similar vein, the statistical results reported in Chapters 3 and 4 indicated that in certain general contexts, (where cultures were dissimilar, geographical distances great or power differentials significant) even when existing patterns of friendship/antagonism were held constant – when the *realpolitik* logic of the situations and the *a priori* probabilities of war were broadly the same – those dyads which participated in co-operative treaty-making strategies were significantly less likely subsequently to go to war than those which did not. Again, this finding indicates that co-operation can have an effect independently of the apparent imperatives of *realpolitik*: a strategy of co-operation (which, even if it fails, is non-fatal) *is* capable of developing an autonomy of its own and of making a limited but nonetheless distinctive and independent contribution to the prospects for bilateral peace.

The specific revision to (concessional) realism that is being proposed, therefore, is that realism should no longer feel quite so secure in its convictions (1) that co-operation is relevant to the cause of peace only to the precise extent that it is firmly underpinned by a convergence of security interest between or among the states involved, and (2) that co-operation is only possible when it appears to improve the power position of the nation-states concerned. Rather, as some game theorists have implied, non-fatal co-operative strategies, such as a commitment to the treaty-making process in areas which do not directly concern matters of vital security, can have an autonomous and independent influence on the relations between states over and above the effects of the calculus of power: such strategies can provide a route out of the dilemma of mutual confrontation which routinely characterises the most critical and important situations in international politics. While this clearly does not in any sense imply a full-blooded return to the overoptimistc idealism of the interwar years, it does indicate that a reconstructed idealism, which emphasises the indirect, political effects of lawmaking, can occupy a relatively minor but nonetheless significant position in a revised version of concessional realism. Treaty-making in the 1920s and 1930s, though it was by no means a guarantee of success, did perform a limited but important role in the transformation of relations between certain nation-states. Even in the difficult and admittedly different conditions of the contemporary international system, it is perhaps a strategy that is still worth trying.

Table A.1 : listing of dyads according to the accuracy of predicted values from the model defined in Table 4.11. **The table opposite summarises the number of dyads which were** (1) correctly predicted as either going to war or avoiding war and (2) incorrectly predicted. In presenting the table it is assumed that a predicted value (from the model defined in Table 4.11) greater than or equal to $\hat{y}_i = .5$ means that war is predicted to occur; a predicted value less than $\hat{y}_i = .5$ means that no war is predicted by the model.

1. Dyads in which no war was predicted and no war occurred. (N = 835)

BELG-SPAI	CZEC-ICEL	ESTO-FINL	SWED-FRAN	EIRE-SWIS	TURK-LITH	INDI-TURK	USSR-USA	CHIL-MEXI
BELG-SWED	CZEC-ITAL	GREK-FINL	SWIS-FRAN	ITAL-LUXE	NETH-NORW	BELG-POLE	SPAI-USA	CHIL-PANA
BELG-SWIS	CZEC-LUXE	HUNG-FINL	THAI-FRAN	ITAL-NETH	NETH-POLE	IRAQ-TURK	SWED-USA	CHIL-PARA
BRIT-ALBA	CZEC-NETH	ICEL-FINL	TURK-FRAN	ITAL-NORW	NETH-PORT	EIRE-TURK	THAI-USA	CHIL-PERU
BRIT-BELG	CZEC-NORW	ITAL-FINL	URUG-FRAN	ITAL-PORT	NETH-RUMA	NETH-TURK	TURK-USA	CHIL-SALV
BRIT-BOLI	CZEC-POLE	JAPA-FINL	YEME-FRAN	ITAL-POLE	NETH-SWED	NORW-TURK	URUG-USA	CHIL-URUG
BRIT-BRAZ	CZEC-PORT	LATV-FINL	YUGO-FRAN	ITAL-SWED	NETH-SWIS	PERS-TURK	VENE-USA	CHIL-VENE
BRIT-CHIL	CZEC-RUMA	LITH-FINL	AUST-GERM	ITAL-SWIS	NETH-SPAI	POLE-TURK	YUGO-USA	COLO-COST
BRIT-COLO	CZEC-SPAI	MEXI-FINL	AFGA-GERM	LUXE-NETH	NETH-VENE	RUMA-TURK	AUST-YUGO	COLO-CUBA
BRIT-COST	CZEC-SWED	NETH-FINL	BOLI-GERM	LUXE-NORW	NORW-POLE	SPAI-TURK	ALBA-YUGO	COLO-ECUA
BRIT-CUBA	CZEC-SWIS	NORW-FINL	BULG-GERM	LUXE-POLE	NORW-PORT	SWED-TURK	ARGE-YUGO	COLO-GUAT
BRIT-CZEC	DENM-EGYP	PERS-FINL	CHIL-GERM	LUXE-PORT	NORW-RUMA	SWIS-TURK	BELG-YUGO	COLO-MEXI
BRIT-DENM	DENM-GREK	POLE-FINL	DANZ-GERM	LUXE-RUMA	NORW-SPAI	SYRI-TURK	BRAZ-YUGO	COLO-NICA
BRIT-ECUA	DENM-HUNG	PORT-FINL	ECUA-GERM	LUXE-SWIS	NORW-SWED	TURK-UKRA	BULG-YUGO	COLO-PANA
BRIT-EGYP	DENM-ICEL	RUMA-FINL	HUNG-GERM	AUST-LATV	NORW-SWIS	AFGN-USA	CAND-YUGO	COLO-SALV
BRIT-ESTO	DENM-EIRE	SAFR-FINL	IRAQ-GERM	AFGA-LATV	POLE-PORT	ARGN-USA	CZEC-YUGO	COLO-URUG
BRIT-FRAN	DENM-NETH	SPAI-FINL	EIRE-GERM	BELG-LATV	POLE-RUMA	AUST-USA	DENM-YUGO	COLO-VENE
BRIT-GREK	DENM-NORW	SWED-FINL	MANC-GERM	BRAZ-LATV	POLE-SPAI	AUSL-USA	EGYP-YUGO	COST-GUAT
BRIT-GUAT	DENM-PORT	SWIS-FINL	PARA-GERM	BULG-LATV	POLE-SWED	BELG-USA	FINL-YUGO	COST-HOND
BRIT-HAIT	DENM-POLE	TURK-FINL	PERS-GERM	CHIN-LATV	POLE-SWIS	BOLI-USA	GREK-YUGO	COST-MEXI
BRIT-HOND	DENM-RUMA	ALBA-FRAN	SAUD-GERM	CZEC-LATV	PORT-RUMA	BRAZ-USA	JAPA-YUGO	COST-NICA
BRIT-ICEL	DENM-SPAI	AUSL-FRAN	SPAI-GERM	DENM-LATV	PORT-SPAI	CHIL-USA	NETH-YUGO	COST-PANA
BRIT-EIRE	DENM-SWED	BELG-FRAN	SWED-GERM	ESTO-LATV	PORT-SWED	CHIN-USA	POLE-YUGO	COST-SALV
BRIT-JORD	DENM-SWIS	BRAZ-FRAN	SWIS-GERM	GREK-LATV	RUMA-SPAI	COLO-USA	RUMA-YUGO	CUBA-DOMI
BRIT-LATV	AUST-ESTO	CANA-FRAN	TURK-GERM	HUNG-LATV	RUMA-SWED	COST-USA	SWED-YUGO	CUBA-ECUA
BRIT-LIBE	AFGA-ESTO	CHIL-FRAN	URUG-GERM	ICEL-LATV	RUMA-SWIS	CUBA-USA	SWIS-YUGO	CUBA-GUAT
BRIT-MEXI	BELG-ESTO	CHIN-FRAN	GREK-HUNG	ITAL-LATV	SPAI-SWED	CZEC-USA	SPAI-YUGO	CUBA-MEXI
BRIT-MUSC	BULG-ESTO	COST-FRAN	GREK-ICEL	JAPA-LATV	SPAI-SWIS	DANZ-USA	TURK-YUGO	CUBA-SALV
BRIT-NEPA	CHIN-ESTO	CUBA-FRAN	GREK-EIRE	LITH-LATV	SPAI-URUG	DENM-USA	ARGE-BRAZ	DOMI-HAIT
BRIT-NETH	CZEC-ESTO	CZEC-FRAN	GREK-LUXE	NETH-LATV	SWED-SWIS	DOMI-USA	ARGE-BOLI	ECUA-GUAT
BRIT-NORW	DENM-ESTO	DENM-FRAN	GREK-NETH	NORW-LATV	SWED-URUG	ECUA-USA	ARGE-CHIL	ECUA-SALV
BRIT-PANA	GREK-ESTO	DOMI-FRAN	GREK-NORW	PERS-LATV	AFGA-USSR	EGYP-USA	ARGE-COLO	ECUA-VENE
BRIT-PARA	HUNG-ESTO	ECUA-FRAN	GREK-POLE	POLE-LATV	BELG-USSR	ESTO-USA	ARGE-CUBA	GUAT-HOND
BRIT-PERU	ICEL-ESTO	EGYP-FRAN	GREK-PORT	PORT-LATV	CANA-USSR	ETHI-USA	ARGE-ECUA	GUAT-NICA
BRIT-PERS	ITAL-ESTO	ESTO-FRAN	GREK-RUMA	RUMA-LATV	CZEC-USSR	FINL-USA	ARGE-GUAT	GUAT-SALV
BRIT-POLE	MEXI-ESTO	FINL-FRAN	GREK-SPAI	SPAI-LATV	DENM-USSR	GHAN-USA	ARGE-MEXI	HOND-MEXI
BRIT-PORT	JAPA-ESTO	GREK-FRAN	GREK-SWED	SWED-LATV	ESTO-USSR	GREK-USA	ARGE-PARA	HOND-NICA
BRIT-SALV	NETH-ESTO	GUAT-FRAN	GREK-SWIS	SWIS-LATV	GREK-USSR	GUAT-USA	ARGE-PERU	HOND-SALV
BRIT-SAUD	NORW-ESTO	HAIT-FRAN	HUNG-ITAL	TURK-LATV	LATV-USSR	HOND-USA	ARGE-SALV	MEXI-PANA
BRIT-SWED	PERS-ESTO	HUNG-FRAN	HUNG-NETH	YUGO-LATV	LITH-USSR	ICEL-USA	ARGE-URUG	MEXI-PARA
BRIT-SWIS	POLE-ESTO	INDI-FRAN	HUNG-NORW	AUST-LITH	MEXI-USSR	IRAQ-USA	ARGE-VENE	MEXI-PERU
BRIT-SYRI	PORT-ESTO	IRAQ-FRAN	HUNG-PANA	AFGA-LITH	MONG-USSR	EIRE-USA	BOLI-BRAZ	MEXI-URUG
BRIT-TURK	RUMA-ESTO	LATV-FRAN	HUNG-POLE	ARGE-LITH	NORW-USSR	LATV-USA	BOLI-CHIL	MEXI-SALV
BRIT-USA	SPAI-ESTO	LUXE-FRAN	HUNG-PORT	BELG-LITH	PERS-USSR	LIBE-USA	BOLI-COLO	NICA-HOND
BRIT-URUG	SWED-ESTO	MEXI-FRAN	HUNG-RUMA	BRAZ-LITH	SWED-USSR	LITH-USA	BOLI-PERU	NICA-SALV
BRIT-VENE	SWIS-ESTO	MOPO-FRAN	HUNG-SPAI	CZEC-LITH	URUG-USSR	MEXI-USA	BOLI-URUG	PARA-PERU
BRIT-YEME	TURK-ESTO	NETH-FRAN	HUNG-SWED	DENM-LITH	YUGO-USSR	NETH-USA	BRAZ-CHIL	PARA-PANA
BRIT-YUGO	UKRA-ESTO	NEWZ-FRAN	HUNG-SWIS	ESTO-LITH	AUST-TURK	NEWZ-USA	BRAZ-COLO	PANA-URUG
BULG-CZEC	YUGO-ESTO	NICA-FRAN	ICEL-NORW	GREK-LITH	ALBA-TURK	NICA-USA	BRAZ-ECUA	PARA-SPAI
BULG-DENM	AUST-FINL	NORW-FRAN	ICEL-POLE	HUNG-LITH	AFGA-TURK	NORW-USA	BRAZ-MEXI	PARA-URUG
BULG-HUNG	AFGA-FINL	PANA-FRAN	ICEL-RUMA	ICEL-LITH	BELG-TURK	PALE-USA	BRAZ-PANA	PERU-URUG
BULG-NETH	ARGE-FINL	PERS-FRAN	ICEL-SPAI	JAPA-LITH	BULG-TURK	PANA-USA	BRAZ-PARA	PERU-VENE
BULG-NORW	BELG-FINL	PERU-FRAN	ICEL-SWED	NETH-LITH	CHIL-TURK	PARA-USA	BRAZ-PERU	SALV-URUG
BULG-POLE	BRAZ-FINL	POLE-FRAN	EIRE-NORW	NORW-LITH	CHIN-TURK	PERS-USA	BRAZ-URUG	URUG-VENE
BULG-RUMA	BULG-FINL	PORT-FRAN	EIRE-POLE	PERS-LITH	CZEC-TURK	PERU-USA	BRAZ-VENE	AFGA-BELG
BULG-SPAI	CHIL-FINL	RUMA-FRAN	EIRE-PORT	POLE-LITH	DENM-TURK	POLE-USA	CHIL-COLO	AFGA-BRAZ
BULG-SWED	CHIN-FINL	SALV-FRAN	EIRE-RUMA	PORT-LITH	EGYP-TURK	PORT-USA	CHIL-CUBA	AFGA-CZEC
BULG-SWIS	CZEC-FINL	SAFR-FRAN	EIRE-SPAI	RUMA-LITH	GREK-TURK	SALV-USA	CHIL-ECUA	AFGA-EGYP
CZEC-DENM	DENM-FINL	SPAI-FRAN	EIRE-SWED	SPAI-LITH	SAUD-TURK	SAUD-USA	CHIL-GUAT	AFGA-SAUD
CZEC-GREK	EGYP-FINL	BELG-RUMA	BELG-PORT	SWED-LITH	HUNG-TURK	SAFR-USA		

	no war predicted 1921 - 1942 ($\hat{y}_i < .5$)	war predicted after 1921 ($\hat{y}_i \geq .5$)	
no war occurred 1921 - 1942	835	64	γ = .864
war occurred after 1921	57	60	τ_b = .431

1. *continued.*

AFGA-JAPA	BOLI-SPAI	CHIN-SWIS	HUNG-JAPA	PARA-SPAI
AFGA-IRAQ	BELG-NORW	COLO-DENM	HUNG-PERS	PERS-NORW
AFGA-PERS	BRAZ-CHIN	COLO-ITAL	HAIT-NETH	PERS-POLE
AFGA-POLE	BRAZ-CANA	COLO-SWED	SAUD-ITAL	PERS-RUMA
AFGA-SWIS	BRAZ-CZEC	COLO-SPAI	INDI-IRAQ	PERS-SWED
AFGA-RUMA	BRAZ-DENM	COLO-SWIS	INDI-EIRE	PERS-SWIS
ALBA-JAPA	BRAZ-HUNG	COST-SPAI	INDI-POLE	PERU-SPAI
ARGE-AUST	BRAZ-ICEL	CUBA-JAPA	INDI-THAI	PORT-SAFR
ARGE-BELG	BRAZ-INDI	CUBA-SPAI	INDI-SAUD	PORT-THAI
ARGE-CZEC	BRAZ-EIRE	CUBA-PORT	VIET-THAI	PORT-URUG
ARGE-CANA	BRAZ-NETH	CZEC-EGYP	IRAQ-JORD	RUMA-JAPA
ARGE-DENK	BRAZ-POLE	CZEC-GUAT	IRAQ-NORW	SALV-SPAI
ARGE-GREK	BRAZ-NORW	CZEC-JAPA	IRAQ-SWED	SALV-SWED
ARGE-ITAL	BRAZ-RUMA	CZEC-PERS	IRAQ-PERS	SALV-NORW
ARGE-NORW	BRAZ-PORT	CZEC-SAFR	IRAQ-SAUD	SPAI-THAI
ARGE-NETH	BRAZ-SWED	CZEC-PORT	IRAQ-SYRI	SPAI-URUG
ARGE-SPAI	BRAZ-SAFR	DOMI-SPAI	IRAQ-YEME	SWED-THAI
ARGE-SWED	BRAZ-SPAI	DENM-EGYP	EIRE-NEWZ	SWIS-THAI
ARGE-SWIS	BRAZ-SWIS	DENM-HAIT	EIRE-SAFR	SWIS-URUG
AUSL-CANA	BULG-MEXI	DENM-INDI	ITAL-MANC	SWED-URUG
AUSL-EGYP	BULG-EGYP	DENM-JAPA	ITAL-PERS	SAUD-SYRI
AUSL-NETH	BULG-SPAI	DENM-PERS	ITAL-PALE	SAUD-PERS
AUSL-BELG	BULG-JAPA	DENM-THAI	ITAL-THAI	SAUD-TURK
AUSL-CZEC	CANA-CUBA	DENM-TURK	ITAL-VENE	ALBA-AUST
AUSL-BRAZ	CANA-CHIL	DENM-VENE	ITAL-YEME	ALBA-BELG
AUSL-NORW	CANA-CZEC	ECUA-JAPA	JAPA-GREK	ALBA-BULG
AUSL-SWIS	CANA-DENM	ECUA-NETH	JAPA-NORW	ALBA-GREK
AUSL-CHIN	CANA-GREK	ECUA-SPAI	JAPA-PARA	ALBA-HUNG
AUST-CHIN	CANA-HAIT	ECUA-SWED	JAPA-PORT	ALBA-RUMA
AUST-BRAZ	CANA-IRAQ	EGYP-GREK	JAPA-PERU	ALBA-SPAI
AUST-CANA	CANA-GUAT	EGYP-SAUD	JAPA-PERS	ALBA-SWIS
AUST-JAPA	CANA-NETH	EGYP-HUNG	JAPA-RUMA	AUST-BELG
AUST-MEXI	CANA-NORW	EGYP-IRAQ	JAPA-SPAI	AUST-BULG
AUST-PERS	CANA-NEWZ	EGYP-EIRE	JAPA-URUG	ALBA-CZEC
AUST-URUG	CANA-PORT	EGYP-JAPA	MEXI-NORW	AUST-CANA
BELG-BRAZ	CANA-SALV	EGYP-NETH	MEXI-SWED	AUST-CZEC
BELG-CANA	CANA-SPAI	EGYP-NORW	MEXI-SPAI	AUST-DENM
BELG-CHIL	CANA-SWED	EGYP-PALE	MANC-SPAI	AUST-HUNG
BELG-CHIN	CHIL-DENM	EGYP-POLE	NETH-MEXI	AUST-ICEL
BELG-COLO	CHIL-EGYP	EGYP-PERS	NETH-NEWZ	AUST-ITAL
BELG-COST	CHIL-CZEC	EGYP-RUMA	NETH-PANA	AUST-NETH
BELG-CUBA	CHIL-ITAL	EGYP-SWIS	NETH-PERS	AUST-NORW
BELG-EGYP	CHIL-NETH	EGYP-SWED	NETH-SAFR	AUST-POLE
BELG-ECUA	CHIL-NORW	EGYP-SYRI	NETH-THAI	AUST-PORT
BELG-GUAT	CHIL-POLE	EGYP-SAFR	NETH-YEME	AUST-RUMA
BELG-HOND	CHIL-SPAI	ETHI-GREK	NETH-VENE	AUST-SPAI
BELG-JAPA	CHIL-SWED	ETHI-JAPA	NETH-URUG	AUST-SWED
BELG-MEXI	CHIN-CZEC	ETHI-NETH	NICA-SPAI	AUST-SWIS
BELG-NEWZ	CHIN-DOMI	ETHI-SWIS	NORW-SAFR	BELG-BULG
BELG-NICA	CHIN-DENM	ETHI-YEME	NORW-THAI	BELG-CZEC
BELG-PARA	CHIN-GREK	GREK-NEWZ	NORW-NEWZ	BELG-DENM
BELG-PERS	CHIN-EGYP	GREK-MEXI	NORW-VENE	BELG-GREK
BELG-SALV	CHIN-INDI	GREK-PERS	NORW-URUG	BELG-HUNG
BELG-THAI	CHIN-MEXI	GREK-PALE	NEWZ-SAFR	BELG-ICEL
BELG-SAFR	CHIN-NETH	GUAT-NETH	NEWZ-SWED	BELG-EIRE
BELG-URUG	CHIN-NORW	GUAT-NORW	NEWZ-SWIS	BELG-ITAL
BOLI-CHIN	CHIN-PERS	GUAT-SPAI	PALE-SYRI	BELG-LUXE
BOLI-DENM	CHIN-POLE	GUAT-SWED	PALE-SWIS	BELG-NETH
BOLI-NETH	CHIN-PORT	CHIN-SWED	PALE-JORD	
BOLI-ICEL	CHIN-SPAI		PANA-SPAI	

2. Dyads in which no war was predicted but in which war occurred. (N = 57)

AUSL-THAI	BRIT-FINL	NORW-GERM	JAPA-THAI
BRAZ-ITAL	BRIT-HUNG	SALV-GERM	CANA-FINL
CANA-RUMA	BRIT-RUMA	SAFR-GERM	CANA-HUNG
CHIN-ITAL	BRIT-THAI	GREK-ITAL	AUSL-FINL
CHIN-THAI	BULG-GREK	ITAL-SPAI	AUSL-RUMA
COST-ITAL	CZEC-HUNG	ALBA-USA	AUSL-HUNG
GUAT-ITAL	DANZ-POLE	BULG-USA	SAFR-FINL
HAIT-ITAL	CANA-GERM	HUNG-USA	SAFR-RUMA
SAUD-YEME	CZEC-GERM	RUMA-USA	SAFR-HUNG
ITAL-PANA	DENM-GERM	HUNG-YUGO	NEWZ-FINL
JAPA-MEXI	EGYP-GERM	ITAL-YUGO	NEWZ-RUMA
JAPA-NETH	ESTO-GERM	BOLI-PARA	NEWZ-HUNG
JAPA-NEWZ	GUAT-GERM	COLO-PERU	
JAPA-POLE	LITH-GERM	ECUA-PERU	
JAPA-SAFR	MEXI-GERM	AUSL-JAPA	

3. Dyads in which war was predicted but in which no war occurred. (N = 64)

AUST-LUXE	AUST-FRAN	THAI-GERM	FRAN-USA
BRIT-AFGA	BULG-FRAN	EIRE-ITAL	HAIT-USA
BRIT-ARGE	ICEL-FRAN	ITAL-RUMA	INDI-USA
BRIT-AUST	EIRE-FRAN	ITAL-LITH	LUXE-USA
BRIT-CANA	JAPA-FRAN	AUST-USSR	SWIS-USA
BRIT-CHIN	LITH-FRAN	BULG-USSR	AUST-PANA
BRIT-INDI	PARA-FRAN	CHIN-USSR	EGYP-ITAL
BRIT-IRAQ	USSR-FRAN	EGYP-USSR	INDI-JAPA
BRIT-LITH	TUNI-FRAN	ICEL-USSR	VIET-JAPA
BRIT-LUXE	ARGE-GERM	SWIS-USSR	IRAQ-JAPA
BRIT-USSR	FINL-GERM	TURK-USSR	EIRE-JAPA
BRIT-SPAI	ICEL-GERM	UKRA-USSR	ITAL-JAPA
BULG-ITAL	ITAL-GERM	ITAL-TURK	ITAL-NETH
DENM-ITAL	JAPA-GERM	JAPA-TURK	JAPA-MANC
AFGA-FRAN	PORT-GERM	POLE-UKRA	JAPA-SWED
ARGE-FRAN	RUMA-GERM	CANA-USA	JAPA-SWIS

4. Dyads in which war was predicted and in which war occurred. (N = 60)

BRIT-BULG	CANA-JAPA	NETH-GERM	DOMI-GERM
BRIT-GERM	CHIN-JAPA	NEWZ-GERM	DOMI-ITAL
BRIT-ITAL	ETHI-ITAL	NICA-GERM	ALBA-ITAL
BRIT-JAPA	ITAL-MEXI	PANA-GERM	
GERM-FRAN	ITAL-SAFR	POLE-GERM	
ITAL-FRAN	JAPA-PANA	USSR-GERM	
SYRI-FRAN	INDI-GERM	YUGO-GERM	
ETHI-GERM	ITAL-NEWZ	ALBA-USSR	
AUSL-GERM	COST-JAPA	FINL-USSR	
BELG-GERM	DOMI-JAPA	HUNG-USSR	
BRAZ-GERM	GUAT-JAPA	ITAL-USSR	
CHIN-GERM	HAIT-JAPA	JAPA-USSR	
COST-GERM	HOND-JAPA	POLE-USSR	
CUBA-GERM	SALV-JAPA	RUMA-USSR	
GREK-GERM	NICA-JAPA	GERM-USA	
HAIT-GERM	CUBA-ITAL	ITAL-USA	
HOND-GERM	NICA-ITAL	JAPA-USA	
LATV-GERM	HOND-ITAL	AUSL-ITAL	
LUXE-GERM	SALV-ITAL	CANA-ITAL	

<u>Table A.2</u> : Illustrative listing of dyads which fall into selected categories of the 4-way crosstabulation between war occurs after 1920/not and Aggregate of Economic Agreements (See Table 4.1 for definition) controlling for (1) "Friendship/Antagonism I" (see Table 2.5 for definition) and (2) cultural difference/no cultural difference (see Table 2.4 for definition). The listing is provided for "antagonistic" and "cultural difference" dyads only. The number of dyads falling into each category is summarised in the Table immediately opposite.

1. Dyads in which no war occurred and which scored zero on the aggregate economic agreements index. (N = 91)

ARGE-SWIS CHIN-ESTO AFGA-LITH CHIN-MEXI BRIT-JORD
AUSL-CZEC MEXI-ESTO PERS-LITH CHIN-PERS BRIT-LIBE
AUSL-CHIN PERS-ESTO TURK-LITH CHIN-SWIS BRIT-NEPA
AUST-MEXI AFGA-FINL SWED-URUG COLO-ITAL BRIT-YEME
AUST-PANA CHIN-FINL MEXI-USSR COLO-SWIS DENM-EGYP
AUST-PERS MEXI-FINL ALBA-TURK DENM-HAIT AFGA-ESTO
AUST-URUG ARGE-FRAN CHIL-TURK DENM-TURK JAPA-SWIS
BELG-COST IRAQ-FRAN CHIN-TURK DENM-VENE NETH-YEME
BELG-CUBA PARA-FRAN SAUD-TURK ECUA-JAPA NETH-VENE
BELG-ECUA PERU-FRAN AFGN-USA EGYP-ITAL PERS-RUMA
BELG-HOND AFGA-GERM DANZ-USA ETHI-SWIS SWIS-THAI
BELG-MEXI ECUA-GERM INDI-USA GREK-MEXI SWIS-URUG
BELG-NICA PERS-GERM FALE-USA IRAQ-JAPA CHIL-POLE
BELG-SALV SAUD-GERM AFGA-BRAZ EIRE-JAPA CHIN-DOMI
BRAZ-SWED HUNG-PANA AFGA-CZEC ITAL-THAI CHIN-GREK
BULG-MEXI AFGA-LATV AFGA-JAPA ITAL-VENE
BULG-EGYP CHIN-LATV AFGA-POLE JAPA-GREK
CANA-IRAQ PERS-LATV AFGA-RUMA JAPA-PERS
CHIL-DENM TURK-LATV ARGE-NORW JAPA-SWEL

2. Dyads in which no war occurred and which scored one on the aggregate economic agreements index. (N = 14

BRIT-AFGA MEXI-FRAN ECUA-SWED INDI-JAPA
BRIT-ALBA MORO-FRAN EGYP-GREK INDI-POLE
BRIT-ECUA NICA-FRAN EGYP-JAPA INDI-SAUD
BRIT-PARA PANA-FRAN EGYP-NETH IRAQ-NORW
BRIT-SYRI PERS-FRAN EGYP-NORW IRAQ-SWED
BRIT-URUG TUNI-FRAN EGYP-POLE ITAL-MANC
BRIT-VENE YEME-FRAN EGYP-PERS ITAL-PERS
JAPA-ESTO ARGE-GERM EGYP-RUMA ITAL-PALE
ARGE-FINL IRAQ-GERM EGYP-SWIS ITAL-YEME
BRAZ-FINL BRAZ-LATV EGYP-SWED JAPA-NORW
CHIL-FINL JAPA-LATV EGYP-SAFR JAPA-PERU
EGYP-FINL BRAZ-LITH ETHI-JAPA JAPA-RUMA
PERS-FINL JAPA-LITH GREK-PALE JAPA-SPAI
COST-FRAN NETH-VENE GUAT-NORW JAPA-URUG
CUBA-FRAN INDI-TURK GUAT-SWED MEXI-NORW
DOMI-FRAN DENM-EGYP HAIT-NETH MEXI-SWED
ECUA-FRAN DENM-INDI SAUD-ITAL MANC-SPAI
EGYP-FRAN DENM-PERS INDI-IRAQ NETH-MEXI
GUAT-FRAN ECUA-NETH INDI-EIRE NETH-PANA

4. Dyads in which no war occurred and which scored three or more on the aggregate economic agreements index. (N=42)

BRIT-CHIN RUMA-TURK URUG-USA
BRIT-COST SWED-TURK VENE-USA
BRIT-EGYP SWIS-TURK ARGE-NETH
BRIT-IRAQ ARGN-USA CHIL-NETH
BRIT-PERS CHIL-USA
BRIT-USSR COST-USA
BRIT-TURK CUBA-USA
TURK-ESTO CZEC-USA
CHIN-FRAN ECUA-USA
INDI-FRAN EGYP-USA
SALV-FRAN ESTO-USA
TURK-FRAN GUAT-USA
URUG-FRAN HAIT-USA
PERS-USSR MEXI-USA
BULG-TURK NICA-USA
CZEC-TURK PANA-USA
DENM-TURK PERU-USA
GREK-TURK SALV-USA
BRIT-CHIL TURK-USA

5. Dyads in which war occurred and which scored zero on the aggregate economic agreements index. (N=24)

SYRI-FRAN SALV-ITAL
ETHI-GERM DOMI-GERM
COST-GERM DOMI-ITAL
ALBA-USA HOND-ITAL
CANA-RUMA
COST-ITAL
ETHI-ITAL
ITAL-MEXI
JAPA-PANA
JAPA-SAFR
INDI-GERM
COST-JAPA
DOMI-JAPA
GUAT-JAPA
HAIT-JAPA
HOND-JAPA
SALV-JAPA
NICA-JAPA
CUBA-ITAL
NICA-ITAL

(For dyads defined as "culturally different" and as antagonistic according to "Friendship/Antagonism I")

γ = −.33

τ_b = −.13

	Score on Aggregate of Economic Agreements				
	None	One	Two	Three or more	
No war 1921-1942	91 (79.1%)	148 (90.8%)	62 (90.1%)	42 (93.3%)	345
War occurred after 1921	24 (20.9%)	15 (9.2%)	7 (9.9%)	3 (6.7%)	49
	115	163	71	45	394

2. *continued.*

NETH-PERS BRAZ-YUGO BRAZ-CZEC CHIN-CZEC
NETH-URUG AFGA-BELG BRAZ-ICEL CHIN-DENM
NORW-THAI ARGE-AUST BRAZ-INDI CHIN-EGYP
PALE-SWIS ARGE-BELG BRAZ-EIRE CHIN-NETH
PERS-POLE ARGE-CZEC BRAZ-POLE CHIN-NORW
PERS-SWIS ARGE-CANA BRAZ-NORW CHIN-PORT
PORT-THAI ARGE-DENK BRAZ-RUMA CHIN-SPAI
SALV-SWED ARGE-GREK BRAZ-SWIS CHIN-SWED
SALV-NORW ARGE-SWED BULG-JAPA COLO-DENM
SPAI-THAI AUSL-EGYP CANA-CUBA COLO-SWED
SWED-THAI AUSL-BRAZ CANA-CHIL CUBA-JAPA
SWED-URUG AUST-CHIN CANA-HAIT CZEC-EGYP
IRAQ-TURK AUST-BRAZ CANA-GUAT CZEC-GUAT
ITAL-TURK AUST-CANA CANA-PORT CZEC-JAPA
JAPA-TURK BELG-GUAT CANA-SALV CZEC-SAFR
POLE-TURK BELG-PARA CHIL-EGYP
GHAN-USA BELG-URUG CHIL-CZEC
SAUD-USA BOLI-CHIN CHIL-ITAL
ARGE-YUGO BOLI-ICEL CHIL-NORW

3. Dyads in which no war occurred and which scored two on the aggregate economic agreements index. (N=62)

BRIT-ARGE MANC-GERM TURK-YUGO EGYP-HUNG
BRIT-BOLI PARA-GERM ARGE-ITAL EGYP-EIRE
BRIT-CUBA THAI-GERM AUST-JAPA GREK-PERS
BRIT-GUAT URUG-GERM BELG-BRAZ GUAT-NETH
BRIT-HAIT ARGE-LITH BELG-CHIL HUNG-PERS
BRIT-HOND TURK-USSR BELG-CHIN PERS-NORW
BRIT-MEXI HUNG-TURK BELG-EGYP PERS-SWED
BRIT-MUSC EIRE-TURK BELG-PERS
BRIT-PANA NORW-TURK BOLI-DENM
BRIT-PERU SPAI-TURK BOLI-NETH
BRIT-SALV AUST-USA BRAZ-DENM
BRIT-SAUD BOLI-USA BRAZ-HUNG
TURK-FINL CHIN-USA BRAZ-NETH
CHIL-FRAN DOMI-USA CANA-CZEC
HAIT-FRAN HOND-USA CHIL-SWED
JAPA-FRAN IRAQ-USA CHIN-POLE
BOLI-GERM PARA-USA CZEC-PERS
CHIL-GERM PERS-USA DENM-JAPA
JAPA-GERM EGYP-YUGO DENM-THAI

6. Dyads in which war occurred and which scored one on the aggregate economic agreements index. (N=15)

CUBA-GERM
EGYP-GERM
GUAT-GERM
HOND-GERM
NICA-GERM
PANA-GERM
SALV-GERM
BULG-USA
AUSL-JAPA
CHIN-ITAL
HAIT-ITAL
ITAL-PANA
JAPA-MEXI
JAPA-NEWZ
JAPA-POLE

7. Dyads in which war occurred and which scored two on the aggregate economic agreements index. (N=7)

BRAZ-GERM
HAIT-GERM
MEXI-GERM
JAPA-USSR
JAPA-USA
GUAT-ITAL
JAPA-NETH

8. Dyads in which war occurred and which scored three or more on the aggregate economic agreements index. (N=3)

BRIT-JAPA
CHIN-GERM
HUNG-USA

Notes and References

INTRODUCTION: LAWMAKING, CO-OPERATION AND PEACE

1. See Herbert Butterfield, *Christianity and History* (New York: Charles Scribner, 1950); *History and Human Relations* (London: Collins, 1951) esp. pp. 20–3.
2. I use this term in the sense defined by Barry Buzan, *People, States and Fear: The National Security Problem in International Relations* (Brighton: Wheatsheaf Books, 1983).
3. For an elegant statement of this kind of 'security dilemma', see Glenn H. Snyder, '"Prisoner's Dilemma" and "Chicken" Models in International Relations', *International Studies Quarterly*, vol. 15, no. 1, (March 1971), pp. 66–103.
4. This theme has some parallels both in the analysis of 'Prisoner's Dilemma Supergames' and in the neofunctionalist notion of 'Spill-over'. On the former, see Michael Taylor, *Anarchy and Co-operation* (New York: Wiley, 1976); on the latter, see J. S. Nye, *Peace in Parts: Integration and Conflict in Regional Organisation* (Boston: Little, Brown, 1971), chs. 1–3. For a major recent study of the potential role of co-operation in the contemporary international system, see Robert O. Keohane, *After Hegemony: Co-operation and Discord in the World Political Economy* (Princeton University Press, 1984); especially ch. 1.
5. Among the other possible candidates which could be cited are diplomatic initiatives such as summit meetings, symbolic gestures such as state visits, and (at the other extreme) unilateral disarmament. None of these, however, constitutes a particularly satisfactory vehicle for a systematic analysis of the potential role of co-operative strategies in international politics. The first two are comparatively infrequent and, on the face of it at least, are rarely pursued with any vigour or much chance of success; the third, certainly in the view of many observers of international affairs, can in no circumstances be regarded as a 'non-fatal if unsuccessful' option and in any case furnishes no empirical examples from which theoretical inferences could be derived.
6. Richard Nixon, *Real Peace* (Boston: Little, Brown, 1984), pp. 12–14.

1 THE IDEALIST TRADITION AND ITS MODERN VARIANTS

1. Kuehl cites Sully and Cruce's 'Grand Design' for a European order (1625) as the source of the crucial principle of arbitration. See Warren F. Kuehl, *Seeking World Order: The United States and International Organisation to 1920* (Nashville: Vanderbilt University Press, 1969), ch. 1. For a recent attempt to provide guidelines for a new world legal order, see Grenville

Clark and Louis B. Sohn, *World Peace Through World Law* (Cambridge, Mass.: Harvard University Press, 1966).

2. The first bilateral arbitration treaty is generally recognised as the 1794 Jay Treaty between Britain and the US, which provided a model for a number of similar treaties throughout the nineteenth century. See A. M. Stuyt, *Survey of International Arbitrations 1794–1970* (Leiden: Sijthoff, 1972).
3. A statement of this position can be found in the Appendix to James Brown Scott (ed.), *Resolutions of the Institute of International Law Dealing with the Law of Nations* (New York: Oxford University Press, 1916): 'Mr. Goldschmidt's Draft Regulations for International Tribunals: Preliminary Remarks', pp. 205–39, especially pp. 207–13.
4. This argument is most strongly associated with Wehberg and Lauterpacht. See Hans Wehberg, 'Restrictive Clauses in International Arbitration Treaties', *American Journal of International Law*, vol. 7 (1913), pp. 301–14; H. Lauterpacht, *The Function of Law in the International Community* (Oxford University Press, 1933).
5. Despite the failure of the US to join the League, American international lawyers continued to play a prominent role in international efforts aimed at building upon the framework of Wilson's 14 points. In response to the question, 'But who were the idealists?' one is tempted to reply – after reading successive issues of the *American Journal of International Law* of the immediate post-war years–'almost everyone in the field of Anglo-American international law in the early 1920s; though some had more profound reservations than others'.
6. Reprinted in Inis Claude, *Swords into Ploughshares: The Problems and Progress of International Organizations* (New York: Random House, 1964), Appendix 1.
7. Alfred Zimmern, *The League of Nations and the Rule of Law 1918–1935* (London: Macmillan, 1936), p. 265.
8. Report of the Study Group of the David Davies Memorial Institute of International Relations, *International Disputes: The Legal Aspects* (London: Europa Publications, 1972), p. 15.
9. The signatories were Belgium, Britain, France, Germany and Italy.
10. Charles G. Fenwick, 'The Legal Significance of the Locarno Treaties', *American Journal of International Law*, vol. 20 (1926), pp. 108–11.
11. The General Treaty was also known as the Pact of Paris.
12. For a brief contemporary juridical critique of the General Treaty, see Edwin M. Borchard, '"War" and "Peace"', *American Journal of International Law*, vol. 23 (1933), pp. 114–17.
13. A more extended review of these developments can be found in Lauterpacht, *The Function of Law*, pp. 372–82.
14. H. M. Swanwick, *Collective Insecurity* (London: Jonathan Cape, 1937), p. 36.
15. Zimmern, *The League of Nations*, pp. 349–50.
16. For a discussion of the so-called 'secret treaties' of 1915, see Swanwick, *Collective Insecurity*, pp. 53–9.
17. Percy E. Corbett, *Law in Diplomacy* (Princeton University Press, 1959), p. 137.
18. Swanwick, *Collective Insecurity*, pp. 211–12.

19. Ibid., p. 144.
20. *League of Nations Treaty Series No. 54*, p. 301, cited in Corbett, *Law in Diplomacy*, p. 191 (Corbett's emphasis).
21. F. P. Walters, *A History of the League of Nations* (Oxford University Press, 1950), p. 709.
22. Ruth B. Henig (ed.), *The League of Nations* (Edinburgh: Oliver & Boyd, 1973), p. 10.
23. Zimmern, *The League of Nations*, p. 187 ff. Henig notes that Anglo-French rivalry throughout the period of the League was partly responsible for its overall failure. The British consistently refused to allow the League to be used as a 'guarantee scheme' for members' territorial integrity and political independence, promoting it instead (unsuccessfully) as a vehicle for achieving peaceful institutional change as international conditions changed. The French, in contrast, regarded this objective as an underhand way of rehabilitating Germany at their expense and by opposing it were able to prevent the League from functioning successfully in the sphere of peaceful change. See Henig, *The League of Nations*, p. 171.
24. Walters, *A History of the League*, p. 500.
25. Henig, *The League of Nations*, p. 173.
26. Walters, *A History of the League*, p. 385.
27. Lauterpacht's most detailed exposition of the arguments justifying the analogy is to be found in his *Private Law Sources and Analogies of International Law* (London: Longmans, 1927).
28. See Lauterpacht, *The Function of Law*, pp. 407–18. The differentiation finds a close parallel in Richard Falk's distinction between 'vertical' and 'horizontal' systems of law. See Richard Falk, 'International Jurisdiction: Horizontal and Vertical Conceptions of Legal Order', *Temple Law Quarterly*, vol. 32 (Spring 1959), pp. 295–320.
29. In Lauterpacht's terms, all systems of law have 'material gaps' (unforeseen contingencies) which can be closed through judicial legislation. No *system* of *law* – if it is to be thus described – can allow 'formal gaps', that is, areas of dispute where judicial decision is impermissible. See Lauterpacht, *The Function of Law*, pp. 60–84.
30. Ibid., p. 64.
31. Uncharacteristically, Lauterpacht was not entirely clear as to what these 'general principles' might be though he does make detailed reference to the following in *The Function of Law*:
    (1) *rebus sic stantibus*: conditions have changed and legal rights must therefore be adjusted (pp. 270–85).
    (2) *ex aequo et bono*: 'in justice and fairness' (pp. 313–24).
    (3) doctrine of 'abuse of rights', derived from continental European jurisprudence: if an individual or group is taking advantage of rights conferred by the community then the community is justified in taking action against the abuser (pp. 286–306).
    (4) the use of analogy from domestic law and existing international statutes (pp. 111–18).
32. Zimmern, *The League of Nations*, p. 98.
33. For Lauterpacht, the principle of nonjusticiability – the 'doctrine of

inherent limitations' – was simply 'a legal cloak for the Sovereign State to act as the ultimate judge in disputed legal rights with other States' (Lauterpacht, *The Function of Law*, p. 7).

34. Ibid., p. 398 (emphasis added).
35. 'It must be a matter for serious consideration whether any possible advantages . . . are not necessarily counterbalanced by the disadvantages, psychological and political, of a system in which a solemn machinery of peaceful settlement is put in motion and maintained in regard to matters of little consequence . . . (that is, justiciable disputes) . . . whereas in major issues defiance of the law, expressed either in aggressive force or in the perpetration of a wrong by passive force, is allowed to have full play.' Ibid., p. 171.
36. Walters, *A History of the League*, p. 465.
37. Quincy Wright, 'The end of a period of transition?', *American Journal of International Law*, vol. 31 (1937), pp. 604–13.
38. Henig, *The League of Nations*, p. 117.
39. Zimmern, *The League of Nations*, pp. 288–9.
40. Henig, *The League of Nations*, p. 146.
41. Singer and Small report that the total number of dead per head of population was greater in this conflict than in any other war since 1815, including the two world wars. See J. David Singer and Melvin Small, *The Wages of War 1816–1965: A Statistical Handbook* (New York: Wiley, 1972), p. 134.
42. Probably the most formidable protagonists of this view were E. H. Carr and Joseph Kunz. See E. H. Carr, *The Twenty Years Crisis 1919–1939* (London: Macmillan, 1961), especially pp. 51–62; Joseph L. Kunz, 'The Problem of Revision in International Law', *American Journal of International Law*, vol. 33 (1939), pp. 33–55.
43. See Hans J. Morgenthau, *Scientific Man versus Power Politics* (University of Chicago Press, 1946); Georg Schwarzenberger, *International Law and Order* (London: Stevens, 1971).
44. Corbett, *Law in Diplomacy*, p. 272–4.
45. For Morgenthau political order itself developed primarily because of the '(existing) . . . order . . . in the social fabric'. See Morgenthau, *Scientific Man*, pp. 116–17.
46. Lawrence Scheinman and David Wilkinson (eds), *International Law and Political Crisis: An Analytic Casebook* (Boston: Little, Brown, 1968).
47. Lawrence Scheinman, 'The Berlin Blockade', in Scheinman and Wilkinson, *International Law*, p. 39.
48. Ibid., p. 14.
49. W. Friedman and L. Collins, 'The Suez Canal Crisis', in Scheinman and Wilkinson, *International Law*, pp. 121–25.
50. Carr, *The Twenty Years Crisis*, p. 8. Carr attributes the story to L. B. Namier. In the 1950s Lauterpacht responded to this specific charge, suggesting that Carr's analogy does not hold. While men have no control over earthquakes, they do, ultimately, have control over their own creations, war included. See Hersch Lauterpacht, *International Law: Collected Papers edited by E. Lauterpacht (vol. 2, The Law of Peace, Part I)* (Cambridge University Press, 1975), ch. 3, p. 62 ff.

51. Carr also relates that whenever Woodrow Wilson was asked 'But what if Collective Security doesn't work?' he consistently responded with a nonexplanation: 'It must be *made* to work'.
52. As Hedley Bull has observed, 'attempts to legislate peace in the absence of . . . (other) . . . factors serve only to bring international law into discredit without advancing the prospects of peace'. Hedley Bull, *The Anarchical Society: A Study of Order in World Politics* (London: Macmillan, 1977), p. 143.
53. This is a dominant theme in the works of Richard Falk. See especially his *Legal Order in a Violent World* (Princeton University Press, 1968), pp. 60–70.
54. See, for example, Rosalyn Higgins, *The Development of International Law through the Political Organs of the United Nations* (Oxford University Press, 1963) pp. 8–9; Falk, *Legal Order*, p. 48.
55. Bull, *The Anarchical Society*, p. 137.
56. Higgins, *The Development of International Law*, p. 8. Bull adds 'Habit or inertia', 'coercion . . . by some superior power' and 'the international law of community'. See Bull, *The Anarchical Society*, pp. 139–140.
57. Falk, *Legal Order*, p. 74.
58. Ibid., p. 67, p. 41.
59. Ibid., p. 68.
60. Richard A. Falk, 'Confrontation diplomacy: Indonesia's campaign to crush Malaysia', in Scheinman and Wilkinson, *International Law* (pp. 127–66), p. 162 (emphasis added).
61. Bull, *The Anarchical Society*, p. 143. It should be noted that Bull assigns a different meaning to the term 'order' than that adopted here. For Bull, international order exists to the extent that there are patterns of activity conducive to the achievement of the 'elementary goals' of the Society of States. See Bull, *The Anarchical Society*, pp. 4–8.
62. Corbett, *Law in Diplomacy*, p. 156.
63. Scheinman, 'The Berlin Blockade', p. 40 (emphasis added).
64. Cited in Lauterpacht, *The Function of Law*, pp. 170–1.
65. Manley O. Hudson, 'The World Court', in Harriett E. Davies (ed.), *Pioneers in World Order: An American Appraisal of the League of Nations* (New York: Columbia University Press, 1944), p. 71.
66. Consider, for example, Falk's first mechanism cited above, that '(nations) . . . avoid a clear violation of law so as to discourage . . . community responses in favour of the victim'. The reference to the avoidance of a 'violation of law' implies as a corollary that in any specific instance, the party avoiding the violation must have decided to *follow* some rule(s) established under extant international law. The crucial point is that the specific rule(s) followed is (are), at the given moment, fixed: the mechanism, if it operates, is thus a static one because it makes implicit reference to international law as a *fixed* set of rules at the particular time point in question. An examination of the remaining mechanisms reveals that each makes a similar implicit reference to a fixed set of rules which can be invoked or followed by either or both parties to a dispute.
67. Thomas C. Schelling, *The Strategy of Conflict* (Cambridge, Mass.: Harvard University Press, 1960); Richard Bilder, *Managing the Risks of International Agreements* (Madison: University of Wisconsin Press, 1981).

68. Abba Eban, 'Camp David – the unfinished business', *Foreign Affairs*, vol. 57 (Winter 1978/79), p. 348, quoted in Bilder, *Managing the Risks*, p. 42.
69. William D. Coplin, 'Current Studies of the Functions of International Law', in James A Robinson (ed.), *Political Science Annual: An International Review Vol. II. 1969–70* (Indianapolis: Bobbs–Merrill, 1970) pp. 149–207; esp. pp. 157–8.

2 BACKGROUND TO THE EMPIRICAL ANALYSIS

1. For a brief review of this approach see Michael Haas, 'International Subsystems: Stability and Polarity', *American Political Science Review*, vol. 64 (March 1970), pp. 98–123.
2. Gregory A. Raymond, *Conflict Resolution and the Structure of the State System: An Analysis of Arbitrative Settlements* (Montclair, NJ: Allanheld Osmun, 1980).
3. Since there were some 60 sovereign nations during the interwar years, there was a total of $(60 \times 59)/2 = 1770$ possible dyads. In fact only 1016 of these pairs had relations with each other (either went to war or signed at least one agreement) in this period. The remaining 754 possible dyads are excluded from the analysis. Since there are no missing data, except where stated total $N = 1016$ throughout the study.
4. See Haas, *International Subsystems*.
5. Kenneth Waltz, *Theory of International Politics* (Reading, Mass.: Addison-Wesley, 1979).
6. Raymond, *Conflict Resolution*.
7. For a recent lucid statement of the need for dyadic analysis in international politics, see Erich Weede, 'Extended Deterence by Superpower Alliance', *Journal of Conflict Resolution*, vol. 27, no. 2 (June 1983), pp. 231–54; especially p. 231.
8. The data in this context were derived from Frank M. Denton, 'Patterns in Political Violence and War' (PhD dissertation, University of Southern California, 1968) and from the *Department of State Bulletin*, 20 December 1941, pp. 551–61. Declarations of war after 1942 were not counted so as to exclude the small number of 'token' declarations of war against the Axis Powers after April 1945 which were provoked by the American threat that those Powers which failed to declare war on Germany and Japan would not be permitted to participate fully in the establishment of the UN.
9. The data for the JUDGEMENTS, ORDERS and ADVICE variables were derived from Manley O. Hudson (ed.), *World Court Reports 1921–42* (Washington, DC: Carnegie Endowment for International Peace, 1943), four volumes. The data for arbitrations were obtained from A. M. Stuyt, *Survey of International Arbitrations 1794–1970* (Leiden: Sijthoff, 1972).
10. Peter H. Rohn, *World Treaty Index: Volume 1, League of Nations Treaty Series* (Santa Barbara, Ca: American Bibliographic Centre–Clio, 1974). Rohn's data, which record all treaties registered with the League between 1921 and 1942, were taken as the basis of the present study. These registered treaties were cross-referenced with the treaties and agreements listed in the *American Journal of International Law*'s 'Chronicle of International Events' (itself the product of an extended bibliographic search which was

published quarterly as part of the *Journal* until the early 1950s). Whenever a treaty or agreement not mentioned in Rohn's index was referred to in the 'Chronicle' this agreement was coded according to Rohn's classification scheme and incorporated into the dataset.

The main emphasis was on bilateral treaties as these were the most common form of treaty commitment made during the interwar years. However, all multilateral *military* treaties and other multilateral treaties involving less than seven nations were also included. Seven was a somewhat arbitrary choice in this regard (though most multilateral treaties in fact did include six or less signatories): it was selected on the assumption that, if any more nations were involved, the possible benefits (of an increase in mutual trust and understanding) resulting from the negotiation and compromise involved in the treaty-making process would be lost in the anonymity of the more general agreement.

11. The signing rather than the ratification of a treaty was considered to be the critical date in any agreement. In part this is because signature constitutes a statement of political intent, and it is the indirect political effects of international law that the present study is seeking to examine. In addition, the focus on signature follows the general principle of international law well established during the interwar years that 'a treaty is binding on the contracting parties, unless otherwise provided, from the date of its signature, the exchange of ratifications having, in such case, a retroactive effect confirming the treaty from that date' (J. Mervyn Jones, 'The retroactive effect of the ratification of treaties', *American Journal of International Law*, vol. 29 (1935), p. 51).

    Account was also taken of agreements that were rescinded or formally revoked by either party though the results are not reported here because the effects of revocation were negligible. 'Violations' of unrevoked treaty obligations, however, are not explicitly included in the analysis since almost invariably in the case of violations of international law either (1) each side accuses the other of violating the treaty first, or (2) the clear violator pleads *rebus sic stantibus* while the violated party pleads *pacta sunt servanda*. The status of a 'violation' in either case is too dependent upon the political judgement of the observer to permit its incorporation into formal analysis.

12. It might be objected that to enumerate only those treaty commitments entered into after 1920 ignores the fact that dyads with a history of longstanding friendship may have had little need to enter into new commitments because they already enjoyed a well-regulated legal relationship born of innumerable past treaties. Law could therefore have an effect on the avoidance of war but the independent variables as measured here would not 'pick up' its effects. This is not in fact a serious problem. As conditions change over time, new forms of legal regulation almost invariably become necessary. As a result, an extensive inheritance of treaty commitments does not inhibit the signing of new treaties and agreements. This conclusion is certainly supported by the data from the interwar period: the US and Britain, for example, which had one of the most extensive sets of mutual treaty commitments prior to 1918, signed more joint treaties after 1920 than almost any other dyad.

13. See, for example, André Gunder Frank, *Reflections on the World Economic Crisis* (London: Hutchinson, 1981), ch. 3; Ernest Mandel, *Late Capitalism* (London: New Left Books, 1975).
14. William D. Coplin and J. Martin Rochester, 'The Permanent Court of International Justice, The International Court of Justice, The League of Nations and the United Nations: a comparative, empirical survey', *American Political Science Review*, vol. 66 (June 1972), pp. 529–50.
15. J. David Singer and Melvin Small, *The Wages of War 1816–1965; A Statistical Handbook* (New York: Wiley, 1972).

3 TREATY-MAKING, WAR AND PEACE: PRELIMINARY EMPIRICAL FINDINGS

1. I use the term 'correlation' to cover all measures of association at whatever level of measurement: in this case, Goodman and Kruskal's gamma and Kendall's tau_b.
2. This characteristic of gamma was particularly important for the present study given that (1) only about 10 per cent of the dyads analysed engaged in warfare in the period under analysis and (2) the majority of the dyads did not sign more than a handful of treaties. Taken together, (1) and (2) mean that there tends to be a preponderance of cases in only one cell of any cross-tabulations undertaken. Reduction in error statistics, which in some senses are more suitable than gamma for tabular data, fail to pick up clear column percentage differences if the row marginals are imbalanced: as a result tau_b is only reported, for comparative purposes, in the later stages of the statistical analysis.
3. It is also worth noting that, because the data constitute a population rather than a sample, tests of significance are not reported.
4. The difference between the values of these two coefficients well illustrates the greater suitability of γ for the purposes of this study. The mutual assistance *vs* war/not cross-tabulation from which they were derived yielded a pattern very similar to that described in Table 3.1, with no cases occuring in the bottom right cell. In these circumstances, γ produces a coefficient of -1, which makes very good intuitive sense: the signing of a mutual assistance treaty was a guarantee that the parties would not subsequently go to war. There is clearly a strong statistical relationship between this particular form of treaty-making and war-avoidance and this is reflected in the magnitude of the negative summary statistic. Tau_b, however, yields a relatively small (albeit negative) coefficient because of the inevitable preponderance of cases in the top left cell (most pairs of nations experience very little contact: they neither go to war nor sign many treaties with one another) which counterbalances the lack of cases in the bottom right cell.
5. David Sanders, *Patterns of Political Instability* (London: Macmillan, 1981), ch. 7.
6. A similar pattern of intercorrelation was also found when controls were applied for ECDIF and ADJACENT, the two other contextual variables defined in Chapter 2.

7. Notably the 'general political' relationship.
8. It will be recalled from Chapter 2 that the 'cultural difference' variable closely corresponds to Coplin and Rochester's concept of 'geocultural region'.
9. Table A.2 in the Appendix provides an illustrative listing of the dyads which fall into each of the theoretically relevant categories of the sort of 4-way cross-tabulation from which the coefficients in Tables 3.5, 3.6 and 3.7 are derived.
10. Specifically, 'Friendship/Antagonism I' yields 19 out of a possible total of 20 negative correlations for the culturally dissimilar dyads. The corresponding figure for 'Friendship/Antagonism II' is 14 out of 18; for 'Friendship/Antagonism III', 15 out of 20; for 'Friendship/Antagonism IV', 12 out of 18; and for 'Friendship/Antagonism V', 15 out of 20.
11. Cross-tabulations among these three variables yielded the following correlations

	tau_b	gamma
cultural difference/not with near/not	– 0.39	– 0.87
cultural difference/not with power differential/not	0.19	0.39
power differential/not with near/not	– 0.07	– 0.18

4 TREATY-MAKING, WAR AND PEACE: FURTHER EMPIRICAL EVIDENCE

1. A number of excellent treatments of the principles behind log-linear modelling are available. See, for example, Graham Upton, *The Analysis of Crosstabulation Data* (Chichester: Wiley, 1976). The notation employed here follows David Knokke and Peter J. Burke, *Loglinear Models* (Beverly Hills, Ca: Sage, 1980).
2. For a general justification of this kind of usage, see Hubert M. Blalock, *Causal Inferences in Nonexperimental Research* (Chapel Hill, NC: University of North Carolina Press, 1964), ch. 3.
3. 'Nonsignificant' means that a given coefficient was less than twice its own standard error; no correlation higher than $\tau = 0.7$ was permitted between predictor variables.
4. It has already been established immediately above that war is more likely when *both* parties are Great Powers.
5. One way of explaining this counterintuitive finding is in terms of Quincy Wright's concept of 'political lag' (see Quincy Wright, *A Study of War*, 2nd edn, Chicago University Press, 1965, ch. 37). Wright argues that any form of contact between different social units – trade between nation-states being an obvious example – is generally accompanied by an increase in social and economic tensions between those units. Such tensions, at the international level, however, need not necessarily produce interstate violence, insofar as the states involved are capable of developing an adequate set of political-legal adjustment mechanisms which can ensure that those conflicts which do arise are peacefully resolved. To the extent that the development of adjustment mechanisms fails to keep pace with the tensions generated by

interstate contact – to the extent that a 'political lag' exists – disputes are likely to be resolved by resort to force. Thus it could be argued that the positive (partial) correlation between trade and war-occurrence indicated by the positive coefficient for VOLUME 28 is simply a reflection of the fact that the political-legal adjustment mechanisms available during the interwar period were largely ineffective as vehicles for peaceful conflict resolution. Such a claim would certainly be consistent with the view (which I would not wish to contradict) that the formal political-legal machinery of the League (the Council and the Court) transparently failed to perform its primary manifest function of sustaining international peace during the interwar years.

6. This is not to say, of course, that the decline in trade on a *global* basis did not generate domestic political tensions in certain countries that might have encouraged aggressive foreign policies at a later date.

5 A CASE-STUDY: ANGLO-TURKISH RELATIONS DURING THE INTERWAR YEARS

1. For a review of this debate, see Anthony R. DeLuca, 'Montreux and Collective Security', *The Historian*, vol. 38, no.1 (1975), pp. 1–20. Documents cited in this chapter are taken from the F(oreign) O(ffice) files at the Public Records Office, Kew Gardens, London.
2. See Chapter 3.
3. W. L. Wright, 'Truths about Turkey', *Foreign Affairs*, vol. 26 (1948), pp. 349–50.
4. Aileen G. Cramer, 'Turkey in search of a protector: 1918–1947', *Current History*, vol. 13 (1947), p. 286.
5. Frank Marzori, 'Western-Soviet rivalry in Turkey, 1939 – I', *Middle Eastern Studies*, vol. 7 (1971), pp. 63–4.
6. French notes in this context: 'Given the Turks' unpreparedness, the British . . . could only explain to themselves the Turks' seeming perversity by reference to bitter internal divisions within . . . (the Turkish leadership) . . . and the machinations of a handful of German conspirators' (p. 213). See David French, 'The Origins of the Dardanelles Campaign Reconsidered', *History*, vol. 68, no. 223 (June 1983), pp. 210–24.
7. H. Kuyacak, 'Anglo-Turkish Economic Relations', *South Asian Review*, vol. 37 (1941), pp. 92–3; Werner E. Braatz, 'Junkers Flugzeugwerke A. G. in Anatolia 1925–1926: an aspect of German-Turkish economic relations', *Tradition*, vol. 20 (1975), pp. 24–39.
8. John R. Craf, 'Turkey, Guardian of the Dardanelles', *Social Studies*, vol. 36 (1945), pp. 157–8.
9. Cramer, 'Turkey', p. 281; Charlotte E. Braun, 'Danger in the Dardanelles', *Current History*, vol. 9 (1945), pp. 225. Marzori observes that as part of the new Anglo-Russian rapproachment,

   [A] hard pressed Britain . . . [reluctantly] . . . permitted Russia to formulate demands . . . which included the annexation of Constantinople . . . [and] . . . a portion of the Dardanelles and

Bosphorus . . . [though] . . . because of the allied defeat at Gallipoli, the presentation of this bill was deferred until the end of the war; because of Brest-Litovsk it was not presented at all. (Marzori, 'Western-Soviet rivalry', p. 63).

10. H. Edib, 'Turkey and her Allies', *Foreign Affairs*, vol. 18 (1940), p. 442.
11. R. R. Kasliwal, 'The Foreign Policy of Turkey since 1919', *Indian Journal of Political Science*, vol. 7 (1946), pp. 387–8; Craf, 'Turkey', pp. 157–8.
12. The Republic of Turkey was proclaimed on 29 October 1923.
13. A. L. MacFie, 'The Chanak Affair (September–October 1922)', *Balkan Studies*, vol. 20, no. 2 (1979), pp. 309–41; Kasliwal, 'The Foreign Policy', p. 389.
14. This was laid down in the Straits Convention annexed to the Treaty of Lausanne and signed on the same day.
15. Ahmed Emir Yalman, *Turkey in My Time* (Norman: University of Oklahoma Press, 1956), pp. 68–71; cited in Robert L. Daniel, 'The United States and the Turkish Republic before World War II: the Cultural Dimension', *Middle East Journal*, vol. 21 (1967), p. 53.
16. P. W. Ireland, 'Turkish Foreign Policy after Munich', *Political Quarterly*, vol. 10 (1939), pp. 191–2.
17. FO 424 263 no. 1, Chamberlain to Hoare, 3/7/25.
18. Geoffrey Lewis, *Turkey* (London: Ernest Benn, 1965), p. 116.
19. Metin Tamkoc, *The Warrior Diplomats* (Salt Lake City: University of Utah Press, 1976), p. 192.
20. FO 424 263 no. 42, Chamberlain to Lindsay, 2/10/25.
21. Tamkoc, *The Warrior Diplomats*, p. 192.
22. FO 424 263 no. 2, Hoare to Chamberlain, 30/6/25; FO 424 263 no. 42, Chamberlain to Lindsay, 2/10/25.
23. Lewis, *Turkey*, p. 116.
24. Philip Graves, *Briton and Turk* (London: Hutchinson, 1941), p. 224.
25. Robert W. Olson and Nurhan Ince, 'Turkish Foreign Policy from 1923–1960: Kemalism and its legacy, a review and a critique', *Oriente Moderno*, vol. 57 (1977), p. 233.
26. Percy E. Corbett, *Law in Diplomacy* (Princeton University Press, 1959), p.205.
27. FO 242 273 no. 89, Henderson to Clerk, 24/9/30; FO 242 274 no. 8, Henderson to Clerk, 5/2/31; FO 242 274 no. 16, Henderson to Clerk, 10/3/31; The earliest advances had in fact been made by Turkey in 1926. See FO 424 265 no. 43, Chamberlain to Clerk, 26/11/26.
28. For a summary of the provisions of the Treaty of Montreux, see 'JR', 'Russian-Turkish relations', *The World Today*, vol. 2 (1945), pp.57–63.
29. D. A. Routh, 'The Montreux Convention Regarding the Regime of the Black Sea Straits (20th July, 1936)', in Royal Institute of International Affairs, *Survey of International Affairs 1936* (Oxford University Press, 1937), p. 584.
30. A. L. MacFie, 'The Straits Question: The Conference of Montreux (1936)', *Balkan Studies*, vol. 13, no. 2 (1972), pp. 203–19.
31. Routh, '*The Montreux Convention*', p. 585.
32. Ibid. p. 606.

33. See, for example, FO 424 264 no. 67, Leeper to Lindsay, 19/4/26; F.O. 424 265 no. 41, Hoare to Chamberlain, Enclosure: 'Report on a Visit to Southern Anatolia, Rhodes and Smyrna', 14/11/26; FO 424 266 no. 7, Chamberlain to Clerk, 28/1/27. The fears of an Italian *coup de main* against Smyrna were further bolstered by a 'most secret' intelligence report on 'Italian Secret Activities in Asia Minor', received by the FO 22/11/25. See FO 371 5471–7127 E6603/G, pp. 168–72.
34. MacFie 'The Straits Question', p. 207.
35. Ludmilla Zhivkova, 'Anglo-Turkish relations 1934–35', *Etudes Balkaniques*, vol. 7, no. 4 (1971), pp. 82–98; Olson and Ince, 'Turkish Foreign Policy', p. 232.
36. Cramer, '*Turkey*', p. 280.
37. FO 424 271 no. 91, Edmonds to Henderson, 20/12/29 (emphasis added).
38. Cramer, '*Turkey*', p. 281.
39. Routh, '*The Montreux Convention*', p. 608.
40. Coming in the wake of the German remilitarisation of the Rhineland and the Italian invasion of Abyssinia, the Montreux negotiations certainly bore all the hallmarks of crisis.
41. As noted in Chapter 1, Scheinman and Wilkinson's study of crisis decision-making found that legal considerations never played anything other than the smallest role in policy decisions during a number of prominent postwar crises.
42. V. K. Volkov, 'The Foreign Policy of Turkey and Greece on the eve of and in the period of the Munich Agreement', *Voprosy Istorii*, vol. 4 (1978), pp. 42–61; Ireland, 'Turkish Foreign Policy', p. 194.
43. Marzori, 'Western-Soviet rivalry', p. 66.
44. Ibid., pp. 66–72. In Marzori's opinion, the Axis coup in Czechoslovakia gave Turkey the opportunity to act on a decision which Ankara had already taken

    [B]efore the Axis coups in Czechoslovakia and Albania . . . Turkey had weighed the advantages of an already tentatively formulated agreement with the Soviets in the Black Sea against an, as yet, unformulated agreement with Britain in the Mediterranean and had decided that the second alternative took precedence. This was a seminal decision from which Turkey would not deviate despite blandishments to do so from both Germany and the Soviet Union. pp. (66–7)

45. 'The obligations undertaken by Turkey . . . cannot compel that country to take action, having as its effect, or involving as its consequence, entry into armed conflict with the Soviet Union' (Protocol 2; quoted in Graves, *Briton and Turk*, p. 243).
46. Cramer, '*Turkey*', p. 283.
47. Tamkoc, *The Warrior Diplomats*, p. 206.
48. David A. Alvarez, 'The Embassy of Lawrence A. Steinhardt: aspects of Allied-Turkish relations 1942–45', *East European Quarterly*, vol. 9, no. 1 (1975), pp. 39–52; G. Jaeschke, 'Turkey's Foreign Policy in World Wars I and II', *Belletin*, vol. 41, no. 164 (1977), pp. 733–43; Tamkoc, *The Warrior Diplomats*, pp. 205–6.

49. Graves, *Briton and Turk*, pp. 239–240.
50. Maria Antonia Di Casola, 'The problem of Turkey's neutrality policy between the end of 1942 and the meeting at Adana', *Politico*, vol. 40, no. 2 (1975), pp. 238–62.
51. MacFie, *'The Straits Question*', p. 207.
52. See below, pp. 122–8.
53. MacFie, '*The Straits Questions*', p. 207–8.
54. Routh, '*The Montreux Convention*', p. 606.
55. Ibid. p. 585.
56. Kuyucak, 'Anglo-Turkish Economic Relations', p. 92.
57. Ibid., p. 93.
58. Ibid., pp. 92–3. Britain's share in Turkish foreign trade fell from 17.3 per cent of total Turkish imports in 1923 to 6.25 percent in 1939 (p. 94).
59. Marzori, 'Western-Soviet rivalry', p. 76.
60. Ibid. p. 173.
61. On the negotiations in 1936 see MacFie, '*The Straits Question*'; for 1939, see Marzori, 'Western-Soviet rivalry'.
62. FO 424 270 no. 23, Clerk to Chamberlain, 14/2/29.
63. Ibid. Enclosure in no. 23: Memo on the Present Position in Turkey by A. K. Helm, 10/2/29.
64. Olson and Ince, 'Turkish Foreign Policy', p. 229.
65. Peter J. Beck, 'A tedious and perilous controversy: Britain and the settlement of the Mosul dispute, 1918–1926', *Middle East Studies*, vol. 17, no. 2 (1981), p. 256.
66. Marzori, 'Western-Soviet rivalry', p. 64.
67. Routh, '*The Montreux Convention*', p. 599; Cramer, '*Turkey*', p. 281; Olson and Ince, '*Turkish Foreign Policy*', p. 227.
68. FO 424 264 no. 4, Lindsay to Chamberlain, 30/12/25.
69. FO 424 264 no. 14, Lindsay to Chamberlain, 4/2/26.
70. FO 424 264 no. 32 Lindsay to Chamberlain, 3/3/26; FO 424 264 no. 35, Lindsay to Chamberlain, 10/3/26.
71. FO 424 265 no. 28, Hoare to Chamberlain, 18/10/26.
72. FO 424 266 no. 13, Clerk to Chamberlain, 9/2/27. British diplomats in the 1920s experienced considerable difficulty in the transliteration of Turkish names. Foreign Minister Tevfik Rüstü was variously referred to as Tewfik Rushdi Bey, Tewfik Rüshdü, Tefvik Rüstü and latterly as Rüstü Aras. For presentational purposes I have employed the version of his name most frequently encountered in the source documents – Tevfik Rüstü – even when the original source uses a different transliteration.
73. FO 424 265 no. 47, Clerk to Chamberlain, 30/11/26.
74. FO 424 265 no. 51, Clerk to Chamberlain, 16/12/26.
75. FO 424 266 no. 1, Clerk to Chamberlain, 29/12/26 (emphasis added).
76. Corbett, *Law in Diplomacy*, p. 203.
77. This interpretation has some parallels in the attempts by social psychologists to understand behaviour in terms of attribution theory. See, for example, D. Bem, 'Self Perception. An Alternative Interpretation of Cognitive Dissonance Phenomena', *Psychological Review*, vol. 64 (1967), pp. 183–200.
78. FO 424 266 no. 7, Chamberlain to Clerk, 28/1/27.

79. See, for example, F.O. 424 266 no. 25, Hoare to Chamberlain, 15/3/37.
80. FO 424 266 no. 29, Hoare to Chamberlain, 30/3/27.
81. FO 424 267 no. 3, Clerk to Chamberlain, 5/7/27.
82. FO 424 268 no. 21, Clerk to Chamberlain, 21/2/28.
83. FO 424 268 no. 23, Clerk to Chamberlain, 22/2/28.
84. FO 424 269 no. 32, Clerk to Cushendon, 31/10/28.
85. FO 424 268 no. 37, Knox to Chamberlain, 8/4/28.
86. FO 424 268 no. 37, Knox to Chamberlain, 8/4/28 (emphasis added).
87. FO 424 270 no. 20, Clerk to Chamberlain, 9/2/29; no. 22 Clerk to Chamberlain 12/2/29.
88. FO 424 270 no. 23, Clerk to Chamberlain, 14/2/29; enclosure by Mr A. K. Helm, 10/2/29.
89. FO 424 270 no. 66, Clerk to Chamberlain, 4/6/29.
90. FO 424 271 no. 66, Clerk to Henderson, 23/10/29.
91. FO 424 271 no. 67, Clerk to Henderson, 23/10/29.
92. FO 424 265 no. 43, Chamberlain to Clerk, 26/11/26.
93. FO 424 272 no. 2, Clerk to Henderson, 14/1/30.
94. FO 424 273 no. 89, Henderson to Clerk, 24/9/30.
95. FO 424 274 no. 40, Clerk to Henderson, 30/4/31.
96. FO 424 276 no. 38, Clerk to Simon, 24/4/32.
97. FO 424 276 no. 53, Clerk to Simon, 3/6/32.

CONCLUSION

1. See, for example, Trevor Taylor, 'Power Politics', in Trevor Taylor (ed.), *Approaches and Theory in International Relations* (London: Longmans, 1978), pp. 122–40.
2. Roger D. Spegele, 'Alarums and Excursions: The State of the Discipline of International Relations', *Politikon* (South Africa), vol. 10, no. 1 (December 1983) pp. 54–7.
3. Ibid., p. 55.
4. Ibid., pp. 55–8.

Bibliography

David A. Alvarez, 'The Embassy of Lawrence A. Steinhardt: aspects of Allied–Turkish relations 1942–45', *East European Quarterly*, vol. 9, no. 1 (1975), pp. 39–52.

Peter J. Beck, 'A tedious and perilous controversy: Britain and the settlement of the Mosul dispute, 1918–1926', *Middle East Studies*, vol. 17, no. 2 (1981), pp. 256–76.

D. Bem, 'Self Perception: An Alternative Interpretation of Cognitive Dissonance Phenomena', *Psychological Review*, vol. 64 (1967), pp. 183–200.

Richard Bilder, *Managing The Risks of International Agreements* (Madison: University of Wisconsin Press, 1981).

Hubert M. Blalock, *Causal Inferences in Nonexperimental Research* (Chapel Hill, NC: University of North Carolina Press, 1964).

Edwin M. Borchard, ' "War" and "Peace" ', *American Journal of International Law*, vol. 23 (1933), pp. 114–17.

Werner E. Braatz, 'Junkers Flugzeugwerke A. G. in Anatolia 1925–1926: an aspect of German-Turkish economic relations', *Tradition*, vol. 20 (1975), pp. 24–39.

Charlotte E. Braun, 'Danger in the Dardanelles', *Current History*, vol. 9 (1945), pp. 222–6.

Hedley Bull, *The Anarchical Society: A Study of Order in World Politics* (London: Macmillan, 1977).

Herbert Butterfield, *Christianity and History* (New York: Charles Scribner, 1950).

Herbert Butterfield, *History and Human Relations* (London: Collins, 1951).

Barry Buzan, *People, States and Fear: The National Security Problem in International Relations* (Brighton: Wheatsheaf Books, 1983).

E. H. Carr, *The Twenty Years Crisis, 1919–1939* (London: Macmillan, 1961).

Grenville Clark and Louis B. Sohn, *World Peace Through World Law* (Cambridge, Mass: Harvard University Press, 1966).

Inis Claude, *Swords into Ploughshares: The Problems and Progress of International Organizations* (New York: Random House, 1964).

William D. Coplin, 'Current Studies in the Functions of International Law', in James A. Robinson (ed.), *Political Science Annual: An International Review Vol. II, 1969–70* (Indianapolis: Bobbs-Merrill, 1970), pp. 149–207.

William D. Coplin and J. Martin Rochester, 'The Permanent Court of International Justice, The International Court of Justice, The League of Nations and the United Nations: a comparative, empirical survey', *American Political Science Review*, vol. 66 (June 1972), pp. 529–50.

Percy E. Corbett, *Law in Diplomacy* (Princeton University Press, 1959).

John R. Craf, 'Turkey, Guardian of the Dardanelles', *Social Studies*, vol. 36 (1945), pp. 157–8.

Aileen G. Cramer, 'Turkey in search of a protector: 1918–1947', *Current History*, vol. 13 (1947), pp. 280–6.

Anthony R. DeLuca, 'Montreux and Collective Security', *The Historian*, vol. 38, no. 1 (1975), pp. 1–20.

Frank M. Denton, 'Patterns in Political Violence and War' (PhD dissertation, University of Southern California, 1968).

Maria Antonia Di Casola, 'The problem of Turkey's neutrality policy between the end of 1942 and the meeting at Adana', *Politico*, vol. 40, no. 2 (1975), pp. 238–62.

A. Eban, 'Camp David – the unfinished business', *Foreign Affairs*, vol. 57 (Winter 1978/79), p. 348.

H. Edib, 'Turkey and her Allies', *Foreign Affairs*, vol. 18 (1940), pp. 442–9.

Richard Falk, 'International Jurisdiction: Horizontal and Vertical Conceptions of Legal Order', *Temple Law Quarterly*, vol. 32 (Spring 1959), pp. 295–320.

Richard Falk, *Legal Order in a Violent World* (Princeton University Press, 1968).

Richard Falk, 'Confrontation diplomacy: Indonesia's campaign to crush Malaysia', in Lawrence Scheinman and David Wilkinson (eds), *International Law and Political Crisis: An Analytic Casebook* (Boston: Little, Brown, 1968).

Charles G. Fenwick, 'The Legal Significance of the Locarno Treaties', *American Journal of International Law*, vol. 20 (1926), pp. 108–11.

André Gunder Frank, *Reflections on the World Economic Crisis* (London: Hutchinson, 1981).

David French, 'The Origins of the Dardanelles Campaign Reconsidered', *History*, vol. 68, no. 223 (June 1983), pp. 210–24.

W. Friedman and L. Collins, 'The Suez Canal Crisis', in L. Scheinman and D. Wilkinson (eds), *International Law and Political Crisis: An Analytic Casebook* (Boston: Little, Brown, 1968), pp. 110–30.

Philip Graves, *Briton and Turk* (London: Hutchinson, 1941).

Michael Haas, 'International Subsystems: Stability and Polarity', *American Political Science Review*, vol. 64 (March 1970), pp. 98–123.

Ruth B. Henig (ed.), *The League of Nations* (Edinburgh: Oliver & Boyd, 1973).

Rosalyn Higgins, *The Development of International Law through the Political Organs of the United Nations* (Oxford University Press, 1963).

Manley O. Hudson (ed.), *World Court Reports 1921–42* (Washington, DC: Carnegie Endowment for International Peace, 1943), four volumes.

Manley O. Hudson, 'The World Court', in Harriett E. Davies (ed.), *Pioneers in World Order: An American Appraisal of the League of Nations* (New York: Columbia University Press, 1944).

P. W. Ireland, 'Turkish Foreign Policy after Munich', *Political Quarterly*, vol. 10 (1939), pp. 185–201.

G. Jaeschke, 'Turkey's Foreign Policy in World Wars I and II', *Belletin*, vol. 41, no. 164 (1977), pp. 733–43.

'J. R.', 'Russian-Turkish Relations', *The World Today*', vol. 2 (1945), pp. 57–63.

J. Mervyn Jones, 'The retroactive effect of the ratification of treaties', *American Journal of International Law*, vol. 29 (1935), pp. 49–54.

R. R. Kasliwal, 'The Foreign Policy of Turkey since 1919', *Indian Journal of Political Science*, vol. 7 (1946), pp. 387–97.

Robert O. Keohane, *After Hegemony: Co-operation and Discord in the World Political Economy* (Princeton University Press, 1984).

David Knokke and Peter J. Burke, *Loglinear Models* (Beverly Hills, Ca: Sage, 1980).

Warren F. Kuehl, *Seeking World Order: The United States and International Organisation to 1920* (Nashville: Vanderbilt University Press, 1969).

Joseph L. Kunz, 'The Problem of Revision in International Law', *American Journal of International Law*, vol. 33 (1939), pp. 33–55.

H. Kuyacak, 'Anglo-Turkish Economic Relations', *South Asian Review*, vol. 37 (1941), pp. 91–100.

Hersch Lauterpacht, *The Function of Law in the International Community* (Oxford University Press, 1933).

Hersch Lauterpacht, *Private Law Sources and Analogies of International Law* (London: Longmans, 1927).

Hersch Lauterpacht, *International Law: Collected Papers edited by E. Lauterpacht (volume 2, The Law of Peace, Part I)* (Cambridge University Press, 1975).

Geoffrey Lewis, *Turkey* (London: Ernest Benn, 1965).

A. L. MacFie, 'The Chanak Affair (September–October 1922)', *Balkan Studies*, vol. 20, no. 2 (1979), pp. 309–41.

A. L. MacFie, 'The Straits Question: The Conference of Montreux (1936)', *Balkan Studies*, vol. 13, no. 2 (1972), pp. 203–19.

Ernest Mandel, *Late Capitalism* (London: New Left Books, 1975).

Frank Marzori, 'Western-Soviet rivalry in Turkey, 1939 – I', *Middle Eastern Studies*, vol. 7 (1971), pp. 63–79.

Hans J. Morgenthau, *Scientific Man versus Power Politics* (University of Chicago Press, 1946).

Richard Nixon, *Real Peace* (Boston: Little, Brown, 1984).

J. S. Nye, *Peace in Parts: Integration and Conflict in Regional Organisations* (Boston: Little, Brown, 1971).

Robert W. Olson and Nurhan Ince, 'Turkish Foreign Policy from 1923–1960: Kemalism and its legacy, a review and a critique', *Oriente Moderno*, vol. 57 (1977), pp. 227–241.

R. C. Plackett, *The Analysis of Categorical Data*, 2nd edn. (London: Griffin, 1982).

Gregory A. Raymond, *Conflict Resolution and the Structure of the State System: An Analysis of Arbitrative Settlements* (Montclair, NJ: Allanheld Osmun, 1980).

Report of the Study Group of the David Davies Memorial Institute of International Relations, *International Disputes: The Legal Aspects* (London: Europa Publications, 1972).

Peter H. Rohn, *World Treaty Index: Volume 1, League of Nations Treaty Series* (Santa Barbara, Ca: American Bibliographic Centre–Clio, 1974).

D. A. Routh, 'The Montreux Convention Regarding the Regime of the Black Sea Straits (20th July, 1936)', in Royal Institute of International Affairs, *Survey of International Affairs 1936* (Oxford University Press, 1937) pp. 584–651.

David Sanders, *Patterns of Political Instability* (London: Macmillan, 1981).

Lawrence Scheinman, 'The Berlin Blockade', in Lawrence Scheinman and David Wilkinson (eds), *International Law and Political Crisis: An Analytic Casebook* (Boston: Little, Brown, 1968).

Lawrence Scheinman and David Wilkinson (eds), *International Law and Political Crisis: An Analytic Casebook* (Boston: Little, Brown, 1968).
Thomas C. Schelling, *The Strategy of Conflict* (Cambridge, Mass.: Harvard University Press, 1960).
Georg Schwarzenberger, *International Law and Order* (London: Stevens, 1971).
James Brown Scott (ed.), *Resolutions of the Institute of International Law Dealing with the Law of Nations* (New York: Oxford University Press, 1916).
J. David Singer and Melvin Small, *The Wages of War 1816–1965: A Statistical Handbook* (New York: Wiley, 1972).
Glenn H. Snyder, '"Prisoner's Dilemma" and "Chicken" Models in International Relations', *International Studies Quarterly*, vol. 15, no. 1 (March 1971), pp. 66–103.
Roger D. Spegele, 'Alarums and Excursions: The State of the Discipline of International Relations', *Politickon* (South Africa), vol. 10, no. 1 (December 1983), pp. 51–72.
A. M. Stuyt, *Survey of International Arbitrations 1794–1970* (Leiden: Sijthoff, 1972).
H. M. Swanwick, *Collective Insecurity* (London: Jonthan Cape, 1937).
Metin Tamkoc, *The Warrior Diplomats* (Salt Lake City: University of Utah Press, 1976).
Michael Taylor, *Anarchy and Co-operation* (London: Wiley, 1976).
Trevor Taylor, 'Power Politics', in Trevor Taylor (ed.), *Approaches and Theory in International Relations* (London: Longmans, 1978), pp. 122–140.
Graham Upton, *The Analysis of Crosstabulation Data* (Chichester: Wiley, 1976).
V. K. Volkov, 'The Foreign Policy of Turkey and Greece on the eve of and in the period of the Munich Agreement', *Voprosy Istorii*, vol. 4 (1978), pp. 42–61.
F. P. Walters, *A History of the League of Nations* (Oxford University Press, 1950).
Kenneth N. Waltz, *Theory of International Politics* (Reading, Mass.: Addison-Wesley, 1979).
Erich Weede, 'Extended Deterence by Superpower Alliance', *Journal of Conflict Resolution*, vol. 27, no. 2 (June 1983), pp. 231–254.
Hans Wehberg, 'Restrictive Clauses in International Arbitration Treaties', *American Journal of International Law*, vol. 7 (1913), pp. 301–14.
Quincy Wright, 'The end of a period of transition?', *American Journal of International Law*, vol. 31 (1937), pp. 604–13.
Quincy Wright, *A Study of War*, 2nd edn (Chicago University Press, 1965).
W. L. Wright, 'Truths about Turkey', *Foreign Affairs*, vol. 26 (1948), pp. 349–359.
Ahmed Emir Yalman, *Turkey in My Time* (Norman: University of Oklahoma Press, 1956).
Alfred Zimmern, *The League of Nations and the Rule of Law 1918–1935* (London: Macmillan, 1936).
Ludmilla Zhivkova, 'Anglo-Turkish relations 1934–35', *Etudes Balkaniques* vol. 7, no. 4 (1971), pp. 82–98.

Index

Abyssinia, 16, 17, 115, 116
'administrative co-operation' treaties, 39, 55, 59, 65, 69, 71, 76
'aliens rights' treaties, 39, 55, 59, 65, 69, 71, 76
Alvarez, David A., 151
anarchical society, 106, 144
Anatolia, 112, 113, 116
Anglo–Turkish relations, 108–34
a priori probability of war, 46, 57
arbitration, 8, 10, 22, 34–8, 52–3, 56
'arbitration/conciliation' treaties, 39, 53, 55, 59, 65, 69, 71, 76
Argentina, 17
Athlone, Earl of, 128
Axis Powers, 27, 112, 117, 118

balance of power, 27, 115
Beck, Peter J., 152
Berlin crisis, 19, 22
bilateral relations, 4, 35, 106, 112
bilateral trade, 37, 40–4, 80–6, 100, 105
  between Germany and Turkey, 120
Bilder, Richard, 23, 144
Blalock, Hubert M., 148
Bolivia, 17
Borchard, Edwin M., 141
Bourgeois, Leon, 13
Braatz, Werner E., 149
Braun, Charlotte E., 149
Bretton Woods, 44
Britain, 12, 19, 28
Brown Scott, James, 141
Bull, Hedley, 22, 144
Burke, Peter J., 148
Butterfield, Herbert, 140
Buzan, Barry, 140

Carr, E. H., 7, 20, 21, 143
Central Powers, 112
Chaco dispute, 17
Chamberlain, Sir Austen, 114, 123, 125, 127
Chile, 17
China, 16
'circumscribed idealist hypothesis', 66, 73, 74, 77, 80, 81, 86–7
Clark, Grenville, 141
Claude, Inis, 141
Clerk, Sir George, 120, 123, 124–5, 127–30
collective security, 9, 10, 12, 117
Collins, L., 9, 143
colonial status, 81–4, 106
conciliation, 9, 10, 52–3
co-operation, co-operative strategies, 1, 4–6, 26–7, 29, 107–8, 119, 131, 133
Coplin, William D., 44, 145, 147
Corbett, Percy E., 11, 12, 18, 22, 141, 143
Craf, John R., 149
Cramer, Aileen, 149
crisis of overaccumulation, 41
cultural dissimilarity, 5, 45, 58–61, 67, 75, 82, 99, 108
'cultural/medical/scientific' treaties, 39, 55, 59, 65, 69, 71, 76

Daniel, Robert L., 150
Davies, Harriet E., 144
Deluca, Anthony R., 149
Denton, Frank M., 145
Department of State Bulletin, 145
Di Casola, Maria Antonia, 152
differences in column ratios, 53–4
'diplomatic agreements', 39, 55, 58, 65, 69, 71, 76

diplomatic negotiation, 24, 33, 39, 49, 51, 106
disaggregation of correlations, 51, 57–62, 72

Eban, Abba, 24, 26, 145
economic nationalism, 42, 81
Edib Bey, 125
Edib, H., 150

Falk, Richard, 19, 21, 142, 144
Fenwick, Charles G., 9, 141
Field, Admiral, 127
'financial treaties', 39, 55, 58, 64, 68, 70, 76
France, 12, 19, 112
Frank, André Gunder, 147
French, David, 149
Friedman, W., 19, 143
'friendship/antagonism', 4, 5, 46–8, 62–71, 73, 74, 77, 78, 80, 86–7, 103, 108
'friendship and co-operation treaties', 39, 53, 55, 59, 65, 69, 71, 76, 116

General Act for Pacific Settlement, 9, 14, 15, 16, 34
'general economic treaties', 39, 55, 56, 58, 64, 68, 70, 76
'general political treaties', 39, 55, 58, 64, 68, 70, 76
General Treaty for the Renunciation of War, 9, 13
geographical proximity/remoteness, 45, 58–61, 67, 75, 82, 99, 108
Germany, 11, 12, 17, 112, 115, 119, 120
Ghazi, *see* Mustapha Kemal Pasha
Graves, Philip, 150, 152

Haas, Michael, 145
Haddow, Mr, 125
Hague Court, 8
Harenc, Major, 126
Helm, Alex V., 125, 126
Henig, Ruth B., 12, 142
Henderson, Sir A., 127
Higgins, Rosalyn, 21, 144
Hitler, A., 17, 40, 72
Hoare, R. H., 114, 122, 125
Hobbesian fear, 2, 24, 106
Hudson, Manley O., 22, 144, 145

idealism, 1, 4, 8, 14–18, 20, 27, 62
Ince, Nurham, 150
Imperialism, 81–5, 122
international crisis, 19, 25, 32
international law, 4, 19, 21
  compared with municipal law, 13–14, 18
  latent function of, 7, 21–3, 33, 38, 39–40, 49, 51, 119
  manifest function of, 7, 20, 27, 31, 37, 49, 55–6, 119
international 'police force', 13, 19
Iraq, 113, 114, 121
Ireland, P. W., 150, 151
Ismet Pasha, 125, 126, 128
Israel, 24
Italy, 11, 16, 17, 115–16, 120

Jaeschke, G., 151
Japan, 16
'JR', 150
juridical 'completeness', 14
jurisprudence: failings of the 'Hague/League' system, 10–15
justiciable disputes, 8, 9, 22

Kasliwal, R. R., 150
Keohane, Robert O., 140
Keuhl, Warren F., 140
Knokke, David, 148
Knox, Mr, 126
Kunz, Joseph L., 143
Kurdistan, 113
Kuyacak, H., 149, 152

Lausanne, Treaty of, 113, 114, 115–17, 119, 122, 124
Lauterpacht, Sir Hersch, 13, 14, 15, 141, 142
lawmaking, 7, 23–8, 32, 39, 61–2
  see also treatymaking
League of Nations, 7, 13, 15, 16, 17, 30, 109, 117, 121, 124
  Council of, 9, 16, 23, 114–15, 124, 128
  Covenant of, 9, 10, 12, 14, 15, 16

legal positivism, 13
Lewis, Geoffrey, 150
Lindsay, Ambassador, 122
Lloyd George, David, 114
Locarno treaties, 9, 11, 12, 14, 17

MacFie, A. L., 115, 150
Manchuria, 16
Mandel, Ernest, 147
Marzori, Frank, 149, 151, 152
Mervyn-Jones, J., 146
Molotov–Ribbentrop pact, 118, 121
Montreux Convention, 109, 112, 115, 116, 119
Morgenthau, Hans J., 7, 18–19, 143
'most favoured nation' treaties, 39, 55, 56, 58, 64, 68, 70, 76
Mosul conflict and settlement, 109, 114, 116, 121–4, 126, 130
Mudroson, Armistice of, 109, 112
Munich crisis, 117
Mussolini, B., 16, 72, 116
Mustapha Kemal Pasha, 113, 122, 124, 125, 128
'mutual assistance' treaties, 39, 55, 56, 59, 65, 69, 71, 76, 102, 104, 109, 117–18

Nady, Younous, 123, 124
Namier, L. B., 143
network of treaty commitments, 24, 76, 77, 100
Nixon, Richard M., 3, 140
'nonaggression treaties', 39, 55, 59, 65, 69, 71, 76, 114, 116, 118
Nye, J. S., 140

Olson, Robert W., 150
Ottoman Empire, 112

Pan Hellenism, 113
Paraguay, 117
partial treaties, 11–12
peace, 4, 6, 7, 13, 20–3, 27, 36, 40, 133
'peace through law', 4, 18
Permanent Court of International Justice, 9, 10, 15, 22, 36, 37, 114
'positivist-empiricism', 132
power politics, 32, 40, 132
  see also realism
power status differential, 5, 45, 58–61, 67, 75, 82, 99, 108

Raymond, Gregory A., 34–5, 38, 145
realism, 1, 3, 4, 5, 7, 17, 18–20, 23, 27, 30, 67, 72, 74, 106
  'concessional' *vs* 'traditional', 132–3
  revisions to, 133–4
realpolitik, 1, 3, 4, 5, 25–6, 28, 30, 40, 49, 109, 117–21, 129–33
'reciprocal neutrality' treaties, 39, 55, 59, 65, 69, 71, 76
'reconstructed idealism', 5, 23, 24, 27–9, 30, 51, 66, 134
Renault, Louis, 22
Rhineland, 7, 115
Rochester, J. Martin, 44, 147
Rohn, Peter H., 38, 145
Routh, D. A., 115, 150, 151, 152
Rumeli, 113
Russia, 112

Scheinman, Lawrence, 19, 22, 143, 144
Schelling, Thomas C., 23, 144
Schwarzenberger, Georg, 7
security, 2, 3, 8, 25, 32, 57, 61, 100, 106
Sèvres, Treaty of, 109, 113, 122
'short-run economic' treaties, 39, 55, 58, 64, 68, 70, 76
Singer, J. David, 47, 143, 147
Simon, Sir John, 128
Small, Melvyn, 47, 143, 147
Snyder, Glenn H., 140
Sohn, Louis B., 141
sovereignty, 8, 113
Soviet Union, 114, 116, 118
'specific economic' treaties, 39, 55, 58, 64, 68, 70, 76
'specific political' treaties, 39, 55, 58, 64, 68, 70, 76

Spegele, Roger D., 153
spurious correlation problem, 5, 44–9, 56–7, 62–71, 73, 77, 106
Spykeman, Nicholas, 7
Straits convention, 109, 115
Stuyt, A. M., 141
Suez Crisis, 19
Swanwick, H. M., 10, 11, 12, 141
systemic *vs* dyadic approaches, 34–5

Tamkoc, Metin, 150, 151
Tardieu, M., 13
tariff barriers, 42
Taylor, Michael, 140
Taylor, Trevor, 153
'territory/boundaries' treaties, 39, 55, 58, 65, 69, 71, 76
Tevfik Rüstü, 123, 125, 126, 127, 128
trade imbalances, 42–4, 81, 83, 88, 89, 100, 105
transformation of bilateral relations, 25, 119, 121, 122–8, 129–30
'transport and communication' treaties, 39, 55, 58, 64, 68, 70, 76
treatymaking, 2, 5, 38, 56–7, 100, 103–4, 128, 130–1
  as an indicator of the state of bilateral relations, 56–7
treaty revision, 10, 11
trust, inter-nation, 5, 6, 24–6, 28, 76, 107, 109, 121, 128, 133
Turkey, 28–9
  and Britain, 108–30
  relations with the Soviet Union, 116–18, 122
  relations with Germany, 118, 120–1, 129
  Turkish nationalism, 113

Upton, Graham, 148
Utopianism, *see* idealism

Volkov, V. K., 151

Wal Wal incident, 16
Waltz, Kenneth N., 34, 145
Walters, F. P., 12, 16, 142
war, 34–8, 49, 52–3, 80
Weede, Erich, 145
Wehberg, Hans, 141
Wilkinson, David, 19, 143
Wright, Quincy, 16, 143, 148
Wright, W. L., 149

Yalman, Ahmed Emir, 150

Zhivkova, Ludmilla, 151
Zimmern, Alfred, 10, 14, 141, 142